Tragic Destiny

George N. Patterson

The Long Riders' Guild Press

www.classictravelbooks.com
www.horsetravelbooks.com

ISBN: 1-59048-187-9

First published in 1959

CONTENTS

'. . . Those who have known a limitless freedom of spirit cannot efface from their souls this experience or deny its existence. FREE-DOM, with its own interior dialectic, THAT TRAGIC DESTINY which it bears within itself, is an experience of a particular order inherent in Christianity itself. A man who has achieved a definite victory over the seductive temptations of humanism, who has discovered the hollow unreality of the deification of man by man, can never hereafter abandon the liberty which has brought him to KNOW God, nor the definitive experience which has freed him from the power of evil . . . . Those whose religion is authoritarian and hereditary can never hope to understand those who have come by this way, through the tragedy immanent in their life's experience . . .

The suffering that has once been lived through cannot possibly be effaced. . . . The man who has travelled far in the realms of the spirit, and who has passed through great trials in the cause of his search for truth, will be formed spiritually along lines which must differ altogether from those pertaining to the man who has never shifted his position and to whom new spiritual territories are unknown. . . . I am enriched by my experience, even if it has been fearful and tormenting, even if, to cross the abyss which lay before me, I have been forced to address myself to powers other than human. . . . '

NICHOLAS BERDYAEV

PREFACE

For a proper appreciation of this book Appendix A (page 189) should be read first. It provides for those who have not read *God's Fool* and *Tibetan Journey* a background of the history of Tibet, what took Geoffrey Bull and me there, some of the personalities involved, and the reason for my hurried dash in 1950 across an unexplored part of Tibet to India. To have introduced all this in the course of the following narrative would have meant tedious digressions for explanations which would have interrupted the flow of events and exasperated the reader.

As I have already indicated, this book is the third in the series beginning with *God's Fool* and *Tibetan Journey*. *Up and Down Asia* was simply a bit of whimsical *divertissement*, written to please some friends and—dare I say it?—to gratify some enemies, who would then have some grounds for their accusations of irresponsibility and unorthodoxy. I promised after finishing *Up and Down Asia* to turn my hand to more serious writing again and with *Tragic Destiny* I resume my attacks on and challenge to my generation.

I launch this new book on its way with a quotation—with reservations which I hope I need not elaborate—from William Blake's *Jerusalem*.

> *Reader! . . . of books! . . . of heaven,*
> *And of that God. . . . . .*
> *Who in mysterious Sinai's awful cave*
> *To man the wondrous art of writing gave;*
> *Again he speaks in thunder and in fire!*
> *Thunder of Thought, and flames of fierce desire;*

9

Preface

Even from the depths of Hell his voice I hear
Within the unfathom'd caverns of my Ear.
Therefore I print; nor vain my types shall be;
Heaven, Earth and Hell shall live in harmony.

G.N.P.

Darjeeling
India

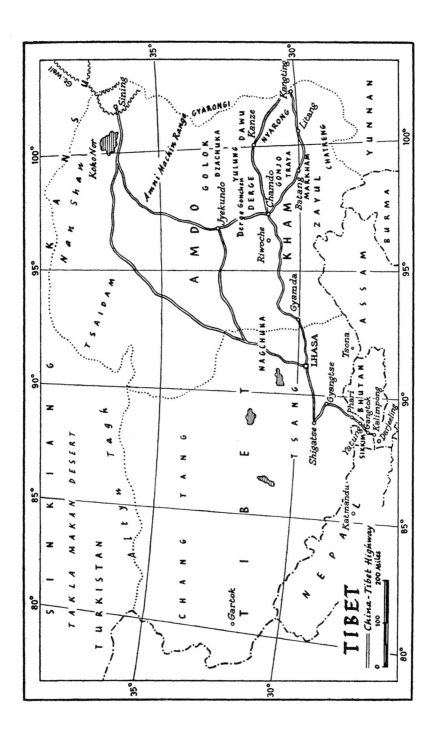

TIBET

China-Tibet Highway

0 100 200 Miles

Chapter One

AN URGENT MISSION

Calcutta, that hybrid monstrosity of architectonics, reared out of the heat-hazed ground like one of the creatures from India's own mythical Sea of Milk. The sun beating back from the white buildings and thousands of white-clothed people, together with the shimmering heat waves which blurred all outlines, increased the impression of milky unreality and over-spilling fecundity of the ancient legend.

In the golden age, the legend ran, Brahma, the creator god, presided over a conference of gods and demons to decide means of securing their immortality. It was finally decided that if they could complete the long and difficult journey to the Sea of Milk, the sixth of the seven which it was believed surrounded the world, in ever-widening circles and succeed in churning it they would obtain a liquor called *amrita* which conferred immortality on all who drank of it. When after many adventures they succeeded in accomplishing the churning of the sea by using a re-volving mountain 77,000 miles high and 77,000 miles deep, certain objects began to emerge from the milky ocean. The first to appear was the wonderful cow, Surabhi, then the goddess of wine, then the goddess of prosperity, Lakshmi, then Dhanwantari, the inventor of the Ayurvedic system of medicine; a horse, a moon, a wonderful gem, then countless millions of beautiful women.

Leaving aside for the moment the goddess of wine, the moon, the wonderful gem and the countless millions of beautiful women, it did not require too much effort of the imagination to span the mythical millennia and see the legend in modern Calcutta. The first impact on the mind was the ubiquitous cow, sauntering un-molested through the arcades sheltering fabulously stacked shops and luxurious hotels, streaming across the six-lane tarmaca-

damed road on to the grassy Maidan already widely covered
with hundreds of the creatures. The goddess of prosperity spilled
her goods in abundance in the shop windows from fashionable
Chowringhee to the smallest bazaar in this teeming city of three
million people. Even Dhanwantari, the physician of the gods, was
still present in the thousands of small chemists, homoeopathic
pharmacies, the Ayurvedic dispensaries, as prevalent as pubs in
England. The Sea of Milk that was India was still being churned
and was still producing delights for the sons of men while they
waited for their *amrita*.

I loved it. I loved the warm, fertile smell of it, like sleeping in
the Tibetan tents beside the young yak calves, or living on a
farm surrounded by prolific nature burgeoning everywhere. The
pulsation of life was almost as visible as the waves of heat, and
served the same purpose of blurring the obtrusive outlines of the
Western pseudo-oriental buildings and streams of gleaming cars,
modifying the first ugly impact and transforming it by some
subtle alchemy into a pleasurable stimulus instead.

Which was all very well, but I was supposed to be on a mission
to save Asia, and in the midst of this proliferating humanity and
abundant evidence of human ingenuity and administration I did
not know a soul. Even the friends with whom I was staying had
only been names to me and as missionaries could hardly be expected to put me in touch with the high authorities I required
urgently to influence the decisions of the Great Powers. What had
seemed natural, if somewhat dramatic, in the mountains of Tibet
now began to appear more than slightly ridiculous when faced
with the polite interest of a British official—if I ever got near to
him.

I moved along Chowringhee dispiritedly in the 100° heat, shirt
already sticking to my shoulders, towards the Office of the High
Commissioner for the United Kingdom. The Victoria Monument and Anglican Cathedral distracted my attention but did little
to lift my depression; if anything they increased it. An administration that could erect buildings like these was hardly likely to have
enough soul or imagination to accept my tale.

The Office of the High Commissioner for the United Kingdom

was all that the Office of the High Commissioner for the United Kingdom should be. As in the reading-room of a public library voices were muted and doors closed softly. Neatly-dressed men and women went quietly and dedicatedly about their business of consolidating Commonwealth solidarity. I don't know whether it was the influence of the Victoria Monument, the Cathedral, Chowringhee or the white blouses of the women and white shirts and trousers of the men in the office, or a heady mixture of the lot, but I found T. S. Eliot rising unbidden from my subconscious:

> *A Cry from the North, from the West and from the South*
> *Whence thousands travel daily to the timekept City;*
> *Where my Word is unspoken,*
> *In the land of lobelias and tennis flannels*
> *The rabbit shall burrow and the thorn revisit,*
> *The nettle shall flourish on the gravel court,*
> *And the wind shall say: 'Here were decent godless people:*
> *Their only monument the asphalt road*
> *And a thousand lost golf balls.'*[1]

I wondered idly if T. S. Eliot himself would have thought of these lines in these circumstances, but decided probably not. It was more likely that he would have said—I pulled myself up, dismissing T. S. Eliot, for the young woman at the 'Enquiry' desk was raising her eyebrows in a polite half-smile of interrogation. I walked across the echoing hall and sat down on the chair in front of her.

'I would like to see someone—the most important possible—about some information I have on Tibet,' I said politely, with an inward frown at my syntax.

'I beg your pardon.' The young woman looked puzzled, as well she might.

I tried again. 'I have some important information about Tibet —I have just arrived from there—and would like to see some highly placed official as soon as possible.'

'Just a minute, please,' she said with weary tolerance, striking a bell—and I suddenly remembered that I hadn't had a haircut for

[1] From *The Rock*, in *Collected Poems*, 1909-1935, Faber and Faber.

about a year, and a shave for nearly three. I stroked my beard contemplatively and thought that that wouldn't help matters any, either.

An elaborately-uniformed Indian stood at my shoulder and the young woman asked him to take this gentleman to see Mr. So-and-So. I crossed the hall to a door in the far corner and was shown into a spacious office where two men were sitting at a large desk. One of them pointed to a chair.

'Sit down. What can we do for you?' he said, not unkindly.

This was going to be worse than I had thought. I took a deep breath and tried again.

'I have just arrived in India from Tibet, and I have important information which I want to pass on to—to—whoever can do something about it,' I finished lamely. I had visions of myself repeating this theme with variations through every office in the building, through every building in the city, through every. . . .

'What sort of information?' the man asked.

'About China taking over Tibet, then Nepal, Sikkim and Bhutan, then India——' I stopped, as I saw the same look pass across the face of this presider over the dissolution of the Empire as had ruffled the surface of the young woman at the desk. He gave me a keen look for some moments, *à la Blackwood's*, then reached over to pick up the phone.

'I have someone here who says he has just come in from Tibet with important information,' he said when he had been given his connection. 'Would you like to see him? All right, I'll send him up right away.' He replaced the telephone and pressed a bell. Another uniformed attendant appeared, and after a few words of instruction to him he turned to me and said, 'If you follow the *chuprassi* he will take you to see someone who can handle this matter.'

We went upstairs and along corridors, and finally entered another, much larger and more impressive, office, with maps on all the walls. A young man, seated behind the huge desk, stood up and pointed to a chair in front of him.

'How d'you do. Have a seat. Smoke?'

'No, thanks.'

16

'Have some tea, then?'

'Thank you.'

'I hear you have just arrived from Tibet?'

'Yes, I arrived last night—or, at least, I arrived in Calcutta from Sadiya last night.'

'From Sadiya? That's rather an unusual way to arrive from Tibet, isn't it?'

'Yes, I came through in almost a straight line from near Batang in East Tibet as I wanted to get to India in a hurry.'

'Why was that? Just a minute, here's the tea. Do you take sugar and milk?'

'Milk and one of sugar, please.'

'Right. We're all set now. You were about to say why you were in a hurry to get to India?'

'Yes. It's a long story, but I'll give you the information I was asked to deliver first, and then fill in the background later. I have been moving about East Tibet for the best part of three years, latterly in the company of the man who is the accepted leader of the largest tribe in East Tibet, the Khambas. This man, Topgyay Pangdatshang, and his brother, Rapga, together with two leaders in the northern province of East Tibet, Amdo, were planning a revolution against the Tibetan Government in Lhasa when the rapid advance of the Chinese Communists in China forced them to postpone their plans. They took to the mountains so that the Chinese would find communicating with them difficult, and then waited to see what would happen in China. I and my friend, Geoffrey Bull, went with them at their invitation. After a bit, as they had anticipated, the Chinese Communists sent word to them to seek their co-operation. However, in one respect it was much bigger than they had anticipated, for the Chinese did not just make overtures to establish friendly relations but issued an ultimatum to them to the effect that they could either co-operate with them, the Chinese Communists, in their plans, or be annihilated in battle. For what they had in mind was not the usual new broom-sweeping of the former Chinese tactics but a plan for the "liberation" of the whole of Asia. First, Tibet would be taken over, then Nepal, Sikkim and Bhutan, then India, in a blue printed plan of

B   17

conquest taking one year, three years, and five years respectively. If the Tibetan leaders of East Tibet collaborated with them in this plan then they would share in the administration; if not, they would be ruthlessly annihilated, for the Chinese Communists would not allow anyone to stand in the way of their ambitions. In furthering their plans the four Tibetan leaders were to keep the revolutionary machinery they had already prepared, but instead of a partisan uprising against the Tibetan Government they would announce it as "an East Tibetan People's Revolution against the corrupt, reactionary Government in Lhasa". The Pangdatshangs reckoned that they could stall for six months in the mountains of Tibet before the Chinese became suspicious at not receiving a reply, and so they asked me to make for India by the shortest possible route to convey the information regarding the Chinese intentions to the outside Governments, and then get them to bring pressure to bear on the Chinese Communists to withdraw, or alert the Tibetan Government of the danger. If Britain or India want them to fight then I have to take back word immediately, before the six months are up. I made the journey to India in under two months, so I have four months left.'

I stopped. The young man was taking it very well, occasionally jotting down some notes, but otherwise following closely with no signs of tolerance or suspicion as exhibited by the others. No lobelias-and-tennis-flannel material here. I prepared to expatiate some more.

'Wait a bit.' He held up his hand. 'I'm afraid I haven't a clue about this area you mentioned. Do you mind pointing it out on the map? I'll be able to follow you a bit more intelligently then.' He pushed back his chair and led the way to a large map on the side wall taking in India, Tibet and China.

'Here is Kangting'—I pointed to a small town on the West China-East Tibet frontier—'where I have been more or less since 1947.'

'What were you doing there?' he interrupted.

'I was a missionary,' I replied.

'Which Mission?' he inquired.

'None. I was—independent, if you like. But that's another story.'

'All right. Go on. Sorry to interrupt.' He turned back to the map.

'Kangting is a frontier town where Tibetans and Chinese are about equally distributed. From Kangting westward the country is completely Tibetan in every way, and is known as Kham by the Tibetans and inhabited by Khambas, the most populous of all the Tibetan tribes and most warlike.'

'About how many would you say?' the official asked.

'No one knows. The figures quoted by various authorities for the whole of Tibet[1] vary from three to seven million, but I gathered from the Tibetans that they probably number four or five million. If this is correct, then the East Tibetans from the two provinces of Kham and Amdo probably number about three million, for they are supposed to account for two-thirds of the population of Tibet.'

'Which is Kham on the map, then?'

'Roughly where the Chinese have marked it "Sikang" from, say, the border of Yunnan and Burma, west of Szechuan, north to a line running through Kantze, De-ge and Chamdo. North of that again, to the Kokonor, is Amdo, or Tsinghai to the Chinese.'

'And where did you say you were?'

'Near Batang here. About three weeks' horse-riding journey west of Kangting. We were actually in the mountains about two days south-west of Batang.'

'And your trip through Tibet?'

'From near Batang here in almost a straight line through Markham Gartok, Draya Gompa, Rima, Denning to Sadiya—and from there to Calcutta by plane.'

'And where are the Chinese forces?'

'One spearhead is reported to have reached Jyekundo here, north-east of Chamdo; another is either in or near Kangting on the east; in the south, just before I left, it was reported that Likiang in Yunnan, here, had fallen to them.'

'Is there any special reason why they have stopped at these particular places?'

'Primarily, because each of them represents the end of Chinese-

[1] See footnote p. 188

19

occupied territory and from there on they face Tibetans; with the exception of Jyekundo where they are in Tibetan-occupied territory, but they had easy access to Jyekundo across indefensible plateaux. That introduces another reason why they have stopped in these particular places, because from where they are now the terrain is over 15,000 feet and very mountainous. Also, Rapga Pangdatshang maintains, and I think he is correct, that the Chinese do not want to fight over Tibet because it is too tricky a political issue. If they can win Tibet by using the Tibetans themselves this will suit them far better than launching a military campaign which could involve them with India and the United Nations.'

'If these Kham leaders—what do you call them? Pangdatshangs —are so sure of this, why didn't they get into touch with their Government right away and get them to appeal officially for help in keeping the Chinese out?' the official asked shrewdly.

'For several reasons. A knowledge of the background of the feudal politics in Tibet is necessary to understand the position fully, with the large official families in Lhasa, the capital, jockeying for power and suspicious of each other, waiting for one family to make some slip and then take over its wealth and influence. But there are other, more understandable, reasons. The Kham and Amdo leaders are known rebels and therefore *persona non grata* with the Government in Lhasa. Also, before the Chinese had moved towards Tibet, and while we were still in Kangting, they broadcast from Peking that they had made an agreement with the four leaders in East Tibet to form an "East Tibetan People's Government" and this effectively drove a wedge between these leaders and an already suspicious Lhasa Government—although this was before the Chinese had made any sort of approach to the Tibetan revolutionaries. Another factor, too, was that they were not prepared to risk their lives and the lives of their people for the devious whim of any Lhasa Government official, for, as I told you about the feudal politics, the Lhasa officials would not be above encouraging the Kham-Amdo leaders to fight the Chinese in order just to see their power and wealth diminished to suit themselves.'

'I can see the force of that reasoning, even if it is all rather confusing,' the official smiled ruefully. 'So they sent you out to see what you could do from this side?'

'Yes, Topgyay Pangdatshang could not come because he is the leader of the Khambas and must remain to lead any fighting. Rapga could not come because he has been expelled from India for his political activities and he was afraid he might be put in jail if he returned without permission. I was the only one who could attempt it on their behalf. It was no use going by Lhasa, for in addition to perhaps not being able to influence the Tibetan Government in any way, it would have taken about three months to get there, and then another month almost to get from there to India, which would have left no time to get word back to Pangdatshang before the Chinese ultimatum expired. Hence the mad dash through that unexplored part of Tibet to get to India in time.'

The official turned away from the map, frowning slightly. 'Of course, you know that we no longer have any influence in Tibet since Independence? It is now India's pigeon, and while we might be able to tender some sort of advice, we are not in a position to do more. That is—to put it quite bluntly—even if your story is believed.' He smiled to take the sting out of his words. 'For quite apart from the general ignorance about Tibet, it seems incredible that the Chinese should contemplate taking on any more than they already have in China. Yet according to your friends they are talking about Tibet, Nepal, Sikkim, Bhutan and even India.'

'It is a bit staggering,' I conceded, 'but they are quite serious about it.'

'Don't mistake me,' the official stressed. 'I don't want you to think that I don't accept your story—even if it is a bit out of my usual daily grind. But I can envisage the reception it will get before it goes very far among our own people—and it still has to convince the Indians. I just don't want to raise your hopes. Have you spoken to anyone else?'

'No—I arrived about nine o'clock last night, bathed, ate and went to bed, and came straight here this morning.'

'Well, I had better arrange for you to meet some of the Indian authorities as soon as possible,' the official said, leaning over to pick up one of the telephones. 'You don't mind, do you? I think it will be better all round.'

'Not at all,' I agreed. 'I am here to get what help I can from whatever source. When I've done all I can in Calcutta I want to go to Kalimpong and if there are any Tibetan officials there get them to pass on the information to their Government in Lhasa.'

The official got in touch with several people on the telephone and then laid it back on its rest. 'I have made arrangements for you to meet one of the top Security officials in Calcutta tomorrow morning. When you have finished with him, perhaps you would get into touch with me again and we'll fix another meeting when I can write down some of the information so that I can pass it on to Delhi and London. After that we'll see what happens. I wonder' —he thought for a moment. 'The Americans have nothing to do with Tibet, but as this news is likely to affect them maybe you ought to get in touch with them—unofficially, of course; what do you think?'

'The more the better as far as I'm concerned,' I replied. 'I know little or nothing about politics, and I am only doing this because I believed God commanded me to do it. I am not interested in imperialism, Communism, neutralism, or American-way-of-life-ism.'

'Are you doing anything tomorrow night?' I shook my head. 'Well, I think I'll get one of the American officials along for a meal and you can tell him your story and then he can take it up from there if he wants to. I think that's about all I can do for you at the moment.' He smiled apologetically.

'Thank you very much,' I hastened to assure him. 'I didn't expect to get so far so quickly. When I arrived here I didn't know who to see or how to go about seeing anyone. At least things are moving in the right direction.'

The official stood up. 'By the way, my name's Anderson—David Anderson. What's yours?'

'Patterson—George Patterson,' I replied.

'Right you are then, Patterson.' He held out his hand. 'I'll be hearing from you tomorrow and we'll fix up another meeting, and a meal. I'd like to hear more of your experiences, quite apart from the political side. Can you find your own way out? Left, right, and down the stairs. Bye for now.'

'Bye—and thanks again.' I smiled and closed the door.

I covered the same ground with the Indian Security official, and more, filling in the history of the various people involved, the character of the country in East Tibet and my route to India.[1] The latter especially was of interest, covering as it did a hitherto unknown and more direct route to the Indian border which, if my account of the proposed Chinese attack on Tibet was true, would bring the Chinese Communists right on to the Indian border in North Assam, an unexpected danger.

The Americans were interested but, as the British official had said, not in a position to do anything even if they had wanted to. Their link with China had been broken when Chiang Kai-shek's Nationalist Party fell, and they had no previous contact with Tibet which would have provided them with an opening for a more direct interest.

Having provided all the necessary information to the British, Indian and American officials, I decided that it was now time to make for Kalimpong to see whatever Tibetan official might be there, who in turn would be able to pass on the news to Lhasa. Also I had letters for the oldest Pangdatshang brother, Yangpel, and for the Pangdatshang manager in Kalimpong, and I had asked that all letters and money which had accumulated over the past year and more should be sent to me there. I had to arrange for fresh supplies of food and medicine to be bought in India and delivered to a Pangdatshang caravan in Kalimpong and sent in this way to our headquarters in the mountains of East Tibet. Medicines especially were essential, for my supplies had run low and if there was to be fighting the medicines would have to be there before the Chinese attacked in only four months from now, and it took a caravan approximately five months to reach the other side of Tibet from Kalimpong.

[1] See *God's Fool* and *Tibetan Journey*.

An Urgent Mission

Loshay, my Tibetan servant, was relieved that we were leaving Calcutta so soon. Not all the novelty that it presented to him, as a nomad from the wilds of Central Asia, could drag him away from under the fan during the day. He had gone out on the first day after our arrival and after a few minutes of the 100° heat and over 90° humidity he had become quite dizzy and breathless. He was a product of 15,000 feet heights, of snows and vast distances and an untainted invigorating air, and only a Calcutta after sunset could interest him.

His powerful figure, draped in the folds of a maroon Tibetan gown, hitched up at the waist to kilt length with a colourful girdle and swinging sword, drew the stares of the perambulating evening crowds, but after a beard and hair trim and general tailoring I faded into the masses.

We had left Bo, in East Tibet, on January 17th and by doing double and treble stages on the way had managed to arrive in Calcutta by March 7th. Within a week in Calcutta I had seen all the officials necessary to set the wheels in motion if anything was to be done for Tibet, and on the 14th Loshay and I quietly slipped away to Kalimpong.

We travelled the 400 miles to Siliguri, the railhead in North Bengal serving Kalimpong and Darjeeling, and in Siliguri we hired a car to take us the forty miles to Kalimpong. The road ran out of Siliguri, across a flat plain, for almost ten miles, then entered the foot-hills of the mighty Himalayas. Far above, the eternally snow-covered Kanchenjunga provided an unparalleled backdrop to an exciting play of ever-changing greens and yellows and browns. The road curved and climbed between thick forests, laced by yellow sunshine across which exotically coloured butterflies dipped and twisted, and sometimes along the face of a mountain above the green and rapid-frothed River Teesta far below. Well up the Teesta Valley an elegant bridge spanned the river, and crossing it the road tilted into an even steeper gradient and snaked its way across the face of the mountain in ten miles of acute bends to Kalimpong.

Kalimpong was situated on the saddle of a ridge, between two mountains, 4,000 feet above the sea. It sprawled lazily from thatched mud *bustees* beginning at about the seventh mile on the road from the Teesta Bridge, across the face of the mountain, and gradually progressed through wood-plaster and corrugated-iron to brick-and-concrete houses and shops. The shopping centre was situated between the ninth and tenth miles—Kalimpong districts taking their delineation from the milestones on the road from the Teesta Bridge—and from the tenth to twelfth miles the two-storied, corrugated roofs of the Tibetan caravanserais took over, before petering away into the thatched *bustees* again. Rising sharply behind the town for another 1,000 feet or so was the Deolo hill on which the church tower and spire of the Scots Mission and Hospital stood out, and disappearing into the distance beyond, the houses and other buildings of Dr. Graham's Homes for Anglo-Indian Children.

I had instructed the taxi-driver to take us straight to Pangdatshang's house (both Rapga and Yangpel had houses in Kalimpong) but he had to stop and ask his way several times. It was to Yangpel's house that we were finally directed in the eleventh-mile district. As we passed through the Tibetan caravanserais, with their milling pack-mules and powerful muleteers, I felt the slow surge of excitement rising up in me again at the thought of the height and distance and majesty and danger that was Tibet, and decided that two months in 'civilization' would be more than enough for me.

The car turned off the main road and after a few hundred yards stopped at a long, oblong building below a large modern house set in a beautiful garden. A Tibetan in European clothing came out of the oblong building and introduced himself as Pangdatshang's manager, Pasang Tenpa. The oblong building was the office, and the house above was Yangpel Pangdatshang's. I introduced myself, handing over the letters from Topgyay and Rapga I had ready, and asked if he would make the necessary arrangements for my stay in Kalimpong.

He glanced quickly at the letters and then invited me into the office while he outlined the situation. It appeared that he had rented Rapga's house to a high Tibetan official who was in Kalimpong at the time, and Yangpel's house was not ready to be occupied. He had stored furniture, rolled up carpets, and sent the servants away because no one was expected. Did I expect to be long in Kalimpong?

No, I told him, a few weeks to recover from the effects of my rapid journey across Tibet and to fix up arrangements for supplies to be sent through him to Kham, see some Tibetan officials and then return to Calcutta for further discussions with officials about the Tibetan situation. I hoped to be away from Kalimpong within a month and India within two months, for I had to be back in Kham before July. That meant leaving India before the rains broke in late May or early June, carried the bridges away in the upper foothills and so stopped my return.

He thought for a few moments and then suggested that I could either stay at the Himalayan Hotel in the town, or go to Dr. Graham's Homes where there was a large European community; he knew both the owner of the hotel and the headmaster of the Homes' school and could fix me up in either place. I opted for the Homes, and after a few minutes' conversation on the phone Pasang Tenpa informed me that Mr. Lloyd, the headmaster, would be delighted to have me as his guest during my visit to Kalimpong.

Before I left Pasang Tenpa I arranged with him to fix an appointment for me with the highest-ranking Tibetan official in Kalimpong. He informed me that that would not be difficult as the highest-ranking official was the one who was living in Rapga's house, Kungo Shakabpa, a 'Tsi-bon' or Minister of Finance, who was the leader of a Tibetan trade delegation on its way to China.

I met Mr. Shakabpa a few days later. As my Tibetan was the Kham dialect, Pasang Tenpa had provided me with an interpreter, a friend of Rapga's, who could be trusted not to divulge what was said. Mr. Shakabpa was a slim, middle-aged Tibetan of average height, with all the charming courtesy so often found amongst the high Tibetan officials. He had been a member of the Trade Delegation which had gone to America and Europe in 1947, in spite of strenuous protests from Chiang Kai-shek's Nationalist Government, in order to try and awaken Western interest in Tibet and expand Tibetan trade. Constant pressure from Chinese representatives in America, Britain and France and elsewhere frustrated them all the way and they accomplished little. Mr. Shakabpa knew a little English but most of the time we talked through the interpreter.

He knew Rapga, had met him in China when the Trade Delegation had passed through, and had also met Topgyay who had come to Nanking to meet his brother Yangpel, who was also a member of the trade delegation, for the first time in nearly twenty years. Rapga was a great patriot and he had given them good advice when the delegation was in Nanking. But underneath the polite interest I could detect a thread of disbelief, an amused tolerance of the foreigner who had permitted himself to be used as a pawn by the astute Kham leaders to further their own interests in Tibet. But he promised sincerely enough to pass on the information about the situation in East Tibet and the proposed Chinese Communist attack to the Tibetan Government in Lhasa. We had tea, and spoke about my travels in Tibet, and after compliments on both sides I left.

I could do no more. I had bowed to the command from God to leave the mountains of East Tibet to carry the news of China's intentions to the outside world. I had seen British, Indian, American and Tibetan officials and laid everything before them, and now the rest was up to God. I was no pawn of the Pangdatshangs, nor tool of any Government, but a servant of the living God. My destiny in His purpose was linked with this land of Tibet with its feuding, fascinating people, its limitless distances and unscalable peaks, its bewildering mixture of fighting priests, feudal politics and myth-entangled history. Like other servants of other times in other countries I could say with Moses, 'I am not an eloquent man,' and be silent as God said, 'Who made man's mouth? Or who maketh a man dumb, or deaf, or seeing, or blind? Is it not I the Lord?'; or like Gideon saying, 'Wherewith shall I save Israel? My family is the poorest in Israel, and I am the least in my father's house,' and hear God say, 'Go in this thy might; have not I sent thee?'; or like David listening to his brother's accusation, 'Why hast thou come? And with whom hast thou left these few sheep in the wilderness? I know thy pride,' and remember David's simple reply, 'Is there not a cause? The Lord will deliver me.'

What more could anyone ask in a generation of hollow men with tired voices? I grinned. T. S. Eliot again. These Penguin books were a godsend to the peripatetic. I grinned even more as another stanza came to mind:

> *When your fathers fixed the place of* GOD,
> *And settled all the inconvenient saints,*
> *Apostles, martyrs, in a kind of Whipsnade,*
> *Then they could set about imperial expansion*
> *Accompanied by industrial development.*
> *Exporting iron, coal and cotton goods*
> *And intellectual enlightenment*
> *And everything, including capital*
> *And several versions of the Word of God:*
> *The British race assured of a mission*
> *Performed it, but left much at home unsure.*[1]

Apposite. Quite a prophet, dry, sardonic, perspicacious. I returned refreshed to the problem of Tibet.

---

[1] From *The Rock*, in *Collected Poems*, 1909–1935, Faber and Faber.

Chapter Two

THE OFFICIALS WERE NOT
CONVINCED

Letters, letters, letters. All the mail Geoff and I had not received during the past year in the wilds of Tibet had been accumulating in India for us. Small gifts and large slowly mounted up until they totalled nearly £1,000. This sum exceeded the amount that we had drawn from Topgyay Pangdatshang during our travels with him in Kham and so our expectation that God would supply all that was necessary to meet our growing debt with Topgyay when the time came to settle was more than fulfilled, and I was able to pay Pasang Tenpa, his manager in Kalimpong, in full. The remainder I set aside to buy supplies of tinned food and medicines to take back to Kham with me on my return. In the meantime problems of a different kind were accumulating for my attention.[1]

My spectacular arrival from East Tibet had coincided with a sudden interest of certain newspapers in this area and I was inundated with requests from reporters for information about the situation in Tibet, particularly in the East, as well as an account of my journey through the formerly unexplored territory I had crossed on my way to India. I had been asked by the powers-that-be not to say anything of political or military significance to the representatives of the press, so the interviews were taken up with a great deal of verbal fencing and the unsporting but politic, 'No comment.' The finished articles in some of the popular papers, liberally padded through the efforts of the reporters' own imagination, were an enlightenment—if not to the millions of readers, at least to me.

[1] See *God's Fool.*

29

The Officials Were Not Convinced

Whether it was the publicity, or a natural concern, or a combination of both, I do not know, but I began to receive letters from friends who spoke of other friends and relatives who were concerned that I should be in India and Geoff in East Tibet; some bluntly accused me of having deserted him, of having broken up a promising partnership for dubious—implied but never spoken —reasons of my own. Even Geoff's letter which I had brought with me and sent home stating quite clearly, 'the Lord has left us in no doubt as to the division of labour at this point' did nothing to suppress the impression of desertion widely held in Christian circles. It was distressing, unfortunate, and unavoidable—except of course, by the exercise of the more apparent Christian virtues extolled in the New Testament Epistles, but as these seemed to be held more in theory than applied nothing could be done to help the situation. In spite of what some good friends said I did not see that it was something to be unduly concerned about, and contended that it would die a natural death when I returned to Kham in about a month's time.

I had already been in India for five weeks, and in Kalimpong for a month of that time, and apart from a slight sickness and diarrhoea had almost completely recovered from the effects of the gruelling dash across Tibet. I had had no definite word from the Indian, Tibetan, British or American Governments about what they were going to do—if anything—about the Chinese Communist danger in Tibet, but the time I had allowed myself for staying in India was running out.

The Pangdatshangs had estimated that the Chinese would attack in about six months, and that had been in January before I left on my trip across Tibet to India. I had been able to do the journey in two months and that left me two months for all the talks, and buying of supplies, in India, before attempting the two months' trip back again. Another factor demanding urgency was the monsoons which usually broke in late May or early June and carried away the light bamboo structures which were used as bridges over the rivers bisecting the trail at various points on the journey. It was now mid-April and time to begin preparations for return.

The Officials Were Not Convinced

Calcutta had a temperature of 105° when I arrived back there. As I went from one interview to another I showered and changed four or five times a day. In addition to the official meetings I had to find time to write out a report on the missionary situation on the Tibetan border for the Brethren Council in Bath, England, and as I held some strong views on this it ran to 35 pages.

Shakabpa, the leader of the Tibetan trade delegation, had also come to Calcutta and I met with him several times to discuss the situation in East Tibet in more detail. While he obviously did not believe my prophecies of doom he was also obviously uneasy at the unknown possibilities the situation afforded. If the Pangdatshangs were powerful enough for the Chinese to want to use them, or even make overtures to them, they were too powerful for Shakabpa's, or the Lhasa Government's, peace of mind. There was too much armed force, too much wealth, too much population, too much anti-Lhasa feeling concentrated in Kham and Amdo to disregard all that was going on there.

It was even more difficult to convince the officials of the other Governments. The Communists still had not consolidated their position in China yet I was asking them to believe that the Communists were about to attack Tibet. Was I certain of my information? Was I sure that the Pangdatshangs and others were not just using me for some local purpose of their own? After all. . . .

The iron entered into my soul. I ought to have known that it was a hopeless venture from the beginning. I had had enough experience of officials and government departments and policies to ensure an adequate cynicism against being believed, let alone being given help. Yet I reminded myself that it was not because I had any great faith in the machinery of democracy or the mental equipment of politicians or minor officials that I had come to India but because I had faith that God was above the machinations of men and could manipulate them to accomplish His purpose, and He had sent me. But maybe I had been mistaken about that. At this distance in time and space, the clarity with which I had heard that voice four months ago in the silence of a remote valley in East Tibet dimmed considerably in the sophisticated surroundings and bureaucratic processes of a civilized democracy. Perhaps I had been too long away from home, or living at a too intense spiritual level, or moving in a too restricted evangelical environment, or. . . .

I applied to the Indian Government for the necessary permits to return to Tibet. I could do no more in India and I wanted to be back in Kham with sufficient medical supplies before the Chinese attacked, and it was now mid-May. It appeared as if I had thrown away everything of a satisfying spiritual experience that I had gained over a period of ten years in a gamble of faith that had involved participation in a politics that I had always held in mildly ridiculed contempt. All I could do now was to return to Tibet and help bind up the wounded Tibetans who would fall in the Chinese attack.

On May 13th I received word that I could apply to Sadiya for my return Frontier Permit, and on the 16th I sent off a cable to my parents to say that I was making final preparations to return to Tibet on May 24th. On the 18th I was asked to go to New Delhi for further interviews on the news I had brought from East Tibet about Chinese Communist intentions and on the 19th I left for New Delhi by plane.

New Delhi had a temperature of 110° when I arrived and I had a series of blackouts while I was there, probably brought on by the heat after the high altitudes of Tibet for three years, which complicated matters a little.

Just before leaving Calcutta I had been introduced at a luncheon to the daughter and son-in-law of the Indian Ambassador to China, Sardar K. M. Pannikar. As Britain only had a chargé d'affaires in Peking who was only allowed to meet a Third or Fourth Secretary of the new Communist Government, and America had no diplomatic representative at all, it was left to India to find out through her Ambassador in Peking, Sardar Pannikar, just how much of the information I had brought was likely to be true. Pannikar sent word to Delhi that it was nonsense. The Chinese Communists had inherited an economically ruined country from Chiang Kai-shek's Kuomingtang misrule and would have enough to keep them occupied in China for the next ten to twenty years. Any movement of troops on the borders of West

China was only to safeguard China's frontiers against Western aggression. Poor Pannikar! He was about to be made to swallow his analyses, not only in Tibet but in Korea as well. I have never discovered who the 'Western aggressors' were whom he and the Chinese Communists feared and were preparing to defend themselves against on the West China border. At the very most there were only five Europeans between India and the West China border—which left India as the only possible aggressor in sight.

However, it was only natural that Pannikar's opinion should be accepted and mine, howbeit courteously, dismissed. I made preparations to leave Delhi but before I could do so I was sent for urgently to meet the American Ambassador, Lou Henderson. It transpired that the American Embassy had just received word from the Lhasa Government that the American Vice-Consul and his party had fled from Urumchi, in Sinkiang, and on reaching the Tibetan border had been fired on by a company of Tibetan soldiers. One had been killed and some were wounded. The Ambassador wanted to know if I would form and lead an expedition to the northern borders of Tibet to rescue the wounded survivors.

I agreed immediately, on condition that I be allowed to leave the expedition in Lhasa on the return journey, instead of coming on to India, and proceed from Lhasa to Kham as I had already planned. Two vice-consuls were appointed to accompany the expedition and I drew up a list of supplies that we would require and which we could buy in Delhi. The remainder could be bought in Calcutta and Kalimpong. It was a difficult expedition to outfit, for in addition to not knowing how many wounded there might be, or what their injuries were, the territory north of Lhasa on the Sinkiang border was completely unexplored.

We left for Calcutta on June 1st to be met there with the news that a wireless message had been received from Lhasa requesting that no expedition be sent. It appeared that the Tibetan Government already held America responsible for the present Chinese Communist suspicions and intentions, due to the unfortunate visit of Lowell Thomas to Tibet in 1949.[1] 'Unfortunate' in the

[1] See *Out of This World*.

sense that there seemed to be misunderstandings on both sides. Lowell Thomas claimed he received an unexpected and surprising invitation to Tibet from the Tibetan trade delegation when they visited America in 1948. On the other hand, the Tibetan Government maintained that he had led the delegation to believe that he had certain official influence and that if he were given permission to go to Tibet to discuss their problems he could take the matter up with the American Government. It was on this understanding that he had been given permission to visit Tibet and been given such an unprecedented official reception. When, on arrival in Lhasa, he had decried any 'official' status or influence, the Tibetan Government had not only been disillusioned with American intentions, suspecting that Thomas's plea of inability was only a cunning political move on America's part, but had also been afraid of the Chinese Communists' interpretation of it as an attempt to establish anti-Communist relations with America. Now, even although the present expedition was obviously a 'mercy' one, they were afraid that the Chinese would use it as an excuse to launch an attack against Tibet. Would we please remain in India and they would bring the wounded to the Indian border and deliver them to the proper authorities there?

There was nothing else that could be done. Disappointed, we cancelled the expedition and the next day I left Calcutta for Kalimpong. It was now June 6th, and dangerously near the six months' time limit I had been given on leaving East Tibet in mid-January, but still the monsoons had not broken and there was a chance that I might get back to Kham in time. I had already sent off the food and medical supplies to be taken by Pangdatshang's mule caravan on the long northern route, and I intended taking the south-east route I had blazed myself earlier in the year, which could be covered in two to three months.

I sent a wire to the Tibetan Assistant-Political Officer in Sadiya, my jumping-off point in North Assam, to hire several Tibetan porters to carry my loads the first 18 days until I got to a place where I could hire horses. Then I left for Kalimpong, where Loshay had remained with our kit, to wind up arrangements.

On Saturday, June 13th, the rains started, and continued in a steadily increasing downpour throughout the night and into Sunday. By Sunday night and through Monday it was falling in such sheets that it was almost impossible to breathe when one attempted to go out into it. The rainfall gauge showed that 43 inches had fallen in 48 hours. On Tuesday the cyclone eased and gradually settled down to the normal showers and drizzle, but the damage had been done. In Kalimpong alone there were 23 dead, and over 400 casualties. Darjeeling had 163 dead and over 1,000 casualties. Houses, roads, cattle, power stations, bridges, railway lines, reservoirs, had been swept away in the landslides throughout the mountains, and we were cut off from the plains by sheer slopes of quivering mud which every few minutes roared down thousands of feet into the raging River Teesta to cause another blockage and then another murderous break-through. The Kalimpong-Siliguri road was down in thirty-one places; at one point ten miles of it had completely disappeared. There was only one week's supply of food left in Kalimpong, and aeroplanes circled overhead to see if it were possible to air-drop supplies, but poor visibility and continuous rain frustrated their attempts.

A few days later I received a telegram from the Assistant Political Officer in Sadiya to say that all Tibetans had returned to Tibet before the rains broke and there were none available and would not be until the end of the year again. And that, as John of nursery days was reputed to have said, was that.

Chapter Three

A REPORT FROM GEOFF

I had come to Kalimpong for a week or two, a month at the most, and it now looked as if I were going to be forced to remain for very much longer. When I discussed the possibility with Mr. Lloyd, the headmaster, he insisted that I stay on in the house with him. His wife was in Britain with the children, and he would be delighted to have my company in the house.

Another guest had arrived just before the cyclone struck, but the house was large and the servants plenty. The new guest was a Dr. Carsun Chang, a political refugee from Communist China. He had been leader of the Social Democrat Party in China, a scholar and statesman of note, and a delegate to the United Nations, but on China being overrun by the Communists he had left for Hong Kong, and then at the invitation of the Indian Government he had come to India to give a series of lectures on political science in Indian universities. These he had completed and he was in Kalimpong to work on a book describing the rise of Communism in China and the need for a party that was neither Communist nor Nationalist, a Third Force.[1]

Right from the start we became firm friends. Dr. Chang was not only interested in politics but also in religion, particularly Buddhism and Christianity, and our interests coincided in Tibet. In recent discussions with politicians in Asia he had been advocating a pan-Buddhistic federation to include Tibet, Nepal, Sikkim, Bhutan, Burma and other Buddhist countries of South-East Asia as a bulwark against further Communist expansion. As a theory I contended that it was unrealistic, and that what Buddhism had not been able to do in China it was hardly likely to accomplish in these other countries. In addition, there wasn't time, and I out-

[1] See *The Third Force* by Dr. Carsun Chang.

lined to him what I knew of Chinese Communists' intentions in Tibet in the immediate future. He revised his opinions in the light of this new knowledge and set about using what influence he had to awaken recognition of the danger to India and the East.

With this in mind Mr. Lloyd invited Shakabpa to tea and we had a long discussion on the subject. Dr. Chang was a more formidable protagonist than I but Shakabpa was more committed than he had been two months previously when I had met him for the first time. Although still leader of the Tibetan trade delegation to India he was now under instructions to proceed to China for exploratory talks with the new Communist Government in Peking. At the same time he had been 'discouraged' from proceeding there right away by authorities in India until the situation clarified itself a bit more, so his earlier confusion was worse confounded.

He asked if two members of his delegation, Shudrun and Dreyul, might be allowed to remain with Mr. Lloyd to study English, so our household increased to four male members and I used the opportunity to study Lhasa Tibetan, my own dialect being the Kham dialect of East Tibet. It was also an excellent opportunity to fill in the blanks in our political knowledge of Lhasa.

I opened up negotiations with the Tibetan Government regarding a probable return to Kham via Lhasa, although in view of what they felt about Lowell Thomas and our earlier expedition I did not have much hope. But I left for Calcutta to collect supplies and see the authorities anyway. I had to walk for fifteen miles across landslides, treacherous with oozy mud, before the road became firm enough to carry cars. None of the authorities in Calcutta held out much hope and they were not too happy about my return to Kham in the circumstances, either—which seemed a bit strange in the light of their belief that the Chinese weren't going to attack Tibet anyway.

When I returned to Kalimpong rumours were filtering through Tibet that the Communists had occupied Kangting and Kantze in Kham, which meant that the northern arm of their forces was closing in on the Pangdatshangs—and Geoff.

On July 27th I had two letters from Geoff. They were brought to me by Pasang Tenpa. The two letters contained recent news for he had written one on April 13th and the other on May 4th, but the third envelope contained no news, since at the time of writing it he had not known where I was or whether I was on my way back, but was addressed 'To Whom It May Concern'. This envelope contained three pages of symptoms relating to Topgyay Pangdatshang's wife who was critically ill and he did not know what to do. With no medical help nearer than the Chinese Communists Topgyay had sent the letter by relays of special riders who had brought it across the northern route to Lhasa and on to India in five weeks instead of the usual five months, and they were all waiting at the various points on the way to carry the medicines back. The special messengers had caught up on the slower caravan which had been bringing the other letters, and brought them on as well.

The first was from Batang:

Dear Brother George,

Greetings from this lonely valley in Jesus' Name—Lord of all. Just about two weeks ago I was sitting in our new room—now fully fitted up as a dispensary, study, bedroom, and little 'gospel' room—when up the path leading to our 'cabin' came that 'great' figure known to us so well, our beloved brother John Ting. Brother Tien came in later—what a reunion! . . .

Politically and militarily things are as follows: After about 2½ months of Communist occupation Kuomingtang troops swept down from the north and recaptured Kangting. The New Year had been gloomy but the entrance of the Kuomingtang troops called forth full celebrations. Reported figures range from 300–3,000 troops having arrived. The Secret Societies were holding Tienchuan, although the Reds had burned half the city, and Sichang was still held by the Kuomingtang. Liu Wen Huie, the Governor, turned over Sikang to the Reds, but they gave him no quarter. He has lost everything and is reported to be like a madman. At this point it looked as if West China might be held. In a few days, however, 1,000 mounted Communist troops from Tsinghai swept the Kuomingtang from the Kangting area. Then

the Red Army burst through on Tienchuan—Sichang fell—and
that was that. The Red Flag with the five yellow stars (under
which I am at present residing!) was planted firmly in West
China. In the few days that the Kuomingtang occupied Kangting
John and Tien slipped out with a caravan and made Bo safely in
21 days.

Then we had a great fire. Five households and Topgyay's meat
storage place were burned to the ground before a hurricane of a
gale. The lamas had been performing some ceremony below the
dwellings and had lit a fire. It was said that a spark from this set a
hayrick on fire, and this was all that was needed. The Pangdatshang lama may be clever, but the murmurings of the people are
sufficient indication that whatever he does now his reputation has
gone for good as far as the religious side of his profession goes.
Two women were nearly burned to death. Burnt flesh, brother!
—it was horrible—like some nightmare. God kept me cool. Both
lived. Soda bic., burn ointment, methyl violet, tannic jelly—all
served their purpose. One woman was not too bad—comparatively speaking, of course—the other woman, I fought for her
life for ten days. Her entire face, ears, a considerable area of her
back, both arms and wrists, just one awful mess. I thought she
might lose one arm completely but I dare not attempt amputation,
I just haven't the experience to know what can be healed and
what can't.

Topgyay has a plan for our house and has chosen a different
site, but more practical and very good. While I am in Batang he
plans to make a start on it. I tried to make him think modestly,
but, to your dismay, you may find some great edifice on your
return! Don't blame me!!

The grey horse I ride everywhere now. With others he still
seems to hold his reputation for fierceness but with me he goes
along nicely. Still quite a few of Topgyay's men won't ride him.
I made the thing a matter of prayer—(don't you laugh, either!!!)
—and really, considering how I was so hopeless and frightened it
is wonderful how God has helped me to learn to ride. A few weeks
before the New Year races he was quite ill but Topgyay said it
would be all right to race him. He lost by about four feet, and

Juga said that he definitely was not up to his former standard. The amusing thing about the whole affair was that no one would believe the grey was beaten fairly—even Topgyay's reputation could not stand beside the grey's and some even suggested that it might have been a put-up job! I myself don't think Topgyay would be bothered, but some hold it, and here in Batang the people collect just to stand and look at it.

Till we meet again,
GEOFF.

The second letter was from Bo, dated May 6th:

Dear George,

I am writing this only half-expecting you to get it. A messenger is leaving here, probably tomorrow or the day after, for Lhasa. He is expected to be in Lhasa in 30 days, so if you are still in Kalimpong you may get this in 1½ months. . . .

Rapga, being the brilliant man he is, and with the very highest interests of his country's complete independence at heart, will compromise no principle and endanger no enterprise by haste or impatience. He has just been reading Marx's *Dialectical Materialism* but, while interested from the point of view of philosophical discussion, he nevertheless repudiates and rejects completely the Communist system. Co-operation with the Chinese, in any form, is obviously repulsive to him and he feels that such a policy must eventually result only in Tibetan extinction. Nevertheless, at the critical time he still waits—events are not a necessary compulsion to him, it seems.

Topgyay is not enjoying good health, and his wife is suffering, almost certainly, from T.B. Together with his kiddies he would gladly, I think, at this juncture lay down everything—as a man who has fought and dabbled in many things, but now has the opportunity of living quietly in comfort in a peaceful valley where he is loved and respected by the local people. Nevertheless, without asking him or approaching him the Chinese Communists have announced some big position for him in connection with the provisional puppet government in Sikang. This mildly amuses him, of course, but no positive action as far as I know has been taken by him to accept such a position. Rather did he suggest to the Reds that as he knew so little Chinese, and also that there were men like Gesang Yeshi about, it would be much better to invite the latter. He declined to go to Kangting on the grounds of his wife's illness, and so he backs down, but how long the Reds will let him I don't know. . . .

Red troops, so far, are not reported west of Kangting except on the Kantze road. Batang flies the Red Flag, but all is peaceful there, being a kind of balance of power below the surface which holds things in check until the Communist forces arrive. The powerful lamaseries and the older element stand opposed by the students. . . .

It would be wonderful if we could meet inside Tibet, which would be a great climax, and no doubt a real seal from the Lord on our separate work in our single mission. I remember you much in prayer. Here I feel somewhat pressed in spirit, at times— but not depressed! and our God is sufficient and shall perform all things for us. . . .

While we were in Batang an urgent note came asking Hsaio, the Christian dispensary worker, and myself to come to Bo, at once if possible, as Mrs. Topgyay was in a desperate condition. On arrival in Bo she was a little better—Topgyay, absolutely desperate, had managed to break into our place and get things together and inject penicillin. I admire his pluck, don't you? I think she had pneumonia. We continued the pencillin injections night and day for a week and the temperature kept roughly between 100°–101°, then put her on to Buffer penicillin, brought from Batang, with the dose eventually reduced. Now, after three weeks, she is far from well, and terribly weak, with a constant temperature of 100°–101° rising in the afternoon. Hsaio is really in charge, so I don't say much, being more or less ignorant, but when she tried to browbeat him over the penicillin dosage suggested I laid down the law more in Pattersonian style than in Bovine, with the result that though she cried she submitted. . . .

Better bring in fresh supplies of all sulpha drugs as gonorrhoea, septic conditions, high fevers and dysentery have made inroads into our stocks. We still have plenty, but a fresh supply for future needs is required.

I have received your note from Walong on the India border. Praise God for your safe arrival.

Till we meet again,
GEOFF.

The third envelope contained only the list of symptoms, three pages of them, together with a rough temperature chart which Geoff had drawn up, and the list of symptoms added up to what to my amateur medical knowledge was obviously like tuberculosis. I had come across very little T.B. in Tibet, but where Tibetans had picked it up in visits to India or China they usually only lived for three or four months afterwards. If Mrs. Topgyay had picked up the disease in China it was now about nine months since she had been there and her condition was critical. To make matters worse for her she was a diabetic and I had been giving her daily injections of insulin all the time I was with her in Kham. Obviously, Topgyay had very little faith in Chinese doctors, and not wishing to place himself in the hands of the Communists had risked sending to India for medicines which might save her life.

I left immediately for Calcutta to consult with leading specialists there, and had my own diagnosis confirmed. It was T.B. When I went onto ask for the best method of treatment we hit several major obstacles. The specialists recommended that she be hospitalized immediately, but she was five months' journey away over the highest and roughest country in the world. Then the treatment that was recommended—streptomycin gm. $\frac{1}{2}$ b.d. for 42 days with P.A.S. 10 gm. twice daily for up to six months—was impossible to obtain in Calcutta—even in India. But even if it could be obtained it would not be issued to me as only an amateur practitioner, for the quota obtained in India from America was rationed to recognized doctors only, and in any case it had to be given to the patient under skilled supervision. Geoff's only knowledge of medicine was what I had been able to show him before I left.

However, I was not put off and decided to tackle one obstacle

A Report from Geoff

at a time. The first was to get hold of the medicine. As I had been in touch with the American Consulate and Ambassador a few months previously in connection with my trip from Tibet I approached them to see if anything could be done about obtaining supplies of streptomycin to save Mrs. Topgyay's life. The problem was finally solved by the Ambassador having adequate supplies flown out specially from the United States to India and then donating them to me for Mrs. Topgyay as a gift from the American people to the Tibetan people.

I now had the supplies but lacked the 'skilled supervision'. This was acquired from the specialist who pointed out possible reactions and treatment. I wrote a long letter to Geoff explaining what I had been taught by the specialist and suggesting that he begin the course of treatment immediately he received the package of medicines.

In the meantime I would make preparations to leave India for Kham by the Sadiya-Batang route as I had earlier planned, and if all went as well as on my previous trip I should be back in Bo inside two months. This would coincide with the arrival of the special messengers who would take at least five weeks to return by the northern route via Lhasa.

I returned to Kalimpong on August 8th and began making preparations to leave for Kham by the 16th if possible. My permits were still in order from my earlier attempts to get away in June, but I had them confirmed after some understandable reluctance on the part of the authorities. The trail from Sadiya was reckoned impassable at this time of year, but I pointed out that it had not been considered negotiable when I had come from East Tibet six months before and yet I had made it. It was now much more important that I get back to save Mrs. Topgyay's life than it had been to come to India with a message from Topgyay. I was finally given the all-clear to proceed and once again sent word to my parents to this effect.

To add to my sense of urgency newspaper reports of Chinese Communist intentions *vis-à-vis* Tibet were growing steadily more ominous. On August 2nd the *Statesman* of Calcutta had reported:

43

A Report from Geoff

Communist China's Commander-in-Chief, General Chu Teh, said today that the 'war of liberation' was not yet ended because 'we still have to liberate Tibet and Formosa'.

On August 6th it was further reported:

COMMUNISTS TO MARCH ON TIBET SOON

Communist China intends marching on Tibet at an early date according to a statement made by General Liu Po-chen, Chairman of the South-West China Military Affairs Commission, quoted today by the official Communist News Agency.

General Liu Po-chen told the Military Affairs Commission that the People's Army would soon enter Tibet with the object of wiping out British and American influence there. When the country had been 'liberated' Tibetans would be given regional autocracy and religious freedom. Lamas would be protected.

The Communists would respect existing customs, he added. Tibetan Government officials would not be removed from their present posts. But the Tibetan Army would be reorganized as part of the Chinese People's Army.

Chinese observers in Hong Kong interpreted the statement to mean that Peking would act while the Western Powers were devoting attention to Korea and Formosa.

Earlier it was believed that the Communists planned to attack Formosa before Tibet, but these plans undoubtedly were upset by renewed American interest in Formosa.

And on August 10th:

COMMUNIST THRUST TOWARD TIBET
REPORTS REMAIN UNCONFIRMED

Reports of a Communist advance on Tibet remain unconfirmed here, but Chinese sources saw significance in a recent official Communist announcement describing how tribesmen of Sikang Province were welcoming members of the People's Liberation Army.

These reports added that they did not think the two columns approaching Tibet could reach this objective of Jyekundo in under a month. It would take another month to reach Lhasa.

The same day (August 10th) an announcement was made from New Delhi in the *Statesman*.

No confirmation of Communist forces invading Tibet is available here.

44

A Report from Geoff

India's Ambassador in Peking has sent no report, nor has Mr. Richardson, India's representative in Lhasa. The Political Officer in Sikkim is also silent.

The Government of India are inclined to discount reports from Hong Kong alleging that Chinese Communist forces are moving towards the borders of Tibet.

Chapter Four

AN EARTHQUAKE

I still was not ready for the 16th but looked as if I might get away by the 18th—one day before my thirtieth birthday.

It had rained steadily for several days and at 7.55 on the night of August 15th Kalimpong was rocked by an earthquake shock which lasted for a full half-minute. I was in the Homes School Assembly Hall at the time and the shock was severe enough to set lights swinging, beams creaking and water in the glasses splashing. In the town itself buildings swayed in the intensity of the shock and there was a time of panic as people rushed out of doors to get away from the dangers of falling masonry.

However, what we had experienced was nothing to what was happening in North Assam and Tibet. The next day's newspapers were filled with reports of the unprecedented catastrophe. The *Statesman's* front page headlines read:

OVER 3,000 BUILDINGS TOTALLY WRECKED IN N.E. INDIA
EARTHQUAKE

The epicentre of the earthquake which shook East and North-East India on Tuesday night has been calculated to be a point in the Eastern Himalayas about 50 miles from the North-East border of Assam.

The tremors which were felt in Calcutta about 7.42 p.m. have been described by meteorologists as being of 'very great intensity'. The severity of the shocks was such that at the Alipore Meteorological Office the pen of one of the seismographs was thrown completely off the recording drum.

Holiday crowds in Calcutta celebrating Independence Day ran for shelter as the city was rocked. Cinema house audiences shrieked and prayed while bewildered shopkeepers shut the doors and windows of their shops.

Records available to the Meteorological Office in Poona show that the earthquake was of greater intensity than the Bihar earthquake of

46

An Earthquake

1934 and much greater than the Quetta earthquake of 1935. Experts there suggested that it may be second only to the great Assam earthquake of 1897 which was felt over an area of more than 1½ million square miles.

In the next few days, as reports of damage caused by the earthquake increased, the imagination boggled at the chaotic devastation. Millions of tons of water, blocked in the upper reaches of the Brahmaputra River by landslides after the earthquake, burst through their barriers and swept over Upper Assam over hundreds of miles of country. The town of Sadiya began to sink, over two thousand villages were swept away, other towns were damaged with six thousand people homeless in Jorhat, and over a hundred thousand cattle cut off.

The epicentre of the raging cataclysmic destruction was between Sadiya and Batang, my proposed route back to East Tibet and the trail down which I had come only six months before. The newspapers reports covered an area that could be observed, most of south of Sadiya, but what was the damage likely to be north of Sadiya on the way to South-East Tibet? At the time there was no means of finding out, but from Jean Kingdon-Ward, wife of the famous botanist, who was in the area during the earthquake, and from reports from Tibetans who were there and later came to Kalimpong, I was able to piece together a picture of the damage.

People were thrown to the ground in the violence of the shocks and with the succeeding paroxysms they could neither stand nor sit, clutching panic-stricken at the madly shuddering earth. After the first shock there was a deep rumbling from the bowels of the earth and then thunderous reverberations in the heavens, pealing through the valleys in unbelievably deafening salvoes.

Throughout the night the earth continued to tremble every few seconds, and towards the north the distant crackle as of heavy gunfire continued to be heard. Mountains poured down an endless cascade of rocks and dust into the river valleys and raging rivers began to dry up. The stars of the early evening were blotted out by an impenetrable cloud of dust which rose higher and higher and then added to the horror of the night when it became shot through with bloody red from unseen and inexplicable fires or volcanic masses. Clear mountain rivers became chocolate-brown floods carrying countless tons of mud and rock and timber, and other valleys through which they had foamed their way became mere savage dry cuts on the ravaged face of the earth.

This was the route I had to take to get through in two months if I was to save Mrs. Topgyay's life and be in Kham before the Chinese Communists arrived—if they had not already arrived; or, perhaps again, having arrived had disappeared in nature's holo-caust unleashed in that area. But I had to make the attempt any-way. Geoff and the Pangdatshangs were depending on me.

By the morning of August 17th I reckoned I had everything ready to leave on the 18th. I would fly to Calcutta, and from there to Dibrugarh, then use whatever means was at hand to by-pass sinking Sadiya and make my way up any negotiable valley to Walong, Rima, and Batang.

I went down to the Homes office to send off my last letter and cables to this effect, and after a short chat with the secretary went back to the house to finish my packing.

On the way I had a sudden twinge of pain in my groin which brought me up short with a catch in my breath. It passed off and I went on, thinking it strange but not unduly worried. As I entered my room it came again and this time it was accompanied by a momentary blackout. Fortunately I was at the bedside and caught at the headboard as I swayed.

This second attack had me worried for I had never experienced anything like it before. I decided, in view of the fact that I was about to tackle a fairly rugged trip, I ought to see a doctor. The Homes had an experienced European medical officer and I went to see him. He was in bed with a mild attack of flu but saw me and diagnosed a possible strain due to the football I had been playing with the Homes masters and senior boys.

I went back to the house, and rising from the lunch table I had another attack and passed out completely. Mr. Lloyd and Dr. Chang put me to bed, with a couple of aspirins, and I went off to sleep. The next few hours—and days—are only a haze of jumbled recollections.

When Mr. Lloyd returned from school at tea-time he came to

my room to find me in a delirium, twisting and turning on the bed. He immediately sent for the superintendent of the local Scots' Mission Hospital, Dr. Craig, and when he arrived at about five o'clock I had a temperature of 103°, was in blinding agony with the pain in my leg, and completely *non compos mentis*. Dr. Craig ordered me into hospital right away, where it was found that I had deep thrombophlebitis, and I was strapped to the bed to keep me from moving lest my agonized contortions should result in a clot of blood breaking away and putting an end to my life.

Chapter Five

A DRAMATIC ILLNESS

It was several days before I was sufficiently recovered to understand what had happened. Throughout that period I had been given injections of pencillin every three hours, night and day, and the pain had eased considerably. My leg was still weighted to the bed, of course, so that I could not move, and it looked as if I would be like that for some time to come. The doctors were puzzled as to why I, a fit young man, should have suddenly gone down with an attack of thrombophlebitis. Their orders were that I was to be perfectly still for another month or so until they saw how the condition progressed. If it was favourable then I could get up, and gradually exercise my leg until I was able to get around again. But I could put any thoughts of ever returning to Tibet or ever riding or climbing again completely out of my head. For some months, if not years, I would have to go very carefully indeed to avoid the possibility of a recurrence with fatal consequences.

Since nothing further could be done I accepted an invitation that had been given to me by friends, Gordon Bell and his wife Millie, to go and convalesce with them. Gordon was the third member of our trio who had gone to Tibet with Geoff and me through China, but he had got married on the way. When Geoff and I left West China for the interior of Tibet he and his wife left for Hong Kong and took up missionary work on the Indian side of the Tibetan border, in Kalimpong. They had another missionary worker staying with them, Dorothy Christiansen, a nurse, and she offered to do all the nursing I would require during my convalescence. My Tibetan servant, Loshay, would attend to whatever other tasks were necessary.

After a month most of the pain had left my leg, although it was still swollen and red in places with occasional twinges of pain. Sickness and nausea increased until I had to be put on a special diet. One of my visitors kindly informed me of a friend of his who had phlebitis and was in bed for 13 weeks, and now if he had to walk any distance he had to wear a special elastic stocking.

The doctors were, if anything, even more pessimistic. There were three of them, and one of them remarked that he had a woman under his care at that time with the same complaint and she had been confined to her bed for four months, and was more or less an invalid. The worst that could happen was that a clot might form in the vein, and then breaking off and reaching the heart would kill me instantly. The least that could happen was that the walls of the veins would inflame and cut off the flow of blood, causing inflammation and intense agony. In undue stress the latter tended to recur more often until one becomes a permanent invalid, or until the former alternative happened when one became a corpse.

Everyone has a morbid curiosity to share the experiences of others—preferably tragic—without being ultimately affected by the consequent suffering involved. The more a person's feelings are exposed, raw and bleeding, to their avid gaze the greater is their delight. In this way they can imagine themselves to be in the same state, they can project themselves into the same circumstances, and while having all the sensual delight of pain and pleasure be sufficiently remote not to be touched.

Many of my visitors were of this category. The publicity attached to my arrival in India, my intended return to Tibet in spectacular circumstances, the dramatic nature and timing of my illness, provided excellent material for analysis, speculation and advice. 'God must have some purpose,'—'It is His Will,'—'You must just accept it as from the Lord,'—were some of the usual stock clichés handed out. That they were all true in their way did not help me any for all of them demanded a passive attitude and I had been living and moving on the assumption that God's will for me at that time was a very active affair. The Communists were moving forward rapidly—Peking Radio had announced that the People's Liberation Army had crossed into Tibet—and decisions were being forced on Geoff with bewildering rapidity. Pangdat-shang and the Khambas were waiting for my arrival, the whole meaning of my life demanded action—and I was bound, immobile, on a bed, with an inexplicable illness for several months, or even for a lifetime.

It was mid-September before I could bring myself to face the situation again and look for answers. I had been content to use as an excuse to avoid some soul-searching the semi-stupor induced by pain and sickness and shock. But I realized it could not go on. Peace of mind, or soul, did not lie in simply *acknowledging* the purpose of God, but in *apprehending* it. Merely to acknowledge His Will was a barren fatalism, or an empty determinism, and could never give satisfaction to either God or myself. His glory could only be encompassed and furthered by an intelligent appreciation and apprehension of His purpose in my present circumstances, and then by following it through to His predisposed conclusion. Only in this way could I be an intelligent instrument to accomplish the Divine Will and to fulfil my own destiny. 'He made known His *ways* unto *Moses*, His *acts* unto the Children of Israel,' the Scriptures had recorded, and this communion was what He desired of every servant of His. 'Shall I hide from Abraham, my friend, that which I do?' showed the eagerness with which He was willing to communicate with His human vessel. It was God's desire to honour Moses and Abraham, and every child of God, with His confidence, but too often those who professed to know Him and serve Him had to learn His purpose from His '*acts*'.

I went back to the point when I could state with confidence that I had been in the purpose of God, where He had honoured me by making known His 'ways' to me, and that point stood out stark and clear as Midian, Horeb or Moriah. He had sent me to India with the message I had delivered,[1] *but He had not sent me back to Kham again*. I picked my way back, step by step, arguing the logical necessity for each decision as I had made it—the need to get back to Kham before the Chinese attacked, the need to be there to save Mrs. Topgyay's life, the need to be in the forefront

[1] See *God's Fool*.

of the battle for the sake of God's testimony. I stopped, silenced by my own argument as it rose up to rebuke me: since when had God ever allowed His actions to be determined by expediency, by 'need' or 'opportunity'? Rather He was a God 'who took vengeance of their inventions', His children's 'presumption', their 'initiative', although He forgave them afterwards. There was 'no wisdom nor understanding nor counsel against the Lord. The horse is prepared for the day of battle; but victory is of the Lord.'

But then another staggering factor reared up. If it had been God's will for me to remain in India, and I had been doing everything to oppose that will until God had finally used this illness to put me on my back and bring me to the point of obedience again, then the cyclone of June and the recent earthquake must also be taken as evidence of His intervention to stop my return. Could such catastrophic devastation and death be interpreted to fit such an explanation? Or were they just incredible coincidences? An earthquake of that magnitude to stop me travelling from Sadiya to Batang? On sober analysis it was too fantastic to be considered, but on equally sober analysis it had to be admitted that even on such a scale the earthquake had not deterred me from considering the attempt to return. And a further coincidence had to be accepted, that immediately I had sent off the cables to Britain announcing my determination to depart for Tibet I had the first twinge of pain heralding the onset of this inexplicable illness.

I turned shudderingly away from the problem. The conclusion of such an argument was not that any one person could be so important to God to occasion such intervention, but that His purpose for a country or a continent, and His glory, should necessitate it. What manner of God was this that I had chosen to serve?

However, if my analysis was correct and the thrombophlebitis which had struck me down was an intervention from God to keep me in India, then now that I had decided to submit myself to His direction again and remain, there should be no further need of the illness. All I had to do was admit my disobedience to God, seek His forgiveness, ask for the removal of the thrombophlebitis as being no longer necessary, and carry on as usual.

When I announced this decision to my friends there was an

immediate outcry. Gordon and Millie accepted the reasoning as spiritual people, but I was amused at the reactions of some of the others. Those who had been most forward with the usual clichés were now most insistent on the use of 'sanctified commonsense', 'not doing anything foolish'. 'God expects you to look after your body.'

I came to my decision on Sunday, September 10th, and decided that I would spend Monday in bed, in quietness and prayer, then get up for a few hours on Tuesday, all day on Wednesday, and then carry on normally from Thursday.

On the Sunday evening I had a visit from Pasang Tenpa, who brought a letter from Geoff which had just been brought by one of the Pangdatshang messengers. It was from Bo, dated July 16th, and read:

Dear George,

Just a line as a messenger is secretly leaving here for Lhasa. I hope to catch you if you are still in India.

So far I have no news from either you or home. I know it is only circumstances that prevent this but thought I had better tell you in case you had sent any letters.

Have spent, in two visits to Batang, some seven weeks in all there. With brother John had much joy in seeing the Lord work, and a case of adultery judged and put right in the church and believers unified in a very real measure. Also one other young brother leave the Communists and go on with the Lord. Spoke about eight times in all with ever-growing liberty and consciousness of God's power.

Mrs. Topgyay still coughing blood and painfully weak. Whether there is any hope for her I don't know.

First Communist troops arrived—about forty; a few still staying in Bo much to the Pangdatshangs' annoyance. First border incident of size occurred some days away. 100 Chinese killed in attempting to cross the Yangtze. Reds seem intent on going to Lhasa which from all points of view is sheer folly for the Chinese.

Myself, God willing, expect to leave for Tibet with A-R shortly. Things very critical now. Great wisdom needed. A-R says that I am under suspicion by the Communists. He was informed from Kangting.

Have built house here, total cost about thirty pounds; five rooms, one storey. When we shall live in it remains to be seen. I am full of confidence and hope that the present peculiar state of affairs is just such to achieve the advance of the Gospel we desire, so do not concern yourself for me other than to maintain unceasing prayer. Health excellent.

Your fellow-labourer in the Gospel,

GEOFF.

On the Monday morning I had an agonizing recurrence of the pain in my right leg, followed by an attack in my left leg, which had been normal until then, and when the doctor arrived he said that both legs were now affected and that I would have to be immobilized for another two months. I told him of my decision to get up, which he dismissed as sheer folly, and when I insisted that I was determined to do so—not disagreeing with his diagnosis but his prognosis—he said he refused to accept any responsibility for the consequences.

I was too sick with pain to do anything, even to open my mail from home which had arrived, and it was evening before I was able to do so. The news which two of them, at least, contained, was startling. One was from the Brethren Council at Bath and read:

'To say that we were appalled to get your letter on August 29th would be putting it mildly. It came just before ten o'clock when we were having the usual Monday morning prayers with all who work in the office. As a result we felt that you were not intended to spend the rest of your life looking after yourself and that the Lord was still going to use you in Tibet. . . .

'In the circumstances we considered how best to stir up believing prayer from the many who are interested and we decided that the best thing to do would be to circulate copies of the letter to the roughly 500 people whose addresses we have for such purposes. . . .

'It so happened that Mr. Stunt was at Bristol yesterday morning in the company of Professor Rendle Short who, as you know, is

55

a well-known medical man. He read through what you said about yourself . . . and promised to post to us a letter on the subject which we enclose. . . .'

Professor Rendle Short's letter read as follows:

'There are two varieties of thrombosis, which in the past have often been confounded. There is thrombophlebitis affecting the superficial veins of the leg, which are often varicose. This is very painful at first, causes great swelling and tenderness, and is accompanied by fever. The pain and fever abate, but the swelling may last a long time, or even be permanent. In the other variety, coming on very quietly, often after an operation, or in bedridden patients, there is no fever, no swelling, very little pain, and the thrombosis takes place in the deep veins of the leg, out of sight. It is difficult to recognize, and indeed has been overlooked till recently. In this condition pulmonary embolism, leading to sudden acute illness with pain in the chest and frequently leading to death in a few minutes, is not uncommon. It comes like a bolt from the blue. In thrombophlebitis, pulmonary embolism and sudden death are extremely rare. In fifty years I have never seen a case, and the risk is negligible. The modern treatment for the first condition, thrombophlebitis, is rest in bed, penicillin and hot foments during the acute febrile and painful stage. When that has subsided the patient should get up and walk about, wearing a bandage from toes upward to control the swelling. This treatment is new, but all modern experience shows that it is both safe and wide. It is unfortunately true that the swelling may persist, the leg may feel heavy, and there may be further attacks, but stopping in bed does not prevent these happening. A bandage may have to be worn for months or years.'

There was also a gift of £100 from Bath to see a specialist about my condition.

As Professor Rendle Short's recommended treatment roughly coincided with my own more dramatic decision, I got up on Tuesday afternoon as I had decided—without bandages—and apart from an understandable initial weakness of the legs felt perfectly all right. On Wednesday I got up in the morning and stayed up all day, and on Thursday went to the Homes.

A Dramatic Illness

The following week I left for Calcutta to see a specialist, walking two miles over a landslide on the way. The specialist asked about the symptoms, the decisions of the other doctors, and then gave me a thorough examination. At the end he said that according to the symptoms I had listed I must have had thrombophlebitis but there was absolutely no sign of it now. There was no inflammation of the veins, no sign of a clot, and only a slight swelling of the right leg and a slight drag on the same. He advised as much exercise as possible, beginning with toe, ankle and knee exercises to running, climbing, riding and playing football.

I sent off a wire to the Homes' sports master to say that I would like to be included in the Homes' football team to play on Saturday first. When we took the field, on the town football pitch, there was complete silence as we lined up, for I was playing centre-forward and kicking off, and the news of my illness had been known in the town for weeks.

The game finished, my leg stood up to the strain, and that was the last I was troubled with it.

Chapter Six

AWAITING GOD'S DECISION

N ow that the decision to remain in Kalimpong until God indicated otherwise had been taken I had to find a suitable house in which to live. This was not so easy for there had been a growing influx of Tibetans into the town as rumours of Chinese intentions increased.

Through Mr. Lloyd, and one of Kalimpong's resident 'characters', the Honourable Mary Scott, I was introduced to Mrs. Pratima Tagore, daughter-in-law of India's famous philosopher-poet, Rabindranath Tagore. Gurudev, as he was popularly known, had been very fond of Kalimpong and had purchased land there on which to build a house for himself. He died before he could live there but his son, Rutinandranath, had completed the building and he and his wife were in the habit of spending part of every year there. However, their duties at Santineketan, where Gurudev had founded his famous 'natural university', only permitted them a few weeks in the year at 'Chitrabhanu', as the Tagore house in Kalimpong was called, and they wanted someone to lease it who would look after the house and the garden.

It was a lovely house in a magnificent situation, on a projecting platform of land that faced out on an uninterrupted view of the 27,000 foot snow-covered Kangchenjunga range, and with the mountains spectacularly dropping away just beyond the garden walls into the Teesta and Rangit valleys beneath. It was only a pleasant walk of about a mile to the centre of the bazaar and with all its advantages I was happy to be there.

I could not take over right away as some Chinese friends of the Tagore's were living there, but they were expecting to leave within a week or two, when I could have complete possession. The Chinese family was a Mr. Liu, his wife and child, until recently the

Awaiting God's Decision

First Secretary of the Chinese Embassy in Lhasa, under Chiang Kai-shek's Kuomingtang Government, who had been ordered out together with the Ambassador, Mr. Shen, when the Tibetans saw an advantage to be won with the imminent defeat of Chiang Kai-shek in China. Mr. Liu hoped to work on a book, on the history of China's relations with Tibet, at Santineketan University and later go on to America.[1] Before he left I was able to obtain the Chinese viewpoint on their sovereignty over Tibet in several conversations. I was not impressed.

On October 25th, 1950, the Chinese announced over Peking Radio that the process of 'liberating Tibet' had begun. On my arrival in India I had said that the Pangdatshangs' assessment was six months from the time I had left in mid-January. They were four months out. The miscalculation was infinitesimal—with none of the tragic overtones, except for the disbelief of Lhasa, India and the West—compared to the mistakes of India's Ambassador in Peking, Sardar Pannikar. He had scoffed at the whole idea, had misled his Government and endangered the safety of Asia and the world through his wishful thinking.

Even with the benefit of his hindsight intelligence Pannikar's statements in his book *In Two Chinas*, published in 1955, make strange reading. Here are some extracts:

'The only area where our (China's and India's) interests over-lapped was in Tibet, and knowing the importance that every Chinese Government, including the Kuomingtang, had attached to exclusive authority over that area, I had, even before I started for Peking, come to the conclusion that the British policy (which we were supposed to have inherited) of looking upon Tibet as an area in which we had special political interests could not be maintained. . . .

'In regard to Tibet, I knew they (China) were a little uncertain about our attitude. I expressed the hope that they would follow a policy of peace in regard to Tibet. Chou En-lai replied that while the liberation of Tibet was a "sacred duty", his Government were anxious to secure these ends by negotiation and not by military action. . . .

[1] See *Tibet and the Tibetans* by Liu and Shen.

Awaiting God's Decision

'To add to my troubles, by the middle of the month, rumours of a Chinese invasion of Tibet began to circulate. Visits and representation to the Foreign Office brought no results. The Wai Chiapu (Foreign Office) officials were polite but silent. Things were certainly moving on that side. The only information that I was able to wring out of them was that certain measures were being taken in West Sikang, that is on the borders of Tibet proper. In India, mainly as a result of messages from America and Hong Kong correspondents, public opinion was already excited. On October 25th, 1950, however, the Chinese announced over the Peking Radio that the process of "liberating Tibet" had begun. The fat was in the fire. The Government of India was troubled about the Chinese action on the Tibetan borders and I received instructions to lodge a strong protest. The Chinese reply was equally strong. It practically accused India of having been influenced by the imperialists, and claimed that China had not taken any military action but was determined to liberate Tibet by peaceful means. . . .

'I had expected a virulent campaign against India in the Press. But for some reason the Chinese, apart from publishing the correspondence, soft pedalled the whole affair. The controversy was seldom mentioned in the Press. But on our side matters were not so easy. The Indian Press, egged on by the sensational correspondents and the blood-curdling stories issued from Hong Kong by Taipeh agents, kept on talking about the Chinese aggression. Even Sirdar Patel, the Deputy Prime Minister, felt called upon to make an unfriendly speech. There was also some support in the External Affairs Ministry for the view that India should act vigorously to protect Tibet. In the meantime Ecuador, which was then a member of the Security Council, threatened to bring up the Tibetan question before the United Nations. Knowing the temper of the Indian public and the attitude of some of the officials I was nervous that the Government might take some hasty step. . . .

'The Tibetan question had also settled itself, for the Chinese after the first military display were content to keep their armies on the frontier and await the arrival of the Tibetan delegation for settlement by negotiations. . . .'

60

The combination of Pannikar's unexampled fatuity and complacency, with his petulant diatribes against Hong Kong and Formosa, and then China's intervention in Formosa, helped him and Sir Benegal Narsing Rao, India's representative to the United Nations, to have Tibet's appeal against the Chinese act of aggression shelved by the United Nations and the whole matter relegated into oblivion.

I left for Calcutta to take part in official discussions following on this new situation in Tibet, and, while there, heard the further announcement from Peking that two Britishers had been captured in a military camp near Chamdo. The only two Britishers in the whole of Tibet at that time were Geoff Bull and Robert Ford, the wireless operator with the Tibetan Government at Chamdo. There was complete confusion in Indian, British and American official circles, for on the one hand there were Pannikar's assurances of Chinese non-intervention in Tibet, and on the other hand there were my informed reports coupled with the Chinese Government's own broadcasts from Peking.

I returned to Kalimpong to find that if any proof were needed it was to be found amongst the Tibetans themselves. High officials from Lhasa were pouring into Kalimpong every day, and my house in the New Development area of Kalimpong was surrounded by Tibetan lessees of the other houses. The Dalai Lama's sister was only a few hundred yards away. Shakabpa had bought a new house for himself, also quite near, after cancelling his proposed trip to Peking to negotiate with the new Communist Government. Other members of the Government quickly bought or rented houses in the district until we might easily have been mistaken for a suburb of Lhasa.

With this exodus of a hitherto remote people into Kalimpong, particularly in the context of the dramatic possibilities the new situation in Tibet afforded, every newspaper editor of note felt that here was the place and the people to get information. Reporters of all kinds, and of all shades of opinions, began to pour into Kalimpong looking for copy.

They were faced with hitherto unencountered obstacles. In the first place the Tibetan officials were not publicity conscious and refused to meet the various representatives of the Press; and when any of them did manage to meet a Tibetan official at some social function they were not able to talk with them because of language difficulties.

It was here that some of Pannikar's complaints had some substance. For, unable to make contact, or obtain information, at an informed level, the correspondents resorted to collecting information in the bazaar through bilingual Nepalis or from even more dubious sources. This information they padded out with a lot of concocted, imaginary claptrap to add up to an article. In this way the world was informed of the completely fallacious 'antiquated weapons' of the Tibetans, superstitious abracadabra to oppose the ruthless might of Communism, and a timid, peace-loving people constitutionally unfitted to put up any resistance. At one period there were 22 reporters, all trying to find some new copy on Tibet to send home to demanding editors.

Lest it might be thought that it was only the 'yellow rag' journalists who indulged in such irresponsible tactics, it might be as well to record that it was the correspondent of a famous news agency who sat in his hotel with map, pencil, paper and ruler, and worked out the Chinese advance across Tibet, at an average of 16 miles a day, until he had them occupying Lhasa— and they had never moved beyond their initial capture of Chamdo, in East Tibet. When I pointed out to him how dangerous his tactics were, without giving any of the information I had and which I had been officially requested to withhold, he promptly accused me of being morally responsible because while I knew the true situation, could speak Tibetan and was in the confidence of the Tibetan officials, I persisted in refusing to divulge any news. When the full extent of methods and imaginative reports was exposed several months later, he was dismissed, but in the meantime the damage was done and Tibet and the Tibetan situation completely misrepresented and misunderstood in the minds of the world's public—and even more tragically in the minds of the world's politicians. By the time the Tibetan Government got around to making an official protest at the amount and character of the false reports being issued from Kalimpong, editors had lost interest and little or no notice was taken of the protest.

I was aware, of course, of how the Tibetans felt about it for I was acting as interpreter and go-between in the many talks that were being held at the time. To add to their sense of frustration, the official in charge of trade talks in Kalimpong, who happened to be the eldest Pangdatshang brother, Yangpel, could not get a satisfactory reply from the Indian Government as to why the Indian Government had suddenly imposed a tax on Tibetan wool, which according to the Geneva Convention ought to have had free access to the sea as it was only bonded through India. Then the possibility of 'liberation' by the Chinese Communists meant that Tibet would be classified as a Communist satellite by America, and as America purchased 80 per cent of Tibet's wool export this would cripple the country economically and throw it right into the hands of the Chinese.

I thought it remarkable that on the very day I learned officially of Geoff's capture from some Tibetan friends I was reading in the parallel passage in Isaiah 37 the same words I had read at the time of our separation:[1]

'Hast thou not heard that long ago I did it, and that from ancient times I purposed it? Now have I brought it to pass, that thou shouldest lay waste fortified cities into ruinous heaps. And their inhabitants were powerless, they were dismayed and put to shame; they were as the grass of the field and the green herb, as the grass on the housetops and grain blighted before it be grown up. But I know thine abode, and thy going out, and thy coming in, and thy raging against me. Because thy raging against me and thine arrogance is come up into mine ears, I will put my ring in thy nose, and my bridle in thy lips, and I will make thee go back by the way in which thou camest. . . .'

I took comfort from the thought that both of us in our radically different circumstances were still under the hand of God, still in the path of a purpose that had been determined from 'ancient times' and that the One who had allowed the Assyrians to over-whelm the Israelites for a period of discipline and then turn them back at the height of their power could equally easily do the same

---

[1] See *God's Fool*.

with these latter-day Assyrians as they swept down on the fold of Tibet.

Not only reporters were attracted to Kalimpong. Scholars of many kinds from all parts of the world took advantage of the situation which had brought so many influential and normally unapproachable Tibetans to Kalimpong and, together with tourists, they made Kalimpong the most popular resort in India. The press of visitors and social engagements became so great that lunches, teas and dinners were soon filled up and breakfasts had to be included in order that people might meet everyone that they wanted to meet. As there were only about three foreign speakers of the Tibetan language in Kalimpong—Prince Peter of Greece and Denmark, leader of the Third Danish Expedition to Central Asia, Dr. Roeriche, a well-known Russian Central Asian scholar, and myself—it meant that I had to put in a tremendous amount of concentrated language study in order to be able to cover some of the topics discussed, for in addition to the political talks there were geologists, naturalists, anthropologists and the many others who wanted to find out about their own particular interests in Tibet.

As I looked back to my despair at being deprived of all active participation in Tibetan work during my illness only two months before I marvelled again, as I had done so on many other occasions, at the wisdom and patience of God.

Page 65 follows
after page 96

along with them in their plan and was then told that his part would be to go into Lhasa with the Chinese, depose his younger brother, the Dalai Lama, and then under Chinese control alter the existing political, social and religious structure in Tibet. In return he would be recognized as the 'President' of Tibet.

Taktser accepted his role and in due course was sent with a five-man Chinese diplomatic delegation to Lhasa ahead of the People's Liberation Army still camped in Chamdo in East Tibet. A few days outside Lhasa, on a pretext, he sent a trusted servant on ahead to acquaint the Dalai Lama and the Lhasa Government of the imminent danger. As he did not go into details the messenger was not believed.

Immediately on his arrival Taktser told the Dalai Lama of the Chinese Communist intentions and urged immediate departure for India to request sanctuary and help. This time Taktser was believed and the Dalai Lama with a large entourage of Government officials left for Yatung on the Sikkim-Indian border to await replies to their appeals for help. Taktser then came on to Kalimpong as the Dalai Lama's special envoy to India and the Western Powers, and carried personal letters from the Dalai Lama to this effect.

However, he was in an extremely dangerous position. The Chinese, on hearing of the precipitate departure of the Dalai Lama for the Indian border, immediately jumped to the conclusion that Taktser had divulged their plans, and sent word to every Communist—Chinese, Tibetan and Indian—that he was to be liquidated before he could do any more damage. In the state of political confusion that existed on the Indo-Tibetan border at the time, with many suspected pro-Communists amongst Tibetan officials, a high percentage of Communists in the local Chinese community, and an Indian Communist representative in power in the Kalimpong constituency, he went in hourly fear of his life, not knowing whom he could trust. Even his mother and sister had no knowledge of the true state of affairs that had brought him to Kalimpong and the Dalai Lama to the Indian border. He dare not go out except under heavy guard and that at night, and he dare not move any farther—as, for instance, to Calcutta where it would be even easier to engineer his death in some apparent accident—yet it was absolutely essential that he contact leading officials of the various Governments quickly in order to save the Dalai Lama, and also Tibet. It was shortly after his arrival in Kalimpong that he had heard his mother and sister speak of me, and after our conversation earlier in the evening he had decided that I was his only hope. Would I help him and the Dalai Lama? and Tibet? He wanted to escape from the present Communist menace, the Dalai Lama wanted sanctuary in India, and Tibet wanted whatever help could be given from any source to deliver her from the Chinese.

He produced the letters and one was his letter of authority from the Dalai Lama requesting every assistance to help him to a place of safety; the other was a much more explosive document authorizing Taktser to make any secret agreement on behalf of the Dalai Lama with any outside Power prepared to help. No wonder Taktser had brought guards and drawn the curtains!

I was silent for some time after he finished talking, and Taktser must have interpreted this as a sign of reluctance on my part for he proceeded to offer whatever I wanted in the way of reward for any help I would give—I could ask whatever I wanted and he and the Dalai Lama would provide it.

My silence was not because of any reluctance to help but because of the stupendous possibilities the situation opened up. My first reaction was to agree wholeheartedly and begin discussing ways and means, for was not this a miraculous answer to prayer and evidence of the sovereign disposition of God in relation to Tibet? Here I held the fate of the country in my hands, as God had said eighteen months before in that remote valley in Tibet—or even more incredible, as He had said almost fourteen years before—as well as the life of the god-king himself. That I could help, and even succeed, I had not the slightest doubt, for my conversation over the past year since arriving in India had brought me into touch with leading Indian officials, the British Deputy High Commissioner and the American Ambassador amongst others. Only—was it of God? Like T. S. Eliot's Thomas of Canterbury in *Murder in the Cathedral* I had to be sure that it was not:

82

The Dalai Lama's Brother Escapes

The last temptation is the greatest treason
To do the right deed for the wrong reason.

And also there was Geoff. Geoff in a Chinese Communist prison, with all that such an escapade might mean to him. If I did this I would place myself in the forefront of anti-Communist activities and no longer would it be accepted that my opposition was merely an ideological affair to be contemptuously dismissed; it involved a political participation that would have a serious, even monumental effect on Communist expansionist intentions. I dare not act like an irresponsible Christian Scarlet Pimpernel gambling audaciously with the lives of friends and the glory of God. I had to be sure.

Slowly I outlined to Taktser what it was that was troubling me, not the question of payment for any services rendered, but my place in the purpose of God. That place and that purpose I knew to be in Tibet, and I loved the country and its people, and if God indicated that it was His will that I go ahead I would be very happy to do so. Once I had this fact clear I was not afraid of what the Communists might do. As to payment, I wanted nothing. This was my task, my destiny, and if I was helping Tibet or the Tibetans in delivering them from an atheistic Communism I could see it as part of my contribution under the hand of God. However, if he would give me a letter once he had reached safety, expressing his gratitude for anything that was done, that would satisfy me for I would present this to him or to the Dalai Lama sometime in the future when I wanted to return to Tibet. If he would leave his letters of authority with me I would translate them, spend some time in prayer to God, and then if I received the command to go ahead I would slip away from Kalimpong quietly in the morning to Calcutta to begin arrangements. When I had everything arranged I would send a telegram to Yangpel Pangdatshang to say that the goods he ordered were ready for collection and this he must take as an indication that everything was arranged and he must leave immediately for Calcutta. Once there we would have to deal with circumstances as they arose.

Taktser was delighted with the suggestion, agreed that we

must have the help of God to be successful, and that it was impossible to return to Tibet just now, but when the Communists were driven out and he could return, the freedom of Tibet would be mine. I would be a friend of the family and the Government for life and could travel where I liked. On that note we parted.

I spent most of the night in prayer, and it was one of those occasions when, as St. Paul says, in Moffat's version, one had to '. . . struggle, not with blood and flesh but with the angelic Rulers, the angelic Authorities, the potentates of the dark present, the spirit forces of evil in the heavenly sphere.' In the early hours of the morning I knew the answer: I was to go on with God. The same God who had looked after me so far would continue to do so in the intensified Communist antagonism of the future. The same God who would look after me would look after Geoff in vastly different circumstances. He had done so in the case of Daniel in the cut-and-thrust of Babylonian politics and the raw physical dangers of the lions' den, and He was still the same—or, at least, it would be a spiritual venture to prove if He were so.

The news I took to Calcutta created a sensation and the diplomatic telephone between New Delhi, London and Washington hummed with questions and answers. Difficulties multiplied as arrangements for Taktser's escape progressed. As it had to be kept absolutely secret only the top officials were informed of what was required and Taktser had no passport. Sufficient money for an extended stay in the U.S. would have to be given with the consent of the Reserve Bank of India, which was out of the question in such secretive procedures; exit permits to leave the country and by-pass customs formalities would have to be obtained. Slowly all those problems were resolved. In the United States the Committee for Free Asia, a non-Communist association of businessmen, invited Taktser to go to America at their expense as their guest. The Indian and U.S. Governments issued affidavits in lieu of a passport, accepting the Dalai Lama's letter as of sufficient *bona fides*. The letter was also accepted by the Indian Government as sufficient to warrant diplomatic immunity from customs inspection and other normal requirements at the airport. The way of escape was now clear and all that remained was for Taktser to come to Calcutta for the final talks on the political aspects of his mission and then escape to America and safety.

Taktser and a companion slipped away from Kalimpong and arrived quietly in Calcutta, but even at that the news must have got around, for we were followed by at least two people wherever we went. We changed taxis in lonely streets, slipped into shops and markets and out through back doors and side entrances to get away from their attention, but this was only successful for short periods. Taktser's terror increased as the talks dragged on, waiting for replies from Washington, arranging for the Dalai Lama's sanctuary in India. Taktser had arranged a secret code with the Dalai Lama and a close trusted adviser, Trichang Rimpoche, and after I had translated the conditions for agreement he would telegraph the outline by secret code to Trichang Rimpoche in Yatung. The terms of agreement with the U.S. were finally drawn up to the satisfaction of both sides, and the Dalai Lama's part was publicly to announce Tibet's rejection of the 17-Point Treaty forced on the Tibetan delegation in Peking the previous month, on which rejection the U.S. would take up the matter of Tibet's independence and Chinese aggression in the United Nations. There were also other items that need not be listed here. On making the foregoing announcement the Dalai Lama would leave Yatang for India within seven days.

There had been suggestions that I accompany Taktser to America as he did not speak any English, but it was more essential that I remain to handle the arrangements in India, and I recommended that Colonel Robert Eckvall, a former missionary to Tibet, be used in America as interpreter. When this was agreed upon we fixed for Taktser to leave India by plane on the night of July 2nd, and for the Dalai Lama to come to India six days later.

At this point word was received from Hong Kong that the Tibetan delegation which had negotiated the recent 17-Point Treaty was on its way to India, accompanied by a Chinese diplomatic delegation to take over Tibet, and both would arrive in Calcutta on Sunday, July 1st.

On the Sunday night Taktser's brother-in-law, Yapshi Sey, who was a member of the Tibetan delegation, secretly visited the hotel where we were staying, but Taktser insisted that we tell him nothing, saying only that he had come to Calcutta for medical treatment. (He had been to see a doctor who diagnosed stress.) We kept away from the hotel all day on Monday to avoid meeting the Tibetan and Chinese officials who were certain to call. When we returned in the late afternoon there was word waiting that the diplomatic delegation wanted Taktser to call at the Chinese Consulate.

As we expected to leave at 9 p.m. that night we did nothing about it, but as we were sitting in our room, waiting for the taxi, in walked Taktser's brother-in-law again. The suitcases were packed and stacked in the centre of the room, Taktser and his companion were dressed in Western-style suits, and we were obviously ready for immediate departure. At first Taktser tried to tell Yapshi Sey that he was going to Delhi for further medical treatment, then finally admitted that he was on his way to America and bound him to secrecy. While we were still talking the news came through that we could not leave as the passport of Taktser's servant-companion was not in order and would require some alteration. The flight had to be cancelled.

The next day we were told that it would be the 5th before we could get away, and during the intervening days on several occasions Tibetans came to the hotel with thinly-veiled threats as to what might happen if Taktser tried to leave India. On Thursday the Chinese Ambassador arrived from New Delhi and a peremptory request that Taktser should attend the Consulate at 6 p.m. for a meeting was conveyed to us; if Taktser was not well enough to attend, or did not find it convenient for any other reason, the Ambassador and other members of the delegation would call upon him at the hotel.

At first Taktser refused point-blank to go to the Chinese Consulate, maintaining that the Chinese would hold him there by force, but when I pointed out to him that the Indian Government was sympathetic and had appointed him Security protection there could be no great risk in going there; also, that it would help to disarm the Chinese suspicion and keep them away from the hotel where we had everything ready for departure. He reluctantly agreed to go, taking with him his brother-in-law as an interpreter to help drag out the proceedings, and we arranged that if he did not phone me shortly after 6.30 p.m. I would call on the Indian Security authorities to take up the matter with the Chinese.

At 6.35 p.m. I had his phone call, and he came straight back to the hotel. The Chinese Ambassador had asked him what he was doing in Calcutta, and when he told him that he was there to get medical treatment the Ambassador had told him that they had excellent hospitals and doctors in China and that he could go there. In any case he wished Taktser to leave Calcutta immediately, either for Tibet or China. As for his defection and betrayal of the Communist plans to the Dalai Lama, he would be forgiven this time and his error overlooked as being understandable since it was his younger brother who was involved. Taktser agreed to leave India immediately and the interview terminated on this assurance.

A Tibetan official was appointed by the Chinese to be in the vicinity of the hotel at all times, but we succeeded in eluding him when necessary. When the time came for us to leave for the airfield I called a taxi to a side entrance where the hand luggage had already been taken by the servant and we left without being seen. We had just got out of the city, on to a lonely part of the road where there was little traffic, when the taxi spluttered to a standstill—out of petrol. The driver managed to get a tin can filled with some from a small shop about half a mile away, while we fumed with impatience, and this was enough to take us to the airfield where all the airport officials were in a mild panic wondering if we had been murdered *en route*. At 11.5 p.m. Taktser and his companion left for London, America and safety.

I left for Kalimpong on the afternoon plane next day as I had discovered that the Chinese and Tibetan delegations were travelling on the morning plane. I took with me letters from Taktser to his mother and the Dalai Lama, telling them of all that I had done and asking them to help me in any way I wanted.

The task of getting the Dalai Lama into India from Yatung on the other side of the Sikkim border was a formidable one. According to Taktser the Dalai Lama trusted no one fully except Tri-

The Dalai Lama's Brother Escapes

chang Rimpoche, and his position was such that he was never alone. Any official who went into his presence had to be accompanied by another official, so that it was impossible to discuss any plans.

At first I discussed the possibilities with Yangpel Pangdatshang who, as Governor of Yatung, was in a position with a strong following of about 200 armed Khambas to take the Dalai Lama from reluctant fellow-travelling officials by force if necessary. On my putting the hypothetical possibility to him he agreed to do it but only if the Dalai Lama personally requested him to do so; he did not trust a single government official.

There were one or two other possibilities but the plan that was finally agreed upon was as follows. When I returned to Kalimpong from Calcutta I found that an Austrian named Heinrich Harrer had arrived in Kalimpong from Tibet.[1] He was an escaped prisoner-of-war who, after a remarkable journey, spent the following seven years in Tibet. He had become friendly with some of the official families but left Lhasa before the Chinese Communists arrived. At that time he made none of the claims he was to make later in his book regarding his influence over the Dalai Lama—in fact, I understood from the Dalai Lama's family that he was rather *persona non grata* and had been asked to leave Lhasa before the Dalai Lama's caravan—but while he had been in Yatung he had made a map of the valley and surrounding areas, and claimed to have left a copy with the Dalai Lama's officials in Yatung. He had approached the Americans with plans for forming an anti-Communist group amongst some of the Tibetan officials, and the Americans viewed it with some hope, until I pointed out that the key-man in the plan was the one the Chinese had used to try and intimidate Taktser with threats in Calcutta.

I suggested that word be sent to the Dalai Lama to take a few of his most trusted officials with him on his customary evening walk and make for a certain point marked on his copy of Harrer's map. I would be waiting at that point with several trusted Khambas and horses and we would ride for the Bhutan border, only a few hours away, and through the narrow neck of Bhutan into

[1] See *Seven Years in Tibet*.

The Dalai Lama's Brother Escapes

India, before any pursuit could be organized. To get word of this plan to the Dalai Lama I suggested that his brother-in-law, Yapshi Sey, whom we had met in Calcutta, be used as a messenger, for being a member of the family he could enter the Dalai Lama's presence alone without being accompanied by another official.

It seemed foolproof, but when Harrer was approached for the use of his map he was naturally suspicious and demanded that if anything was going on he wanted to be in on it. I wasn't too happy about it but there was no way round and I finally agreed, on condition that he was subject to my orders all the time. We planned to slip out of Kalimpong late one night, with several Khamba companions, and cross the border away from the police check-posts. Each would carry a rucksack with the bare essentials —bowl, tsamba, dried meat, knife.

About 10.30 p.m. on the night we had agreed to leave I was sent for to come to the Dalai Lama's mother's house. There I found his mother, his sister, her husband, Yapshi Sey, and Harrer. Yapshi Sey had come back post-haste with a letter from the Dalai Lama requesting us to cancel all arrangements for his coming to India. He would have to return to Lhasa.

It appeared that the three Abbots of the three chief monasteries of Lhasa—Drepung, Sera and Ganden—had arrived in Yatung and requested the Dalai Lama to return to Lhasa. He had been disinclined to do so and they had insisted on a consultation with the State Oracle. The State Oracle was the medium who, when any important decision had to be made, became possessed by the requisite spirit and under spirit-possession gave the decision of the gods.

The Dalai Lama had had to submit to this regular Tibetan custom and under possession the State Oracle had directed that he must return to Lhasa. The Dalai Lama had refused to accept this direction, an unheard of occurrence, and demanded an unprecedented second 'possession'. Again, under possession, the State Oracle said he must return to Lhasa and, when the seventeen-year-old Dalai Lama looked like rejecting this also, the three Abbots reminded him that if he did not accept the commands of the gods in heaven how could he expect other Tibetans to accept his com-

89

mands on earth? So he had no alternative but to return to Lhasa, he said in his letter, and I who knew Tibetan customs would realize why this should be so. He would never forget about the help I had given and would remember what the Governments had offered. He could not now make the agreed rejection of the 17-Point Treaty as planned but would keep in mind all that had been discussed for use in the future. He had asked his brother-in-law to read the letter to me and then burn it as it was too dangerous to keep. I watched the flames slowly eat it away.

Next day the newspapers carried the story of the Dalai Lama's brother's surprising arrival in America, and a few days later I received a letter from him written in English by his interpreter, Colonel Eckvall:

Dear Mr. Patterson,

Ten days ago I arrived in New York City and am now in hospital having a careful check-up which may take some days longer. On the journey I thought often of your helpfulness in acting as my interpreter, but fortunately one of the persons who met me at the airfield, like yourself, speaks Tibetan and has been helping me in my plans and problems having to do with getting settled and getting started on my studies.

The things which I have seen and learned since my arrival are of great interest. Soon I shall be hard at work on the English language.

Please accept my thanks for your great interest in my people and myself and for your many efforts on our behalf.

With very best wishes,
Most cordially yours,
TAKTSER.

Chapter Nine

I WAS TO BE LIQUIDATED

The news of Taktser's escape and arrival in America had an explosive effect in Kalimpong. The tensions which inter-family, party and international intrigue had built up in the past year increased to breaking point. Was Taktser's arrival in the United States to be interpreted to mean that America was about to take a direct interest in Tibetan affairs? Would the Dalai Lama follow his example? Rumours multiplied by the hour and as it was locally known that I had been in Calcutta at the same time as Taktser Rimpoche I became the object of close questioning.

The persons who were hardest hit by Taktser's escape were the members of the Chinese 'advisory' delegation to Tibet, led by Chang Chung Win. He, together with the Ambassador, had already informed Peking that the situation endangered by Taktser's divulging of their plans and subsequent escape to India had been recovered when he had promised in Calcutta to return to Tibet or China. Now that he was in America their plans were more upset than ever and Tibet, instead of being quietly annexed and isolated, had an important link with the West. Just what Taktser was authorized to say and do they had no means of knowing, but obviously there would have to be a radical change of plan.

Chang Chung Win, and the advisory delegation, had only intended staying a few days in Kalimpong *en route* to Yatung and Lhasa, but now they dare not move lest they be made an international laughing stock by meeting or just missing the Dalai Lama and his officials on the way to India, for they had no means of knowing as I had that the Dalai Lama had been forced to change his mind by the decisions of the State Oracle. The much trumpeted 'advisory' delegation might arrive in Lhasa with no one to 'advise'. Or again, if they insisted on entering Tibet as the supposed advisory delegation in those circumstances this might be the act used against them by America or others to label them as blatant aggressors.

Chang Chung Win was livid, and his fury was mostly directed against me. I heard from two sources that he had given orders that I was to be liquidated so that I could no longer interfere. I had a friend who was in the local Communist Party and he warned me that at a secret meeting to discuss the new situation created by the Chinese Communist take-over in Tibet and its significance for India, it had been decided that I must be removed. I was also approached by local Security officials, who had heard from their sources of information that I was a marked man, and asked if I wanted the 'protection' of an escort or a permit to carry arms. I sent word to Chang Chung Win through both channels that no follower of Jesus Christ was afraid of any amount of followers of Karl Marx and that I would carry on as I had been in the habit of doing. I would go out after dark for my newspaper at my usual time, would visit friends all over the mountainside including the notorious tenth mile area, and I would take no escort and carry no arms. I was 'immortal till my work was done', and would yet stand in Tibet when he and the Chinese Communists had been thrown out.

One of the most disturbing factors in the advisory delegation's prolonged stay in Kalimpong was the opportunity it provided for contacts with Indian Communists. I knew of at least one group of influential Indian Communists who came to Kalimpong as 'tourists' and had clandestine meetings with the delegation. Their meetings and discussions for proposed infiltration into India were made easier by the stupidity of a local official. For some obscure reasons of his own this official, who was a Bengali and unacquainted with Nepali hillman politics, thought that if the Gurkha League representative of the Nepalis was got out of the way, it would be a straight fight between the Congress candidate and the Communist candidate with the former certain to win. With a more blatant than usual 'fixing' of the nomination procedure he succeeded in disqualifying the Gurkha League candidate, but found to his horror and consternation that the hill people were so furious at this political fixing by Congress that they voted solidly for the Communist candidate. The result was, of course, that Kalimpong, the most strategic point on the Chinese Communist route to already heavily Communist-influenced Calcutta, became a Communist constituency at the most critical period of the Indo-Tibetan crisis, thus making it easy to further Chinese Communist intrigues for future take-over.

An interesting factor that emerged from the intrigues was the conflict between the Russian and Chinese Communists' aims in the area. I was told by several high Tibetan officials of the separate approaches and offers made to them by the Russian intelligence agent in Kalimpong who had pointedly told them that if they were not satisfied with the Chinese offers they could always take up the matter with Russia direct through him. This counter-counter-espionage had one amusing outcome on one occasion when the Russian agent accompanied Chang Chung Win and some other members of the delegation for a visit to the Dalai Lama's mother and sister, and Dr. Carsun Chang and I who had been invited there earlier to discuss and advise on the Tibetan situation had to slip out of a rear bathroom door and over the hillside to avoid being caught there by them.

It was a most difficult time for the Dalai Lama's mother for she had to make several momentous decisions, and whatever she decided involved a break with some members of her family. Her son, the Dalai Lama, was in Yatung, and about to return to Lhasa, and another son, also a lama, was there with him. Outside Tibet there was one son, Taktser, in America, and another son, Gyalu Thondup, in Formosa, with her daughter's husband, Yapshi Sey, a member of the Tibetan delegation which had signed the 17-Point Treaty in Peking and who was on his way back to Lhasa with the advisory delegation. In her dilemma she turned to Dr. Chang for advice for he, too, had members of his family on either side of the Bamboo Curtain.

The local Tibetans were becoming more and more disillusioned with the activities of Indian officials, and impatience was giving way to animosity. Although Mr. Nehru, the Indian Prime Minister, had given verbal assurance to the Dalai Lama that he would be given sanctuary in India, the local Political Officer put obstacles of his own creating in his conversations with Shakabpa, the Dalai Lama's appointed representative at that time, and amongst the higher Tibetan officials the impression grew that India was collaborating with China over the absorption of Tibet as the price of non-aggression against India. The contempt for such *naïveté* that this supposed attitude induced amongst the Tibetans did not help matters any. At the same time I was shown a letter by Yangpel Pangdatshang and Liu Sha, the Tibetan Foreign Minister, which was the official reply of the Indian Government to the Tibetan request for an explanation as to why their wool, which was being bonded through India for export, should suddenly be taxed in violation of the Geneva Convention that gave inland countries the right of access to the sea. The letter contained only one paragraph and was a summary dismissal of the Tibetan protest without any explanation, and to add insult to injury was written on the ordinary Residency notepaper of the Political Officer.

At a lower level amongst the Tibetans there was impatience and animosity due to the activities of a corrupt Indian official who was taking bribes in return for permits to buy Indian cotton. Had he kept his bribe-taking within bounds perhaps nothing more than animosity would have arisen, but he issued more permits than there was cotton within the quota so many Tibetans were left with useless permits after having paid considerable bribes. Again, inept handling by a local official produced a crisis when the Sub-Divisional Officer pompously appeared and pointed a gun to dismiss the Tibetan traders and muleteers. He only escaped with his life when Yangpel Pangdatshang unceremoniously bundled him through back doors into a nearby car and got him away from the infuriated Tibetans.

To crown all, the U.S. Consulate sent an official to tell the Tibetans that America would no longer be taking Tibetan exports of wool since Tibet must now be considered a Communist satellite and as such was forbidden trade with the United States. As 80 per cent of Tibetan export of wool went to the U.S. this meant that Tibet's economic independence was shattered and handed over to the Chinese Communists.

I was to be Liquidated

There was nothing more could be done. Tibetan officials were forced into having more and more discussions with the Chinese advisory delegation, and plans went ahead for the meeting with the advisory delegation and the Dalai Lama in Yatung, after which they would return to Lhasa together.

While the majority of Tibetan officials and traders were disillusioned with India and the West, there were still many who were bitterly anti-Chinese, particularly the burly, fighting Khambas from East Tibet who had a long history of Chinese hatred. Since most of the caravans which came into Kalimpong were composed of Khamba muleteers there were many local disturbances as groups of them belonging to some patriotic Tibetan official or overlord fought or poisoned others who belonged to some other official suspected of being pro-Chinese. Then there were many others who, either deprived of their legitimate living as traders and muleteers or having retreated before the advancing Chinese Liberation Army, took to the mountains in roving bands of two hundred or more and attacked the pro-Chinese officials' caravans as they left India for Lhasa. Rumours that some of these Khamba bandits were lying in wait between Phari and Lhasa for the Chinese advisory delegation infiltrated into the Kalimpong bazaars and increased the tension there.

I became aware of plans for such an attack through a Khamba friend of Loshay, my Tibetan servant. He wanted Loshay to leave me and join in the venture which was expected to be extremely lucrative. The object of attack was an official who had done a spell of duty in Kham, where he had become notorious for bribery and oppression and who, after fleeing before the Chinese to Kalimpong, was now returning to Lhasa with a heavily loaded caravan of goods hoping to make enormous profits from the Chinese occupation.

Everything went as planned. The Khamba bandit conspirators got themselves hired as muleteers on the official's caravan and then in a lonely spot they seized the official and his son, killed them both and threw them over the cliff edge, then made off into the mountains with the booty. It was as easy as that. I found out through Loshay when the bandits, after some time, returned by a roundabout route to Kalimpong to sell some of the stolen goods.

However, the advisory delegation finally got to Lhasa safely, and was joined by the Army of Liberation which had moved on from Chamdo to Lhasa when they saw that there would be no opposition or even protests from India or the West.

In the meantime in Kalimpong I was being closely watched and followed by several interested parties. My servant was a deadly fighter who had built up a reputation for himself by defeating several opponents in brawls in the tenth mile area. I had warned him shortly after our arrival in India that he must not kill anyone in India or he would be put in jail. He grumbled at this for it placed him at a distinct disadvantage, he claimed, when he had to alter his sword stroke to hit with the flat of the blade or the haft. With all the restrictions he still managed to emerge victorious from several battles, and my collection of swords as trophies mounted. When he heard that I was marked down for liquidation by the Communists he was filled with delight, for he claimed that now no official in India could object if he killed anyone while defending me, his master. He was bewildered to find out that he would still be liable for jail. After brooding over my explanation for some time he decided that he would follow those who were following me and then if they tried to attack me he would attack them and if anything serious happened claim that it was in self-defence.

He found out that I was being trailed by two different people, one from the police and one from the Communists. This complicated matters as he was not always sure which was which. After several frustrating episodes—during one of which he heard plans for my murder—when his plans for a counter-ambush went awry he decided that he would carry the war into the enemy's camp. When the local Communist second-in-command was haranguing the Tibetans at an open-air meeting one day, and calling them running dogs of the imperialists, he thought his chance had come. He pretended to take exception to what was said, claiming that the speaker had insulted the Tibetans, and provoking a fight he beat him up so badly that he had to be admitted to hospital. Then he calmly issued a warning that if his

Page 97 follows after page 80

Chapter Seven

MY INNER STRUGGLE

W hen God sent me to India from the wilds of East Tibet He accompanied His command with a mysterious statement: 'There is no living without dying, there is no dying without living.' At first hearing it was only a trite truism unworthy of record as a conversational gambit, let alone as a momentous divine pronouncement.

Now and again it would rise up to confront me and when it did I reckoned that it had a significance yet hidden but which was to mean much to me in the divine ordering of events in the future. It was only during my illness that its spiritual significance dawned. Ironically enough, it was while reading one of Oscar Wilde's essays, *The Master*, that the moment of enlightenment came. It is short enough and significant enough to bear repeating:

'Now when the darkness came over the earth Joseph of Arimathea, having lighted a torch of pinewood, passed down from the hill into the valley. For he had business in his own home.

'And kneeling on the flint stones of the Valley of Desolation he saw a young man who was naked and weeping. His hair was the colour of honey, and his body was as a white flower, but he had wounded his body with thorns and on his hair he had set ashes as a crown.

'And he who had great possessions said to the young man who was naked and weeping, "I do not wonder that your sorrow is so great for surely He was a just man."

'And the young man answered, "It is not for Him that I am weeping, but for myself; I too have changed water into wine, and have healed the leper and given sight to the blind. I have walked upon the waters, and from the dwellers in the tombs I have cast out devils. I have fed the hungry in the desert where there was no

food, and I have raised the dead from their narrow houses, and at
my bidding, before a great multitude of people, a barren fig tree
withered away. All things that this man has done I have done also
—And yet they have not crucified me." '

It was a paraphrase of the words of Christ: 'He that hoardeth
his life shall lose it; and he that loseth his life shall save it.' Until
we too have been crucified any inheritance of power we may pos-
sess will be but 'torment of thorns and crowns of ashes' to us. I
had to 'die' to returning to Tibet, 'die' to everything I would have
chosen for myself, before I could experience a new 'life' with God.
There could be no experience of this 'life' without a constant
'dying'; but on the other hand there could be no 'death' until I
had first 'lived'.

In the society into which my generation has been born there is
only one way in which we may be permitted to exist and that is if
we are willing to be spiritually dead. Rules as to the conduct of
living exist to which we must conform; rules as to the conduct
of eating exist to which we must conform; rules as to the conduct
of dressing exist to which we must conform; yes, even rules as to
the conduct of dying exist to which we must conform. Only let us
be dead to sense and we shall be considered educated. Let us be
dead to value and we shall be considered civilized. Let us be dead
to God and we shall be considered religious. To show any signs
of life is to forfeit immediately one's place in the society of the
living.

All the above preamble is simply to underline the struggle I
was passing through at the time. I was the product of a generation
that was disillusioned in religion and cynical in politics, and yet
now I was thrown into a vortex of political intrigue and seeking
to find a God-directed path through it. It was difficult enough dis-
ciplining one's self to giving only such advice or recommendations one felt God wanted to be given, but decisions became
much more difficult when a choice had to be made between the
devious political tight-rope and a straightforward spiritual
commitment.

During one of my flying visits to Calcutta a well-known missionary and Bible expositor, J. M. Davies, was holding a series of

special meetings. I not only attended the meetings but lived in the same house with him during his stay in Calcutta. He was of the old imperialist, 'paternalist-compound' school of missionaries, believing that it was necessary for the white Christian to be in a position of authority over the natives to administer the affairs of the church properly. Not even the parlous condition of Brethren assemblies in Bengal, Bihar and South India could shift him from his entrenched belief.

However, this controversy apart, we got on well together. He was very insistent that I should join him at a conference of missionaries from Brethren Assemblies to be held later in the year in South India to protest against the formation of Brethren missionaries into a Society to be called 'Fellowship of Christian Assemblies'. This he felt strongly was a violation of the scriptural principles which Brethren were supposed to hold, and should not be countenanced. I agreed with him on this point and as I had determined to do all in my power to break the anachronistic system that was stultifying Christian activity and bringing it into disrepute in an awakening Asia I promised to consider joining him in his protest at the conference.

This was one of the circumstances that contributed so much to my inner struggle. The overthrow of the antiquated paternalist system, with its imperialist overtones, would release the dynamic power latent in an unorganized Christ-centred community and do far more than any amount of political finaigling could ever do— even if one were only to measure the contribution in terms of anti-Communism.

But the time was not yet. The proposal to further sectarianize Brethren activities was passed by a majority of Brethren missionaries and the 'Fellowship of Christian Assemblies' was duly registered under the Societies Act with the Government.

It hardly seemed credible to me that missionaries who had watched the recent débâcle in China could perpetuate such unmitigated political folly, let alone such scriptural malpractice. In an issue of *Time* magazine dated January 8th, 1951, there was a report which read:

My Inner Struggle

The Bamboo Curtain fell harshly last week on a century of good works in China. Red China's Vice-Chairman of the State Administration Council, Kuo-Mo-jo charged:

'American imperialism has, over a long period, placed special emphasis on . . . cultural aggression in China.'

Kuo recommended and the Peking régime approved:

1. A ban on U.S. subsidies for China schools and churches.
2. A take-over by the Red State, or by puppet 'people's' enterprises, of all U.S.-subsidized educational, medical and relief institutions.
3. A transfer of U.S.-subsidized 'religious bodies' to the control of the Chinese believers (whom) the Government should encourage to become independent, self-sufficient, and self-preaching [sic].

Kuo reckoned that the properties had been worth $41,900,000 (41,000,000 U.S. dollars). U.S. religious bodies had supported and operated 506 hospitals, 905 dispensaries, 31 leprosariums, 320 orphanages, 6,000 odd schools. Their missions and schools had trained scores of prominent Chinese, including many officials of the present Communist Government.

The above was only the U.S. contribution, and did not include the British, Continental, Scandinavian and other Mission contributions. An analysis of the spiritual implications of the Chinese débâcle made even more tragic reading. A cross-section of opinions from many societies who had worked for many years was as follows:

'Missions should not be so confident that medical, educational and social services are going to build the Church.'

'Missions should try as soon as possible to merge with the Native Church organization and cease to exist independently.'

'Do not acquire property and plants far beyond the power of the Native Church to upkeep.'

'The goal should be "new men" rather than "nice people".'

'There has been over-emphasis on organization far beyond the ability of the local Church to carry in the forseeable future.'

'Much *talk* about self-support, but not enough action in that direction.'

'There was too much foreign-owned and controlled property in many places, including large houses in high-walled residence compounds.'

'Too many missionaries kept too much control too long over institutions, funds, policies, methods and activities.'

My Inner Struggle

'In China we dallied and the end of an age has come. A new age has begun. What will be done elsewhere?'

'What will be done elsewhere?' In India—nothing. With a history of imperialistic control and missionary domination far in excess of anything in China the senior missionaries had no intention of changing their outlook or practices and young missionaries were too intimidated by them to do anything drastic about it.

I had given the matter lots of thought over the past few years and particularly during the recent few months since my illness. If there was to be any opening up of Tibet or Central Asia to the spread of Christianity it certainly could not be in an imperialistic context that was already thoroughly discredited throughout Asia and other countries of the world. I definitely could have no part in it. What form, then, could any programme of Christian expansion take in any of these countries in the years ahead which would not carry with it the stigma of 'cultural aggression' or 'creeping colonialism'? Purchasing of land and control of property was definitely out, but as these usually involved the social aspects of the Christian responsibility—the institutional work—such restrictions presented no great hindrance to the spread of the gospel in themselves. The function of the 'apostle', the 'evangelist' and the 'teacher' was essentially an itinerant one, according to the teaching of Scripture, and the denial of land and property to propagators of Christianity would actually be a powerful stimulus to expansion. But the Christian responsibility could not be restricted to the purely evangelical, the simple 'spiritual' aspect.

Too much damage had already been done to the Christian witness in the past century through the artificial distinction sustained by Fundamentalists and Modernists between an 'evangelical' gospel and a 'social' gospel. The Fundamentalist shied away from the purely secular connotations which had become increasingly attached to the latter, and the Modernist felt that the former was only a blinkered interpretation of out-dated hot-gospellers. The ideal, of course, from both a scriptural and pragmatic standpoint was an inter-related combination of both; not in the inherited 19th-century tradition where both were vitiated through being ultra-compartmented but in giving proper emphasis to each of their functions.

The 'apostle', or 'missionary' as the Latin equivalent was, would again be an itinerant messenger of God, with no fixed abode, with temporary pastoral responsibilities as the Holy Spirit indicated in any given locality, as with Paul's three weeks in Thessalonica or three years in Ephesus. The 'evangelist' likewise preaching for conversions in places till that time unchurched. The 'teacher' following to 'build up their faith' until it was 'enlarged' and then moving on. The transient, or pilgrim character, of such a ministry would remove all preconceived grounds of suspicion in newly-born, touchy national governments, and also place the persons concerned in such activities in self-evident subjection to the national churches, thus removing all connotations of 'paternalism'.

With the 'spiritual' responsibilities thus observed—and I use the term advisedly, with the definition already mentioned in mind —the ground would be cleared for the discharge of the Christian's social responsibility in meeting the physical, cultural and material needs of one's fellow men. Just in case there are those who still object that it is not the Christian's responsibility to meet those needs—and I know only too well that there are many who do—let me point out again that it was Christ Himself who told the parable of 'The Good Samaritan' with its underlined emphasis on 'social' responsibilities, that it was Christ Himself who placed loving one's neighbour next to loving God. In addition Paul accepted the injunction of the apostles in Jerusalem that he help the poor, to which end he made an appeal and collection from the believers.

By removing the 19th-century gobbledygook which has cluttered up missionary enterprise until it has become almost as sacrosanct as Scripture itself—particularly amongst those who classify themselves as 'Faith Missions' or 'those who live by faith'—a new sense of responsibility could be driven home in the matter of giving more money and not merely by leaving it to some vague emotional impulse to denote magnanimously an occasional half-crown to some good cause. It would also provide a new incentive to those with business flair to use their accumulating profits or latent talents in extending the work of the Kingdom of God to the limit of their abilities in a challenging way instead of an apologetic, surreptitious pound-in-envelope gesture at a poorly-attended missionary meeting patronized mostly by middle-aged spinsters.

Some like Robert Le Tourneau in America or, in a smaller way, John W. Laing in Britain, have already given a lead in this. Le Tourneau especially has provided a spectacular innovation that, if followed by several others, either separately or together, would have a dynamic impact of Christian witness in hitherto untouched and uninterested areas.

Beginning as a small-time engineer he entered into a contract with God to give away nine-tenths of his earnings in whatever way God indicated. In a meteoric rise in the business world he now has to give away millions of dollars. Instead of pouring this into Mission Societies to repair leaking roofs of missionary compounds, or to provide rice in exchange for attendance at churches, or a wholesale distribution of old-fashioned religious clichés in gospel tracts, he has formed a 'Foundation' to administer his wealth in a responsible and God-honouring manner.

A 'Foundation' is a peculiarly American institution, and the specification of a 'Foundation' according to the standard work on the subject, *American Foundations and Their Fields*, is: ' "Foundation" in the American sense of the term; that is to say, one which is a non-profit, legal entity having a principal fund of its own, or receiving the charitable contributions of a living founder or founders, which is governed by its own trustees or directors and which has been established to serve the welfare of mankind.'

Within this framework the Le Tourneau Foundation is a discretionary perpetuity incorporated in California in 1935 with its donors, Mr. and Mrs. R. G. Le Tourneau. The purpose is 'to teach, promulgate and disseminate the gospel of Jesus Christ throughout the world, and also to unite in Christian fellowship the large numbers of consecrated Christians in the various evangelical churches, and for such purpose to appoint and engage ministers, evangelists, missionaries and others actively to pursue and accomplish the foregoing purposes.'

The methods used are 'grants to other organizations, grants to individuals for research or for study, scholarships; grants of a relief nature to individuals; operation of a religious camp for young people and conference grants where religious groups of all denominations are permitted to hold week-end meetings; maintenance of a national evangelistic centre in New York; publication and distribution of religious tracts.'

With some modifications—particularly in the matter of 'appointing and engaging ministers, evangelists, missionaries, etc.' which is simply a variation of the 19th century tradition!— there is no reason why, say, Brethren, with their high percentage of wealthy business men amongst their members, should not follow some similar approach. It might be argued that the Brethren councils in Bath and Glasgow, as well as in other centres throughout the world, are carrying out such a programme, but with all due respect to those who give so much of their time to this work they have neither the vision nor the ability to carry out such an undertaking on a world-wide scale. Retired bank clerks and small town lawyers are not the type of men to think in terms of, for instance, contracting with the Peruvian Government to clear one million acres of land with the aforementioned purpose in view to 'teach, promulgate and disseminate the gospel of Jesus Christ'. What is required is technically experienced men in each field who will administer such funds donated by a 'social-responsibility'-conscious community (if one may be forgiven such a cumbersome expression) fired by a dynamic Christianity.

The concept is not just an airy-fairy pipe dream occasioned by too much reading of second-rate Christian biographies but a practicable possibility already being carried out by some individuals and with a strong appeal to many others. Many who are tired of giving their hard-earned money as pensions for a lifetime to missionary mediocrities in some obscure village backwaters in Asia would be only too pleased to bend their energies into a more productive channel of missionary expansion. Others not so much concerned with surplus wealth might only be interested in reducing their taxable income by increasing their gifts to charitable, educational and similar causes—a group that could be further stimulated by reminding them of Ananias and Sapphira.

My Inner Struggle

Such Foundations, or whatever name the bodies might be given, would be in a position to approach Governments direct to negotiate agreements suitable to both—as, for instance, the Ford and Rockefeller Foundations in Asia in their 'aid to under-developed countries' scheme—thus eliminating suspicions of incipient colonialism and any other attributed ulterior political motives.

Only Christ-centred, vision-filled armigerents can produce a forward policy that will be sufficiently dynamic to transform existing conditions of obscurantism and arithmocracy and by its very utility destroy the parasitical political growth that goes by the name of Communism. Democracy is a discredited term of debased coinage in any language in the world today. It contains no comprehensible form, presents no inspiring challenge to satisfy the intellect or fire the imagination. It is a collection of negative expedients which can only be held together by an appeal to supposedly vague moral principles which by their very character they inevitably contradict. This merely serves to induce a spirit of cynicism in the young individual or young nation instead of a revolutionary spirit of crusade.

Just as Confucianism and Taoism, Buddhism and Mohammedanism plus billions of American dollars and democracy was not sufficient to keep China from turning Communist, so neither will Hinduism and Buddhism, Mohammedanism and Secularism, plus Colombo Plan, American Aid and democracy keep India from going the same way. The same ominous factors exist in India as in the last days of the Kuomingtang régime in China—corruption in Government, frustration amongst the intelligentsia, iconoclasm, cynicism and discontent in a massive student class that is being educated for unemployment. Irresponsible politicians are forced to the desperate expediency of exploiting the explosive emotional content of the masses by appeals to ancient communalist beliefs or modern linguistic divisions. And all the time the students and intelligentsia restlessly watch China, watch China, watch China—and talk increasingly of actions not words.

Sterile politics, a vitiated missionary approach—or a forgotten, classic, apostolic Christian dynamism that had overthrown world empires in the past, re-energized government policies, even given

73

birth in pseudo-form to new world religions by its impact. In China the trappings of a specious Christendom were swept away with the other empty ritualistic forms, but a new powerful force was emerging that the Communists were having to reckon with—'the independent, self-supporting, self-preaching groups of believers' of which Kuo Mo-jo had spoken, but the implications of which he could not foresee.

In India these groups were also gathering momentum and thousands of converts were being steadily added to the Church. There were no church buildings, no ordained ministers, no Bible colleges, no organization for any antagonistic Government to attack. As in China these groups emerged in an Asian context, without Western influences, from a simple study of the Bible. M.P.s, professional people, merchants, students and sweepers remained in their jobs, but met together for prayer, Bible study and discussion and spiritual upbuilding.

One of the spiritual leaders of the movement, a man called Bakht Singh, came to Kalimpong and for three days we met together for discussion. He had just come from Hyderabad where six hundred converts had been integrated into a local church for the first time. He was a remarkable man.

A Sikh of good family, he had gone to England for advanced studies in engineering. In England he shaved off his beard in defiance of Sikh beliefs when he became an atheistic Socialist. Finishing his studies in England, he decided to continue them in Canada. On board ship he joined in all the activities of the sophisticated Westerners—dancing, drinking, cards, sports—and on Sunday saw no reason why he should not go to the ship's service with the others. While on his knees during the prayer he had a sudden startling vision of Christ and heard His voice saying to him, 'The Lord Jesus Christ is the Living Christ.' He thought over the remarkable occurrence a few times, then gradually it faded from his mind and he carried on as usual. He was travelling in a train one day in Canada when a well-dressed man sitting opposite him took out a Bible and began to read it. He remembered his experience on board ship and asked his fellow-traveller if he could tell him where to get a Bible. The fellow-traveller offered him his own and within the next few months Bakht Singh had read it through *six* times and become a convinced Christian.

He knew nothing at all about churches or denominations and attended any place that was open in London when he returned there after his studies in Canada were finished. His parents refused to send him money when they heard he had become a Christian, and for several months he lived in London without friends or money but was miraculously looked after by God. This left a deep impression on him so that when God commanded him to return to his own land of India to preach he felt no necessity to join any church or missionary society—on the contrary, from his early knowledge of missionaries and missionary societies he held them in very poor esteem.

When he arrived in Karachi in 1943 and began preaching he was asked by a Hindu on one occasion, 'Show me one good Christian and I will believe,' and the point went home to Bakht Singh, who knew there were several thousand Christians in Karachi but most were nominal or backsliding. In the next five years he saw many hundreds converted to Christ through his preaching, but on his return to the various places found that many had drifted back into their old ways. From that time he began to insist that Bibles be bought, studied and preached from, and that Christians should meet together for prayer and instruction. Since then these groups had proliferated all over Pakistan and India, growing in numbers and strength, as many more joined him in a full-time preaching and teaching ministry.

He had come to Kalimpong to visit a small group of converts who met together there, and after our talks he asked me to join them, pointing out my responsibility to meet with them and give what spiritual contribution I could. He went further and pointed out the tremendous opportunity in India, the hunger for something real and the contribution I could make on a national scale with him and the others, especially now when another close European friend of his, Wilf Durham, had just recently died.

I looked toward Tibet, I looked toward India, I looked toward China, I looked toward Russia—and my mind was in a turmoil. Of all the influences that contributed to my mental conflict this one held the greatest appeal. Audiences of thousands waiting and hungering to hear and be taught the Word of God, a constructive ministry in making and forming 'new men' so that whatever the future held there would always be an intelligent core of witness, a nucleus from which there would grow a work to join with that already burgeoning rapidly in China, to lay a foundation of Christian truth in the great new nations that were already coming to the forefront in Asia and the world.

The conflict was intensified by reading at that time J. Burnham's book, *The Coming Defeat of Communism*, in which he showed the strength of the Soviet position:

'First and foremost they enjoy an incomparable geographical position. There is, literally, no position on earth which can in any way compare with that of the Soviet Union and its puppet states. For the first time in human history the Eurasian Heartland, the central area of the earth's great land mass, has both a considerable population and a high degree of political organization.

'This Heartland, with its vast distances and huge land barriers, is the most defensible of all the regions of the earth. Sea power cannot touch it. Conquerors are swallowed up within its enormous confines. Yet raids in force can issue from it East, West, South-west and South.

'Before the coming of airborne and atomic weapons, it was an axiom of geopolitics that if any one power succeeded in organizing the Heartland and its outer barriers, that power would be certain to control the world. As Sir Halford Mackinder expressed it in his *Democratic Ideals and Reality*, "who rules the Heartland commands the World Island (by which he meant Europe, Asia and Africa); who rules the World Island commands the world."

'Air power and atomic weapons have upset the certainty of this axiom. The Heartland is no longer inviolable. None the less the Soviet position is still the strongest on earth. If the Communists succeed in extending their full control to the Atlantic, and in maintaining or extending their position on the Pacific, the odds on their victory would advance close to certainty.'

With the Chinese Communists already in Tibet, and their intention to move into Sikkim, Bhutan and Nepal next, then into

India, it would bring international Communism within reach of its goal. Kalimpong was on the way from Peking to Calcutta, Lenin's blue-printed route for Communist world domination. God had brought me to Kalimpong and until He moved me on elsewhere I could only remember the recent lesson He had had to teach me for making independent decisions of my own. I had to crucify my own desires, and stay.

Chapter Eight

THE DALAI LAMA'S BROTHER ESCAPES

In the new situation that had been created by the Chinese attack on Tibet, Dr. Carsun Chang's interpretations and advice were sought not only by some of the non-Communist Powers but also by the Tibetans. The Dalai Lama's mother particularly held him in high esteem and consulted with him on many occasions. Although about forty years separated us we had become very close friends and met twice or three times each week, sometimes at Mr. Lloyd's house and sometimes at mine.

He arrived one day in March 1957 bringing with him a small, thin Mongolian in Western-style suit, and introduced Mingwang, Prince of Mongolia, and asked if I would help him in any way I could.

Mingwang was a prince of the great Mongol tribe of Torgut, a 'Tsagor Yasse', 'White Bones' noble of the first class, descendant of Genghiz Khan. He and his mother and sister had been educated in Moscow, Paris and Peking, and could speak Russian, French, German, English and Chinese, as well as several Central Asian dialects. His sister, Princess Mme Bréal, was married to the French Consul in Peking, he himself had been a Vice-President of the Council in Sinkiang, a representative to the Nationalist Legislative Yuan of the Chinese Nationalist Government, and a member of the Commission for Mongolian and Tibetan Affairs.

When the Chinese Communists turned towards Sinkiang in 1950 and Russia began moving troops from Mongolia to safeguard her interests in the area, Mingwang and his Torguts gathered to defend themselves against the hated Slavs and the advancing Chinese. It was a hopeless battle, and they retreated before the overwhelming forces. From the Gobi desert through

The Dalai Lama's Brother Escapes

Sinkiang into Tibet, across the vast unexplored wastes of North Tibet they fought, broke up, fought again, their numbers steadily depleted as the fighting and the savage country took ruthless toll of lives in cold, exhaustion and starvation. By the time Mingwang reached Kalimpong there were only 23 survivors with him, and they were destitute.

Although he arrived ahead of the Chinese Communists, the agents of the Russian Communists were waiting for him in Kalimpong and he had already been warned by them that if he tried to communicate with any Western Power he and his family and relatives would suffer. If he required help of any kind the Russians were prepared to pay for any information he was prepared to give for an account of his journey through the unexplored parts of North Tibet. In order to gain time he had already met with the Russian agents on several occasions and given them some information but had stalled them off by taking time over the earlier and less important part of his travels, and he wanted to get away to Formosa quietly before they could bring any further pressure to bear on him.

It seemed as if I was being drawn irrevocably into a political commitment, whether I wanted to or not. I tried to keep my lines of communication with God clear so that He might have full freedom to direct each step to bring His purpose to fruition, but it became increasingly difficult as one became increasingly isolated.

The third brother of the Pangdatshang family, Yangpel, had arrived in Kalimpong and he sent word to me that he had received news of Geoff. He had been captured in the Communist advance on Gartok and taken to Batang. From there he had been taken under escort to Kangting, and then down country to China. He was accused with Ford of being an imperialist spy. A happier piece of news was that the medicines had arrived in time to save Mrs. Topgyay's life and she was not only able to get up but had been able to travel the several days to Chamdo.

Tension increased amongst Tibetans in Kalimpong when members of a delegation arrived from Lhasa *en route* to Peking to discuss Tibet's relationship with the new Government in China.

The Dalai Lama's Brother Escapes

They were not authorized to negotiate any agreement, being simply a delegation to initiate exploratory talks, and there was a rising hope amongst officials—Indians, Westerners and Tibetan —that this was an indication that the Chinese Army intended coming no farther into Tibet. Even when the completely un-expected and startling announcement was made from Peking that the delegation had entered into a 17-Point Treaty with Com-munist China there was a feeling that while it was a bare-faced political coup accomplished under duress it probably meant that the Chinese wanted a political hold and not a military occupation of Tibet.

But it was accorded the same fate as Pannikar's earlier assess-ments. The Treaty was signed at the end of May 1951 and in the second week of June I was asked to go to tea at the house of the Dalai Lama's mother and sister to meet the Dalai Lama's eldest brother who had just arrived in Kalimpong. There was the usual exchange of courtesies in the course of which Taktser Rimpoche, the Dalai Lama's brother, commented favourably on my use of the Tibetan language. We talked about Kham and my interest in Tibet and the Tibetans for an hour or so, then I rose to go. Taktser Rimpoche then suggested that he call on me sometime. I agreed, and said that I would be delighted if he would come for a meal with his mother, sister and the others.

Two hours later, just as it was getting dark, there was a knock at the door and when I opened it Taktser Rimpoche stood there surrounded by several armed servants. I invited him in, bewil-dered by the unexpected visit, the heavily armed guards, the air of watchfulness and secrecy. My bewilderment increased as Taktser questioned me closely as to the trustworthiness of my Tibetan servant, then asked for all the curtains to be closely drawn.

However, what he had to say clarified the situation more than somewhat. It appeared that he had been taken prisoner in the early stages of the Chinese Communist advance in 1949, and taken to China for indoctrination. There he was told that if he did not agree to collaborating with the Communists in their plan of con-quest of Tibet he would be declared expendable. With no alterna-tive to sudden, and probably unpleasant, death he agreed to go

page 81 follows after page 64

master was going to be pestered any more by the Communists, and if any harm came to him, he would seek out all the leading local Communists and do the same to them, or more. Whether it was this threat, or the restraint imposed from a more spiritual realm, I was never to know. I only know I was not molested.

Chapter Ten

THE CHINESE TREAD WARILY

Although on arrival in Lhasa the advisory delegation had gone about its work quietly and mildly, promising no interference in Tibet's religious, political and social structure, it was not long until their advice became couched in stronger terms. The only Tibetan official to take a stand against the Chinese occupation, an elderly statesman called Lukhang, stood up in the Kashag, the Tibetan Parliament, and publicly denounced the Chinese for aggression, pointing out that they had no political claim to Tibet whatever. He wanted, he said, to place his protest on record, although he knew that he might lose his life and would certainly lose his position in doing so. He was right, for shortly afterwards he was 'retired' and more or less isolated by house arrest in Lhasa.

However, the Chinese had to tread much more warily than they had anticipated for they knew that they could not completely plug the leak from Tibet to the outside Powers, and were afraid to apply too much pressure lest events should blow up in their face. The 'leak' which they suspected, but did not know for sure, was that the Dalai Lama was in constant communication with Taktser Rimpoche in America through me. The method was simple. The Dalai Lama gave his letters to Trichang Rimpoche who sent them by trusted messenger to me in Kalimpong. I sent them to Calcutta where they were included in the U.S. despatch bag and delivered to Taktser in the States. Replies from Taktser came by the same channel.

The threats against my person not having been successful, the Chinese shifted their tactics and warned me that if I did not refrain from indulging in anti-Communist activities it would have serious repercussions on my friend, Geoff Bull, in prison in China.

The Chinese Tread Warily

This was a more difficult problem and only my earlier assurance that if we both remained in the will of God no more could happen to Geoff in China than could happen to me in Kalimpong sustained me.

In the meantime, Dr. Carsun Chang had finished his book on *The Third Force* and was ready to leave India. A few months previously a Chinese friend had arrived from Peking, a Dr. B. L. Liu, a former member of Chiang Kai-shek's 'Shadow Cabinet' who had remained in China after the Communist take-over but who had become disillusioned, with appeals from many of Dr. Chang's former colleagues who had also remained and were in influential positions. They had collaborated to get Dr. Liu away from China in order that he might contact Dr. Chang and get him to form a 'Third Force'. While they were disillusioned with Communism and their new Russian overlords, they had also no illusions about a Chiang Kai-shek return, and as Dr. Chang was known for his political integrity, had drawn up the earlier Chinese Constitution, was the respected leader of the Social Democrats and advocate of a temporary coalition government, they appealed to him to take the lead in this matter. They would remain in their positions of influence in Peking until he was ready, when he should get word to them and they would seek to overthrow the Communist Government from the inside.

Dr. Chang left India on his mission early in 1952, travelling first of all to Australia to visit his brother, a former Minister of Finance, and then to various centres of external Chinese influence such as Singapore and the Philippines, on his way to America for further consultations with Li Tsung-jen, former Vice-President of Nationalist China, who was living there.

The Chinese Liberation Army wasted no time in consolidating its position in Tibet and quickly moved into strategic positions on India's border on the south, west and north, concentrating the bulk of their forces in Yatung on the Sikkim border, just north of Kalimpong, and in Rima on the Assam border, just north of Sadiya. No attempt was made at internal development or road-building throughout the country, but gangs of soldiers and highly paid local labour were used to drive the one main road from

The Chinese Tread Warily

Chamdo through Lhasa to Yatung on the Sikkim-Indian border.

Seventy thousand troops were already in the country and there was talk of putting 200,000 troops there within a short time. Morale was kept high by a constant stream of propaganda to the troops telling them of the impending 'liberation' of Sikkim, Nepal, Bhutan and then India. Many young Tibetan officials were wooed by the offer of government positions and a share in the programme of conquest, and this unheard-of opportunity coupled with their bitterness at Indian betrayal brought many into collaboration with the Chinese. Even those who were not deceived with China's promises willingly threw themselves into the various reforms being instituted throughout the country, such as hospitals, schools, dispensaries, town roads and airfields, for they were keen to get away from the priests' reactionary hold on their country and see these reforms so firmly established that when the Chinese ultimately left Tibet the institutions would remain. But such an influx of Chinese into a poorly cultivated country like Tibet brought the country dangerously near to famine conditions. The Chinese had thought that if they introduced agricultural reforms the country would support the army, but they found out the high altitude ground was not able to produce sufficient, and it was not long before the ordinary Tibetan had had enough of Chinese occupation.

While in Lhasa the Chinese has been punctilious in respecting the property and wealth of the priests and nobles, no matter how incriminating and anomalous their position was; in the east they had no such scruples. Making Taktser Rimpoche's escape the excuse, they first of all confiscated the property and land belonging to Kumbum monastery, of which he had been High Priest, and then extended their requisitioning to the other monasteries in Kham and Amdo. It was a very shortsighted move for the Chinese had overlooked the fact that as Kham and Amdo contained 80 per cent of the Tibetan population it followed that the large central monasteries in Lhasa must also have that percentage of representative priests from the eastern provinces who heard from relatives and friends all that was going on in their home areas. Distrust of the Chinese, therefore, increased and no amount of blandishments in Lhasa could win over the ordinary Tibetan.

Jigme Pangdatshang, Topgyay's son, arrived unexpectedly in Kalimpong from Kham bringing news of Geoff. According to his report, Geoff had been with the Prince of De-ge, Commander-in-Chief of the Tibetan Army, in East Tibet when the Chinese Communists had arrived. For a month or so the Chinese Commander, the Prince of De-ge and Geoff had remained on friendly terms, then Geoff had been sent to Batang. Here for a little while he had been well treated, although kept under constant surveillance by an armed guard, and then he had been taken from Batang to Kangting. The last news Jigme had heard was that he had left Kangting for Chungking.

I found it extremely difficult to write home to friends who were interested, for on the one hand I could not write a chatty letter without mentioning Geoff, or the situation in Tibet, yet on the other hand I could not write on either of these subjects without getting Geoff or Tibetan friends into dangerous trouble. I decided that the best thing to do was not to write letters at all. But for the first time I tried my hand at newspaper and article writing. The Chinese had a monoply of news on Tibet and used it to their advantage with the usual Communist claims of welcome from the people, sweeping reforms, abundant prosperity. Under various pseudonyms I contradicted these claims, giving facts and figures as I learned them from Tibetan friends. After a series of articles had appeared in the Communist newspapers *Blitz* and *Crossroads* attacking various people in Kalimpong as imperialist spies, I told the Communist reporter in Kalimpong that another article of that character and I would do a series on the Russian and Chinese spies whom I knew were active in Kalimpong. There were no more articles, and an uneasy truce was maintained with only occasional news reports being issued from Peking and Hong Kong.

Early in 1952 another of the Dalai Lama's brothers, Gyalu Thondup, arrived with his wife in Kalimpong from Formosa, and after a short stay he and his mother left for Lhasa, leaving his wife in Darjeeling. A few months later Gyalu Thondup made a dramatic escape from Lhasa through South Tibet into Assam and so back to Darjeeling.

Chinese Communist activity on the Indian border at last began to worry India, and in May 1952 Mr. Nehru, with a large entourage of political and military advisers, paid a visit to Kalimpong and Gangtok, in Sikkim, to see what was happening for himself. He was bluntly informed by his advisers that in the event of a Chinese attack there was nothing India could do to stop it, either militarily or politically. China's claim to the border States was based on the same assumptions as for Tibet and the Indian acceptance of Chinese occupation of Tibet was a diplomatic defeat that looked like leading them into losing Nepal, Sikkim, Bhutan and parts of Bengal and Assam.

Headlines in the newspapers read: 'We Are Next on Mao's List' as Chinese propaganda against India increased in intensity in China and Tibet and movements and preparations of troops built up on the borders. A political commentator in India, Dr. Takarnath Das, wrote a warning article on the vulnerability of India's frontiers:

> It may be pointed out without fear of contradiction that if Soviet Russia decides to move southward, Pakistan, with her present hostility towards India, cannot defend herself. Neither is it possible for India to defend herself from such an onslaught single-handed. I may be permitted to remind Indian statesmen that a far less peaceful Persia, under Nadir Shah, during the early eighteenth century, invaded and sacked Delhi and took away Mogul India's peacock throne.
>
> If Sino-Russian forces move towards Northern India—especially North-Eastern India—India, with her present relations with Pakistan, especially Eastern Pakistan where millions of Hindus are denied human rights, cannot defend herself. It is no secret (and the Government of India must have more adequate information than I have) that from Lhasa, as well as from Peking and Moscow, movement for cession of certain parts of North-Eastern India—particularly Nepal, Bhutan, Sikkim and adjoining regions—and Chinese expansion into North Burma and Malaya are in full progress.
>
> I venture to assert that the idea that India has nothing to fear from a Soviet Russian-Communist China alliance is *mere wishful thinking*.

Robert Trumbull, of the *New York Times*, on a visit to Kalimpong and Darjeeling, was able to collect quite a bit of information and published an article on his analysis of the situation in Tibet headed, 'Chinese Plan To Dominate Border States'.

Chinese Communists in Tibet plan to move 200,000 troops into the realm of the Living Buddha in order to dominate India's Himalayan borders.

In a long-range scheme Communist infiltration into Afghanistan, Nepal and Indian protected States of Bhutan and Sikkim will be followed by penetration into India itself. Meanwhile the Communists have been unable to gain control over Tibet, except in the military sense, in a year of occupation by the 15th Division of Mao Tse-Tung's army. Real power is held by the anti-Communist secret 'People's Committee' whose recommendations are followed by the 17-year-old Dalai Lama, Tibet's spiritual and temporal ruler, in defiance of the Chinese.

Already the Tibetans had become tired of Chinese 'liberation' and the 'People's Committee' was a secret group known in Tibetan as Mi-mang Tsong-du with influential membership. Tibetan officials were collaborating with the Chinese principally out of a feeling of helplessness and frustration but were in no doubt that they would turn against their captors when the time was ripe. The Chinese announced from Peking with a great fanfare that the Dalai Lama had accepted the chairmanship of the proposed 'Political Military Committee' that was to rule Tibet under direct orders from Mao Tse-tung, but in Tibet they could not get it functioning even with cajolery added to threats. With the knowledge of his people's support conveyed to him by the Mi-mang Tsong-du the Dalai Lama continued to stall off the Chinese and the Chinese dared not tamper with his authority.

Meanwhile isolated clashes between Chinese soldiers and Tibetan civilians became so frequent and violent in Lhasa that the Chinese were forced to segregate their troops. A great deal of the local resentment over and above the traditional hatred of the Chinese was caused by the severe food shortage and inflated prices brought on by the influx of thousands of the Chinese troops.

Three high-ranking Tibetan groups who went to Peking for consultation on the implementation of the enforced Sino-Tibetan Treaty let it be known that they did so with the understanding amongst themselves that they were merely affording the Peking

Government an occasion to carry out propaganda, and that they did so under duress.

It was about this time that the Chinese gave up their proposed grandiose schemes for linking up the principal cities of Tibet with a network of roads connecting them with China. Instead, they announced that they intended to build the first motorable road from Chengtu through Chamdo to Lhasa and from Lhasa to the Natu Pass on the Sikkim border of India. They were having great difficulty supplying their troops in Tibet, and with the rising tide of discontent against the occupation in the country, they hoped to supply Lhasa and their occupation troops by this easier route through shipments from Shanghai to Calcutta, to be transported from there to the border via Kalimpong.

Chinese garrisons were mushrooming every five miles along the proposed motor road, the ancient Silk Road of the caravans, but the greatest build-up was on the border nearest India. They made no attempts to disguise their ultimate purpose that after gaining military domination of the Indian border area they would infiltrate into the whole of the Himalayan area from Afghanistan through Kashmir, Nepal, Sikkim, and Bhutan, and then India.

In the meantime Dr. Chang had travelled throughout Southeast Asia having his consultations with the external Free Chinese leaders, and after arriving in America and having talks with Li Tsung-jen and others there he released the text of the Third Forces' political manifesto on October 16th, 1952. The *Chinese World* made it front page news:

FREE CHINESE FORCES ISSUE MANIFESTOS

Organization of the Chinese Anti-Communist Forces was given a tremendous impetus today when Ku Meng-yu, spokesman for the newly formed 'China's Fighting League for Free Democracy', released the complete text of a Manifesto issued by the League on the occasion of China's commemoration of the Double Tenth anniversary date of China's Independence Day. The founders of the new organization, in addition to Ku Meng-yu, include such notable figures as Dr. Carsun Chang and General Chang Fang Kwei. . . .

The League's platform was such as might have been drawn up by any group of Liberals in any part of the world. 'Resolved to overthrow the totalitarian and party dictatorship as practised by the Chinese Communist régime . . . to realize and safeguard the inviolability of the right of religious worship . . . the freedom of thought, the freedom of speech, the freedom of the press. . . .'

It was addressed to their compatriots on the mainland of China, in Formosa, and in all other places where Chinese lived and worked, and sought their support and co-operation. They suggested that Chinese everywhere should sever all relations, social, economic and otherwise with the Communists, and, co-operating with the Governments of the countries where they were residing and with all local leaders and public bodies interested in combating Communism, seek to overthrow the Chinese Communist régime on the mainland.

That these were platitudes no one would dispute but that they were also expressions of the desires of millions of people was equally true. The man who had drawn them up, Dr. Carsun Chang, was the man who had, some years before, drawn up the Chinese Constitution, and who was known for his political integrity and incorruptibility even to the Communists in his own country. Whether they would ever see accomplishment at the hands of their creator only time would tell.

In the meantime a much smaller event had occurred in Kalimpong, but one that was to fit into the jigsaw pattern of Tibetan history and which should be recorded if only for that reason. I had met and become engaged to be married to Margaret Ingram, a surgeon on holiday from the Ludhiana Christian Medical College, regarding whom her former chief, Norman Tanner, one of the world's leading surgeons, had said: 'When she left us there was no doubt that she was a very accomplished surgeon of great ability.' When I returned to Tibet it would be with the company of one whom God had given outstanding gifts to be used in a skill that the Tibetans desperately required.

Chapter Eleven

THE MISSIONARY CONTROVERSY

From 1952 onwards the Chinese Communists in Tibet intensified their programme of take-over of Tibetan governmental and administrative institutions, not only with a view to absorbing Tibet within China's political structure but, more ominous, with a view to infiltrating and taking over Asia.

In Lhasa, under the 'Asiatic Section' of the International Communist Intelligence Bureau, they established a large Communist Intelligence Branch with an impressive administration under the following seven offices:

1. Foreign Affairs Office
2. Border Affairs Office
   (a) Yatung Office
   (b) Lammo La Office
   (c) Tsona Office
   (d) Gartok Office under Tihwa (Sinkiang) control
3. Training Academies
   (a) Staff Training Academy
   (b) Tibetan Languages Training Academy
   (c) Commercial (Traders) Training Academy
   (d) Infiltrating Academy
      1. India Infiltrating Class
      2. Nepal Infiltrating Class
      3. Bhutan and Sikkim Infiltrating Class
4. Espionage Office
   (a) Transfer Section (Movement Control)
   (b) Conference Section (Meetings, etc.)
5. Mines Research Office
6. Land Survey Office
7. Meteorological Office (Air and Climate Survey)

The Missionary Controversy

'Foreign Affairs' came under the control of the 'Advisory Bureau' and was directed from Peking through its head, Chang Chung-win.

The 'Border Affairs Office' was concerned with intelligence related, as the name implies, to the Border States of Bhutan, Nepal, Sikkim and India, and methods of infiltration into these areas. Yatung is a strategic point on the main trail into Sikkim and India, only a day's journey from Gangtok and Kalimpong. Lammo La is on the Tibet-Nepal border, a village about eighty miles from Khatmandu, capital of Nepal, and a trading post between the two countries. Tsona Dzong is a town in a district between Tibet, Bhutan and Assam.

Members of the various intelligence and infiltration groups were taken mostly from bi-lingual border provinces between China and Tibet, such as Kham, Amdo, Yunnan, Kansu, and Sinkiang; they studied English, Hindi, Bengali, Nepali, and Tibetan, as well as subsidiary intelligence pursuits. With such well-organized activities to further their plans for take-over in Asia the outlook for India and the Border States looked bleak indeed.

Early in 1953 I was asked by the Dalai Lama's brother, Gyalu Thondup, if I would help a Tibetan who had arrived in Kalimpong and who was looking for someone with influential contacts to assist him in something.

The Tibetan was from Amdo Province and I had already heard about his arrival in Kalimpong through the town's usual grapevine, but apparently I still had more to hear. What the town knew was that after he had arrived in Kalimpong someone had tried to poison him and he had gone temporarily out of his mind. The Dr. Graham's Homes' medical officer had treated him, and a Swedish missionary in town had taken him into his home and his life had been saved. At that point I came into the picture. When he knew that I was the person who had helped Taktser Rimpoche to escape to America he opened up with his full story. He was Gompo Sham, the son-in-law of one of the top four leaders in East Tibet, Hou Wan Seiling of Amdo, a General of the People's Army. He had been sent by Hou Wan Seiling to India to contact Taktser Rimpoche and try to get help for a large-scale revolution against the Chinese Communists in East Tibet. He had crossed Tibet as a mendicant monk, dodging the Chinese who were on the lookout for him, and slipped into India without a permit. The landlord of the inn in which he was staying in Kalimpong knew this and was blackmailing him, and Gompo Sham suspected he had gone to the local Chinese Communists who had given him the poison to kill him. All this, coupled with the news that Taktser was not in Kalimpong but in America, had served temporarily to overcome him and drive him out of his mind, but he had since heard of me, and that I was the one who had helped Taktser and perhaps could also help him.

After pointing out that there were several differences between his position and influence and Taktser's I agreed to do what I could for him, and he went on to tell his story. Apparently the Chinese in East Tibet had become exasperated by the intransigence of the Amdo and Kham tribesmen and decided to wage an all-out campaign of extermination. Up to that time the Chinese had kept to the main road, the chief monasteries and the occasional towns and villages, leaving the tribesmen in the mountains severely alone. But the great fighting tribes would not leave the Chinese alone and rode out in sudden attacks on the Chinese, slaughtering garrisons and then taking to the mountains again where they were completely unapproachable.

Some tribes were worse than others, and the Goloks who ranged the mountains between Amdo and Kham were the most intractable and warlike of all the fighting tribes of East Tibet. The Chinese had ordered Hou Wan Seiling and Gompo Sham to go to the Golok area and subdue these tribesmen, teaching them a lesson that would bring the other tribes to heel. Hou Wan Seiling, a Vice-President of Tsinghai, or Amdo, Province, had been fighting a skilful delaying action since the Chinese occupation, keeping the reins of power over his Amdo tribesmen in his own hands, but he knew that he had not sufficient power to control the Goloks. Not only were they naturally warlike but they were so fiercely anti-Chinese that any suggestion coming from Hou Wan Seiling or Gompo Sham of collaboration with them would mean their immediate death.

With such a choice before them they decided to precipitate a mass revolt. There were several groups of rebels, anyway, throughout East Tibet, and together with the arms they had brought with them in retreat from the Communists and supplies which had since been dropped by Chinese Nationalist planes operating from Formosa, they were in a position to more than hold their own against the scattered Chinese Communists. Three thousand Chinese Communists had been sent into that particular area of Amdo but in the mountains nearby there were about 80,000 anti-Chinese rebels. He claimed that 8,000 troops from General Ma Bao-Feng's Nationalist Army, and 6,000 from General Ma Feng-kwai's Nationalist Army had escaped into the mountains of Tibet, had taken refuge there and settled in with the Tibetan tribesmen. But they didn't want a long drawn-out time of guerrilla warfare and he had been sent to get into touch with Taktser Rimpoche to see if he could get help from any of the outside Powers.

I passed this news on to the Dalai Lama's brother to be forwarded to the Dalai Lama in Lhasa, and then left for Calcutta and the round of interviews with officials again. As I had anticipated, it was more difficult to arrange an escape for comparatively unknown Gompo Sham than for the Dalai Lama's brother, and passport and financial obstacles which had been overcome for the latter did not apply to the former. He had brought with him, secreted in his clothes, several gold bars amounting to some tens of thousands of rupees but this would hardly be sufficient to keep him for an indefinite time in America.

As I had now been away from home for about seven years, and had been contemplating a short leave to get married anyway, I sent word to the Brethren Council in Britain to ask them to place £200 at my disposal to cover the fares for Gompo Sham, his wife and myself, with sufficient left over to take them to America; he could then return this when he arrived in America and got his affairs sorted out there. He agreed with this and I booked passages, only to be informed at the last minute that the U.S. Government recommended that he go to Formosa and they would use their influence to get him a visa to go there. This was a blow not only to him but to me, for I had obtained the money and booked the passages, and in asking for the money from the Brethren Council, strictly against Brethren principles as well as my own, had considerably compromised my standing with them in relation to my former attitude to the Scriptures.

However, as the money had arrived and the passages were booked I decided to carry on with my plans to go home anyway. British and American indifference in relation to Tibet's predicament was frustrating and in addition to getting married I thought I might be able to stir up some interest on Tibet's behalf.

It was a vain hope. I had plenty of talks with people at different levels, who were polite and seemed interested, but nothing was ever taken up and nothing was ever done. Tibet was too hot a situation to handle, not only because of the implied interference with a touchily independent India, but also because it meant tangling with a powerful, aggressive China. It was much easier to let an unknown, unrepresented Tibet slide into oblivion.

On the religious issues I had more ground for hope. I began and carried on, as I had planned, an all-out attack on an antiquated anachronistic missionary system. I did not confine myself to Brethren churches, but went to every denomination to which I was invited. The reputation acquired through the earlier newspaper reports of my trip across Tibet opened many doors which would have been closed to me in less spectacular circumstances, and at least I was able to get my foot inside, although each time I spoke I came away convinced I had preached my benediction.

It was not that there wasn't interest, or even enthusiasm, but this was usually confined to the young of my own age, or the middle-aged and elderly 'spiritual' who were averse to 'revolution' in spiritual things. There had been too many divisions in the past over obscure issues, and even if what I said regarding the missionary situation was true—and it was difficult to believe that so many sincere people could be quite so foolish and so blind—if left alone it would sort itself out.

Before I had left Britain, several times during missionary talks at home a tenuous thread of doubt had crept into my mind about the methods used by Brethren missionaries which seemed at variance with what was generally accepted and taught in Brethren circles, but the impeccable phraseology of the speakers, their sound knowledge of 'Scriptural principles', their unassailable evidence on the screen of large assemblies, or churches, had served to lull the suspicions aroused.

The 'compound-paternalist' system of missionary activity—the religious equivalent of the political 'white man's burden'—was a system evolved from an imperialist attitude of mind where the foreign missionary condescendingly brought the benefits of a Western Christianity to the natives. The missionary was the responsible fountain-head for the financial as well as the spiritual activities of his particular community, if not always in a clergy-laity relationship then certainly in a superior-inferior relationship with the people of the country. He was the 'great white father' in his district dispensing the benefits of a Western-conceived system of church-gathering and practice, Western forms of worship, musical instruments and hymn tunes, and as often as not despising and denouncing all forms of national culture as inferior to his own. The elders of the churches might be invited to his house on Christmas Day for a celebration meal, but again as likely as not they would only be permitted into the compound garden or on to the veranda. It was necessary to maintain one's standing.

The practice was, of course, only a question of policy in many instances among the denominational and inter-denominational missions, and was merely an inevitable development from the accepted premise of denominationalism in an imperialist era. However, when practised as a system by those from Brethren assemblies it constituted a violation of the very principle on which they gathered together as a separatist group. The Bible taught a missionary sent out from a local church only to preach the 'whole counsel of God', build up autonomous, self-supporting, self-propagating churches in whatever locality the Holy Spirit might lead him to, and then pass on to some other place to continue the same work. Yet I had seen missionaries, sent out from assemblies which were established on these very principles, building homes, anticipating permanent residence in the locality, purchasing land, and even building halls at their own expense, thereby making the indispensable centre of the Christian community themselves, around whom every activity revolved and without whom it could not exist. The final unbelievable folly was committed when the deeds of their houses and halls were filed with a company floated in Britain for that purpose. It was not only violation of Scriptural principle of the most flagrant kind—it was political suicide.

I did not help my case any by attacking on all fronts at once the empty hypocritical attitude that could hold public prayer meetings for Geoff Bull while 90 per cent of those who attended asked, 'Do you think he's alive?' 'Do you think the Chinese will ever let him go?' Believing prayer, forsooth! Also, the interest was principally a selfish and chauvinistic one. There was no question that God might have a purpose for him in prison—God *must* release him because it was a good thing to get as far away as possible from the Communists—or that John Ting, our Chinese fellow-worker, was also in prison, and Watchman Nee and thousands of others. These were Chinese and it was their problem, but Geoff was an Englishman and it was necessary to get him to England. What was to happen afterwards, of course, was something that could be shelved for the present—Geoff's ministry, Chinese Christian believers under Communism, expanding Communism itself, retreating apologetic Christianity.

I took at least one meeting a day, sometimes two, three, and even four. I talked well into the night with many who had been shocked, many who were antagonized, many who wanted something done. But those who I felt had the most to contribute to the situation because of the context in which they moved—religious, social, political, economic—namely, those associated with so-called Plymouth Brethren groups, were strangled by a creeper growth of control that had accumulated over the past fifty to a hundred years and the dynamic contribution that Brethren could have made in the present generation was stunted by this reactionary parasitical growth that had fastened on the movement.

The major difficulty was that the reactionary group could not be pinpointed, separated, and cut off as the constitution of Brethren churches professedly permitted. Henry Fairlie, the political commentator, has defined a similar group functioning in English political life as 'the Establishment', and it was just such a grey amorphous body that throttled Brethren vitality. 'The Establishment', said Fairlie, 'is a useful phrase because it denotes, not the oligarchs, but those who create the pressures which sustain the climate of opinion within which they have to act. The Establishment, as a concept, is concerned with the meteorology of power. For purely descriptive (and, of course, not pejorative) purposes one could show the Establishment today and on one of those fascinating meteorological maps, as a vast depression centred over the British Isles, only occasionally disturbed by a ridge of high pressure. The further outlook is that the depression will continue indefinitely.'

How it worked in a claimed non-sectarian group such as Brethren was that in each local church or 'Assembly', as they termed it, one or two of the 'oversight' or elders, would represent the local assembly in a district group of assemblies formed to make the holding of campaigns or conferences easier for all. From these district groups delegates would emerge—appointed by the nebulous pressures of power at various levels, never by open vote which was, of course, frowned upon as non-Scriptural —who would represent their areas either at 'elders' meetings' held in Netherhall Christian Guest House, in Largs, or on the Council of Brethren for Home and Foreign Missionary Work in Glasgow for Scotland; or on the Brethren Council at Bath, the Committee for Missionary Prayer Meetings and Westminster Missionary meetings in London, or the High Leigh Conference for Brethren in England. When any major Brethren event took place two Brethren from amongst the Scottish groups would be 'appointed' to travel to England to carry the mind of Scottish Brethren. At an international level, when any matter was to be discussed or when any missionary problem arose, members from the Scottish, English (also representing Wales and Ireland), American, Canadian, Australian and New Zealand assemblies would get to-gether to settle the issue raised. The remarkable fact was that none of these men were ever 'appointed' by Brethren assemblies in the accepted sense of the term, and the groups and committees which gave them their authority were not supposed to exist. They settled issues and formulated policies affecting the whole of international Brethren witness yet had no body who could dismiss them for incompetence, replace them, or to whom they were ultimately responsible. The slightest deviation from the climate of opinion generated by this 'Establishment' meant recall from the missionary vocation, subtle derogation of character, forbidden use of any platform as an 'undesirable', being cut off from financial support of gifts from individuals or assemblies, dismissal into the wilderness.

I have gone into the 'organization' in some detail because a knowledge of the set-up is necessary for a background appreciation of the difficulties involved in trying to eliminate the anachronistic, imperialist, 'paternalist-compound' missionary approach which was absorbing millions of pounds every year in useless activity. It presented just as big a problem as the removal of a reactionary Government in Tibet or the removal of a Communist Government in China. Further, it involved for me a question of association based on Scriptural principles. What Brethren taught conformed completely to Biblical teaching so I was happy to be with them in a spiritual structure that had enlightened the tyrannies and darkness of history, but what they now practised was categorically opposed to what they taught. If this impossible dichotomy could be exposed and dealt with in one way or another then there would be a release of energy that could once again turn the world upside down.

I received a letter in due course from the Brethren Council at Bath: 'We have been grieved to hear from many of the bad impression of your own character given to many by your attacks upon the work of others and for your own sake, as well as for the sake of the Lord's work, we do request you will desist from making them. We think we have said before that in our view it would be far more in accordance with the mind of Christ for you to show by your work in India how much better such work can be carried on than for you to criticize the work of others. We shall be glad to have your proposals for the repayments of the loan.'

I sent a cheque to cover the latter, which was the £200 sent for the passage money for Gompo Sham, his wife and myself, and the abrupt demand for which my sensitive mind interpreted as a subtle form of intimidation—and a letter clarifying my position, which I contended was an attack upon a *system* denounced in theory by Brethren themselves but practised nevertheless, and not upon individuals who were perfectly free—more free than I apparently was—to uphold its virtues or factually prove my allegations wrong if such were the case. As to my spiritual activities, if statistics were to be the criterion—which I did not concede—I could point to many converts in China, the founding and building up of several Scriptural type churches functioning without my presence, a wide ministry of preaching to thousands all over India, and the building up of the local churches in Kalimpong and district. If that didn't prove my argument that the old-school approach was unnecessary as well as unscriptural, then nothing would.

The Scottish Brethren were even less courteous and scriptural. In conversations the 'Establishment' let it be known to the various representatives that in the future I was to be considered *persona non grata*, a dangerous young man, and to be refused the platform of Brethren assemblies everywhere. They sent no letter, did not call me before them, sent no older person—although many were acquaintances of many years standing—to see me, talk with me, or reprimand me. The 'Establishment' was in danger and had to draw together to safeguard itself, and to do so I should be forbidden access to possibly responsive ears.

Of course, it did not work out this way. Many Brethren groups and individuals disliked the authoritarian and centralized control that had developed over the years, and agreed with what I expounded from the Scriptures even if they disagreed with my suggestions for rectifying the situation. I had liberty to say what I liked in many influential places. Also, the 'Establishment' could only shut the doors of houses against me by publicly proving me guilty of heresy, false doctrine or division, and I was guilty of none of these things. The favourable reactions and response to what I had to say was much beyond what I had expected or even hoped for in my most sanguine moments, and, had I so wished, I could have built up an impressive following throughout the country to 'do something' about the situation. But I was not prepared to establish a divisive group; what I wanted was to change the climate of opinion throughout all the Brethren assemblies in Britain and the world, and to appeal for a return to the practice of what they preached. Then all the other errors and deviations would be righted in a Scriptural manner that would not necessitate another division with further weakness. What I was saying was perfectly Scriptural—as witness the fact that I had never been approached and put under discipline as I would most certainly have been had there been any suggestion of Scriptural deviation—and could easily be put into practice given a proper condition of mind and spirit before God. The machinery was there; it only required an influx of divine power to set it moving.

On December 19th, 1953, the B.B.C. news bulletin carried the information that Geoff Bull had been released from imprisonment and had arrived in Hong Kong. I cabled him:

> 'PRAISE GOD STOP HAVE JUST HEARD NEWS STOP
> COME HOME IMMEDIATELY STOP WILL SHARE ANSWERS
> TO PRAYER GEORGE.'

His reply read:

Dear George,

Four years' greetings! I can just hear your Gaelic saying to me, 'David Livingstone, I presume!!' Well, brother, I have been a long time walking into the morning but I have wrestled until the breaking of the day and what does it matter if we limp into the dawning provided our name is Israel? Having come out in the miraculous Grace of God I just feel like shouting from the mountain tops: 'Jesus never fails.' I think I am beginning to understand the precious word, 'When the Lord turned again the captivity of Zion we were as them that dream.'

Dear brother, how often have I thought of you and all our plans for Tibet, wondering how you felt, but He not only 'appointeth the times' but 'changeth appointed times' (Daniel Darby Version) and He knoweth the way that He takes.

You will be longing to know everything, but of course it is

absolutely impossible in a letter to cover all these years. . . .
Gradually, I hope to be able to tell you all but it will take time. . . .

You just don't realize, George, after practically three years
without a Bible or any religious freedom whatsoever, shut up for
about three years two months (including escorted travelling) and
subjected most of the time to intensive Marxist education of a
more or less compulsory nature, on top of which for about 18
months I didn't know in my own mind whether I would be exe-
cuted or not and for most of the time the very least I could expect
was indefinite imprisonment. I was in solitary confinement for
about ten months of the time, but thank God the food I was given
for most of the time was about the same as the Liberation Army's
officers, the conditions I was housed in were hygienic. I had
medical attention when required . . . so physically I am remarkably
well. . . .

As to the Liberation Army, of course Topgyay could only let
them through, it would have been madness to resist. We arranged
that the second time I went back to Batang, as soon as the news
came through of the approach of the first detachments of the Red
Army, then I would get straight back to Bo. At that juncture
Rapga and I planned to get across the Golden Sand river into
Tibet proper. The Batang Magistrate, an old Kuomingtang
official, called me secretly and gave me the news at the time and I
got back, but met the advance detachments of the Red Army
on a 15,000 foot pass. They were tired to death and could hardly
speak with fatigue so I got past them. . . .

The Kuomingtang sympathisers were in connection with each
other in Batang. A courageous Tibetan, Puntsok Wangje, who
had done underground work in Lhasa, headed the Communist
uprising in Batang. I must say I admire their pluck. It's a wonder
we didn't all lose our heads (literally) in one way or another. At
Bo, in the end of July, the Pangdatshangs fairly obviously had
their new plot, but in the circumstances it was difficult to say
anything. Our plans were obviously falling through, but they
wanted to hold in with Lhasa, and yet must play a card with the
Communists, and the result was that Rapga and I left for Tibet
and Topgyay for Kangting. Rapga suggested leaving three days

before me to avoid suspicion and possible interception. He is a wizard, because he was, as he suspected, intercepted but permitted to pass on. It was a miracle his escort and the Batang Communists who intercepted him did not open fire on one another. Three days later I got clean through the mountains. We met inside Tibet at a place called Ja Gag, a Pangdatshang agency off the track from Bum Ting and Lha Dun, then we moved together to Gartok. A great time with De-ge Sey in Gartok and some great opportunities medically and in the Gospel. With Rapga's help later at Chamdo, and also Bob Ford, I was able to continue at Gartok and permission to go to the north looked very hopeful indeed. Then came the earthquake which was quite an experience —but we survived; I guess the wind and fire was to follow. Practically all those two months skirmishing continued along the Golden Sand river and the Red Army piled up on the Jyekundo, De-ge, Batang, Atunze and Tsakaio fronts. Arms came down from Chamdo but obviously preparations were inadequate. Moves were made secretly by the Batang Communists to get De-ge Sey to make a separate surrender of South-east Tibet. (I am racing through the facts; all described in detail is just like an adventure story but suffice the sketch for the moment.) Early in October reports from the front came in. First, from the south, the Konko Lama country. They lost a pass almost at the first assault. De-ge Sey was greatly disturbed. I think he feared treachery. Then came news from the north saying that 300 Chinese had passed across the river in a most remote spot between Batang and Chamdo. Things looked grim. De-ge Sey sent out a detachment of cavalry in that direction—other reports came in—things were moving—then the great blow, 1,800 Communist troops had forced the river on the Batang front and were advancing on Bum Ting. This meant the river defences were broken. (I learnt of the strategy used for this later—all very interesting.) Of course we thought maybe advance units would penetrate to Gartok on the next day. De-ge Sey thought if he could gather sufficient forces he could fight a big battle on the plain of Gartok—but it was impossible. I was with him and the Depon at the most critical moment and he was at a loss to know what to do for the best.

The Missionary Controversy

That night they conferred all night. I had thought they would fight in Gartok and hold the fort to the last man, and envisaged the place being burnt over our heads, but his decision was to make an immediate withdrawal to the north.

An hour later amidst great confusion in fort and district he came in. As the Communists advanced the local people were going over to banditry, the magistrate fled for his life, administrative control broke down, people started to steal, the army was disintegrating—resistance was becoming impossible. The General, De-ge Sey, stood before me with his six-foot odd and magnificent clothes. He looked a giant—exceedingly courageous and really very calm, but of course feeling the tremendous strain. He said, trying to control the break in his voice, 'I have decided to go out and surrender. I must go for my men's sake.' I considered this a great action on his part, because he could escape, but in order to save the lives of the men of his scattered army he was willing to sacrifice himself. . . .

I paused a moment to learn what God's will was. I simply said to him, 'Would you like me to come with you? I will interpret for you in Chinese.' He looked at me. I don't think he thought I would go all the way through the crisis with him. He said, 'Yes, come.' So we went. Six hours riding—then we sent out a man. The advancing Red Army was just round the brow of the hill about 500 yards away. Our man went forward and announced the fact of the General's presence, and we were asked to go forward. We met the ordinary soldiers, then in a few minutes the officers came up. Darkness fell. In the evening we gathered in a Tibetan house in the village near the Pangdatshang's big house. A not too big room—Chinese, Tibetans, English—we talked in the flickering light of the pine drips. The General was asked why he resisted. He replied that he was obeying his Government's order, but when further loss of life was useless he surrendered. I tried to speak for him to some extent. They accepted his unconditional surrender. He had thought they would kill him but their policy was quite different. The next day we went in with the Liberation Army to Gartok. Two days later I was interviewed, transferred to a private house in the village, and placed under arrest. From that time, October 1950, to December 1953 I was in their hands. That is another story. I learnt much of the other world—learnt that there are two sides to every question. Spiritually it was an immense trial; physically I've come through tolerably well. . . .

I have given you a mere frame of what transpired. You can imagine what is in the gaps, for instance, travelling under escort —passing through prisons—under interrogations. Years and years of indescribable mental experiences which can never be described adequately on paper—but, George, 'Jesus never fails.' Think of the past and think of the future—we must search out all in our work not after CHRIST, then go on again towards the mark. I have known triumph and failure—sorrow and joy—have passed through every mood of disappointment and elation— passed through death, I guess, all but the stopping of my heart-beat and passed through life in its reality as I have never known it before—passed through it all, George, but God forbid that I should boast save in the Cross of Christ my Lord. I have been brought back with my armour hacked to shreds, but, brother, I am standing—that's just about all I know. . . .

You, brother, more than anyone can understand what a miracle it is my life has been spared. Of all that one did and planned in the end, there is nothing that the People's Government of China do not know—but I am alive in Hong Kong. In my prison room I prayed that if it would take 20 years to make me the man God wanted me to be, then to keep me till that day: but in three years two months He has let me go. I need to seek His will and enable-ment for that new service. . . .

I want to say how thrilled I was to hear of your marriage. Knowing you so well the course of events was not really surpris-ing to me and I am sure the Lord has given you and your wife the very best He had for you both. Accept my very heartiest con-gratulations. . . . Just carry on with your original plans and I will fit in when the time comes. . . .

Chapter Twelve

THE TIBETANS GROW BITTER

I returned, married, to Kalimpong early in 1954. Anti-Chinese feeling inside Tibet and amongst Tibetans in Kalimpong had strengthened. The Mi-mang Tsong-du ('People's Party'), or Tibet Reorganization Committee, had grown considerably and were sufficiently powerful to stage public demonstrations in Lhasa against the continued occupation by the Chinese. Whenever the demonstrations looked like becoming too out of hand the Chinese would complain, more arrests would be made by the army, but the Communists were afraid to push matters too far and usually handed over the leaders of the demonstrations to the Tibetan officials for punishment. Needless to say, they were normally freed after a few days.

Although anti-Chinese feeling was high and public intransigence the order of the day, Tibet made no attempt to appeal to India or other outside Powers for help. They were bitter against India on account of the betrayal they had suffered, and believed that India was both afraid of the Chinese, inept in her diplomacy vis-à-vis China and disillusioned with other countries and the U.N. because her appeals had been ignored. All that was left to them was Chinese-baiting, occasional demonstrations, and sometimes a flare-up into a local armed revolt.

India had gradually become aware of the anti-Indian feeling in Tibet, and the difficulties which might accrue from it, and began to take hesitant measures to counteract the flow of anti-Indian propaganda amongst the Tibetans. I was approached and asked for suggestions as to how this might be accomplished without involving India in too open an anti-Chinese attitude which might precipitate a Chinese attack, or even embarrass India's relations with China. I had no confidence in the majority of Tibetan officials I had met during my stay in Kalimpong, and said so. They were small-time feudal intriguers, opportunists, afraid of any suggestion that demanded an open commitment, fearful of their wealth and property, suspicious of each other. Even the Mi-mang Tsong-du in Lhasa had no open official connections, and the supposed 'leaders' were only middle-class traders, 'front-men' to hide the identity of officials who were either too scared or too highly placed in Chinese Communist councils to commit themselves to an open anti-Chinese Communist stand. Any attempt to form an anti-Communist group out of them was bound to end in failure. In any case, even supposing such a group could be got together purely on the ground of selfish interest, they could do little against the Chinese. In Lhasa, and Central Tibet, mass demonstrations could be held with the help of the discontented masses, but they could put up no effective opposition to the well-armed and disciplined Chinese Communists.

The only ones who were capable of doing this were the Khambas and Amdowas of East Tibet. They had the arms, the courage and the ability to take on the Chinese and defeat them. What they were not prepared to do was do it for the useless figure-head officials of the Lhasa Government. But any plan for overthrowing the Chinese would have to have Kham and Amdo representation and participation to succeed. If the Indian Government was prepared to rescind their expulsion order forbidding Rapga Pangdatshang to enter India I would send for him to come to India and guarantee his anti-Communist sincerity. He, and his brother Topgyay, had twice lost everything they possessed in fighting for Tibetan independence, and with Hou Wan Seiling and Geshi Sherab Gyaltso in Amdo would be prepared to risk wealth and life again, I was certain.

When I was given assurance that Rapga would be permitted to enter India I sent him a secret message on the direction folder of a bottle of medicine asking him to come to India. I reckoned it would take six months, at least, for the parcel of medicines to reach him in Kham and for sufficient time to elapse for him to open the requisite bottle and send a reply. In the meantime, with a great blaring of trumpets, India signed a 'Trade Pact' with

The Tibetans Grow Bitter

China. The significance of this agreement did not lie in the handing over of telegraphic and postal communications in Tibet to China, or the mutual agreement to have three representative trade agencies in Yatung, Gyantse and Lhasa in Tibet, and Kalimpong, Calcutta and Delhi in India, but in the small print at the bottom that in the future India would recognize that Tibet was an 'integral part of China', to be known as 'the Tibet region of China'. What India was to have in exchange was not made clear. In India it was rumoured that Nehru had hoped to get a fixed delineation of the Macmahon Line as the recognized border between Tibet and India, so limiting China's expansionist designs, but if this were so it was another diplomatic defeat for India for nothing of this was included in the agreement.

However, the Trade Pact was acclaimed in India and China with a great fanfare of trumpets and the principles outlined by Mr. Nehru in this matter, 'The Five Principles of Peaceful Co-existence', or 'Panch Shila', became first of all a slogan, then the basis of India's foreign policy, and were later taken up at Bangdung as the theme of the conference of the nations of the Afro-Asian block and later by Russia and Poland. The 'Five Principles' were:

1. Non-aggression.
2. Non-interference in another's internal affairs, for any reasons of an economic, political or ideological character.
3. Mutual respect for one another's territorial integrity and sovereignty.
4. Equality and mutual benefit.
5. Peaceful co-existence.

While Mr. Nehru and Mr. Chou En-lai were being acclaimed throughout Asia for their magnanimous and enlightened approach to relations between nations, Tibet, which had been the object of discussion and agreement, had been invaded, intimidated, and exploited, and was in the process of being absorbed, took a somewhat different view. Unfortunately it was not publicised in Delhi, Peking, Bandung, or elsewhere outside Tibet. Inside Tibet the official view was as expressed in the Tibetan newspaper *Tibet*

The Tibetans Grow Bitter

Mirror published in Kalimpong, vol. XXII, No. 2, dated June 1st, 1954:

To most Learned Tharchin-la, Printer and Publisher of World News:

I have some very important information for you. Having read the detailed news of the recent Sino-Indian Trade Pact, I enclose copies of the two Simla Treaties of 1914.

As you have the fixed interests of Tibet at heart I request that you publish the enclosed. (Name given but withheld.)

To Leaders, Officials, Monks, Soldiers, Traders, Craftsmen, Agriculturists, Nomads—the People of Tibet:

This is to alert you to the great danger threatening our common cause, the independence of Tibet, regarding which I feel compelled to speak a few words.

1. The last edition of the *Tibet Mirror* carried translations of articles from Indian papers of a trade pact signed at Peking between India and China regarding Tibet. There was a statement that 'discussions in Peking related only to procedural matters and not to the substance of the issue'. Neither was there any mention of which particular Treaty formed the basis of the talks. Further, no full copy of the agreement was made public.

2. Were the talks based on the Trade Regulations of 1893 or of 1908, both of which were mentioned in regard to the Peking Trade Agreement? If so, it is a violation of the Simla Convention of 1914 whereby both of those Trade Regulations are declared revoked in Clause 7.

3. The Peking Trade Pact refers to Tibet as 'an integral part of China', and there are many mentions of the 'Tibet region of China', those being terms unprecedented in the history of Tibet and also another violation of the terms of the Simla Convention, Clauses 3 and 9 of which first of all recognized the virtual independence of Tibet, inasmuch as the Tibetan Government kept her existing rights, which until the time of the recent invasion of Tibet included the management of her external affairs; secondly, guaranteed the non-violation of Tibetan territory, Great Britain and China agreeing to abstain from sending their troops, stationing civil and military officers, or establishing colonies in Outer Tibet. (Part nearer India.)

4. The Simla Convention was signed by the fully empowered representatives of the three Governments of Tibet, India and China, whereas the Peking Pact was concluded between India and China, *the wishes of the Government and people of Tibet being completely ignored.* This makes it clear that China intends not to only absorb Tibet but to destroy our culture, religion and eventually our race, by intermarriage, as is shown by their moves to try and get in, in addition to the 220,000

in the Liberation Army already in Tibet, a further two million Chinese for the so-called economic development of our country. It is only too obvious how our two neighbours are willing to come to private arrangements in favour of aggression so as to serve their own inter-Asian imperialist policies.

5. Please read carefully the second Independent Treaty signed at Simla between Tibet and the British Government in India, on the same day, and immediately after, the Tripartite Simla Convention, as it recognized not the autonomy but the complete independence of Tibet.

'Copy of the Treaty signed between Great Britain and Tibet at Simla Convention on the same day and immediately after the failure of China to affix her official seal to the signatures of her official representative to the now widely known Tripartite Treaty between Great Britain, Tibet and China; *Nota bene*: This being the Independent Treaty entered into by the Government of Great Britain in India and Government of Tibet by mutual agreement.

'The Government of China refusing to fix her official seal thereto, and in default of which, all rights and privileges claimed by the Government of China in and with regard to Tibet, are hereby declared revoked.'

But this plaintive protest was lost in the busy market-place of power politics, particularly in the Afro-Asian clamour of applause for 'Panch Shila', the 'Five Principles of Peaceful Co-existence'.

In June 1954 the Dalai Lama received an invitation from the Chinese Government to visit Peking and other places in China. The invitation raised an immediate protest in Tibet and there were many demonstrations to protest against the Dalai Lama leaving the country, the general suspicion being that he would not be permitted to return. In addition to protesting, the Mimang Tsong-du in Lhasa secretly organized a mass revolt on the day scheduled for the Dalai Lama's departure, when thousands of Tibetans were to throw themselves in the Dalai Lama's path so that he could not pass through them without having to walk over their bodies. The Chinese got word of the plans and several days before the scheduled date of departure moved the Dalai Lama to a relative's house and on his way to China. However, the Chinese were considerably sobered by the intensity of the feeling shown by the Tibetans and went out of their way to assure them that the Dalai Lama would be well treated in China and returned to Tibet safely.

The Tibetans Grow Bitter

For some time the Chinese had been building up the Panchen Lama's influence in Tibet, both to undermine the Dalai Lama's spiritual prestige and to divide the Tibetans into two camps so that they could be more easily dealt with, and he was invited to Peking at the same time as the Dalai Lama. The Panchen Lama, as a reincarnation of the Dhyani Buddha Amitabha (of whom the Avalokitesvara is merely an emanation), is spiritually more important than the Dalai Lama in Tibetan Bhuddism, although historically the Panchen Lama had merely been the teacher of the Fifth Dalai Lama, who out of gratitude and reverence created the position of 'Panchen Lama' and gave him his monastic seat at Shigatse. The Dalai Lama, as a reincarnation of the Bodhisattva Avalokitesvara, wields the political power which for generations has been recognized by the Tibetans themselves and the outside world.

After Britain, China and Tibet had signed the Tripartite Treaty in 1914, the Panchen Lama, who had been very pro-Chinese, had to flee in 1920 to China where the Kuomingtang Government had just come to power. As soon as he could the Panchen Lama began scheming with Kuomingtang officials to support him with money, arms and men to re-enter Tibet, but as the infant Kuomingtang Government was in no position to indulge in adventures, the scheme was dropped.

In 1933 the thirteenth Dalai Lama died. During his reign it had been virtually impossible for a Chinese national, civil or military, to enter Tibet, but as it usually took several months or even years to discover a reincarnation of the Dalai Lama the ageing Panchen Lama prevailed upon the Kuomingtang Government to assist him in liberating Tibet. This time help was given, and while the Chinese forces were converging on Tibet's eastern borders, a Chinese goodwill mission was sent to Lhasa to persuade a leaderless Tibetan Government to accept a permanent Chinese legation in Lhasa on grounds of common cultural and religious ties. In 1935, as a direct result of this offensive, a meeting was called in Lhasa and it was decided that the Panchen Lama should be allowed to re-enter Tibet accompanied by his household and a few followers. Whether from disappointment or old age, the

The Tibetans Grow Bitter

Panchen Lama died in China before he could accept even this meagre offer.

When the new reincarnation of the Dalai Lama was discovered in 1938 in Amdo Province, in that same year and same province was discovered a new reincarnation of the Panchen Lama. The position of this reincarnation was confused by the simultaneous discovery of two other claimants in Lhasa. The authorities in Lhasa understandably ordered the Amdo claimant to appear in Lhasa for verification, but the Chinese authorities, for reasons of their own, refused to comply with this request and some years later officially installed their protégé as the new Panchen Lama. When the Kuomingtang Government fell and fled to Formosa the Chinese Communists took over Amdo Province and, with it, the Panchen Lama.

In 1950, 'at the request of the Panchen Lama', Chinese Communist forces marched on Lhasa, and in 1951 the Panchen Lama was present for the talks conducted by the Chinese Communists with the Tibetan goodwill mission on the special initiative of the Chinese Communist Government. The pact which recognized China's suzerainty over Tibet acknowledged also the Amdo reincarnation as the true Panchen Lama. Soon afterwards the newly declared Panchen Lama, escorted by a strong force of Chinese troops, visited Lhasa, and from that time the Chinese made every effort to build him up politically; but the Tibetan Government consistently refused to recognize him as anything more than a spiritual leader. Even that token recognition was not accepted by the Tibetan people, who identified him with Chinese imperialist policies, and also pointed out that he still had not been accepted according to their religious customs.

The Chinese in Tibet ignored the objection of the Tibetans and on every occasion introduced the Panchen Lama as an equal to the Dalai Lama, listing him as a co-member of the Political Consultative Committee which they set up, and seeking to have all the members around a conference table on ordinary chairs so that the Dalai Lama's prestige would be diminished to equality with the Panchen Lama and other members of the committee—including the Chinese themselves. Needless to say, after the first discussion the Tibetans opposed any further meetings of the committee until this point had been settled.

In China the Peking Government went out of its way to show preference for the Panchen Lama on every occasion, presumably to indicate to the Dalai Lama how they were prepared to treat friends who co-operated with them. This rather naïve policy had exactly the opposite effect on the strong-minded Dalai Lama and as he went about the country saying the proper things his bitterness against the Chinese Communists crystallized into antagonism. When his visit to China looked like being unduly prolonged mass protests were organized from Kalimpong on the Indian border all the way across Tibet to Kangting on the Chinese border, and if the Chinese had any ideas about holding on to him permanently they were forced to forego the policy and let him return to Tibet and his people.

There were great celebrations everywhere, but the most significant factor to emerge from the Dalai Lama's return was the hardening official attitude to the Chinese in Tibet. Schemes which the Chinese confidently announced in the world press as being initiated in Tibet with the people's approval were quietly shelved after blunt refusal to accept them. The Tibetan Army was to be integrated with the Chinese Army, but this was withdrawn. Tibet's economic system was to be linked with China's and Chinese currency used instead of Tibetan, but the Tibetans refused to accept Chinese paper money. The Chinese announced that only traders with letters of credit from the Bank of China, negotiable in Kalimpong and Calcutta, would be allowed to trade, and found themselves with a monumental leakage of Chinese silver coins, minted into silver ingots, being smuggled into India by Tibetan traders, and they had to let the matter drop. They noisily resurrected the idea of the People's Political Consultative Committee and found that it had to be quietly postponed indefinitely. The Mi-mang Tsong-du became more vociferous, more reckless in anti-Chinese demonstrations, and local groups of Tibetans either flared up into fights with Chinese soldiers or officers or discriminated against them to such an extent that the Chinese began to grumble and complain of their lot in Tibet.

On the social welfare level only did things go comparatively smoothly. The more enlightened Tibetan official, and the new enthusiastic younger Tibetan official, willingly worked with the Chinese in building new roads in Lhasa, new schools, dispensaries and hospitals in the various towns throughout the country. These were things they had wanted for many years but had not been able to introduce into Tibet because of the feudal, bigoted, superstitious hold of the priests over the country. Now the new generation were determined to push ahead with the building when they could, irrespective of whether the providers of them were Chinese or Communist, on the assumption that the Chinese would have to leave eventually and that by that time the schools, hospitals and dispensaries would be so strongly established that they could not be removed.

Chapter Thirteen

AN AMERICAN PROPOSAL

In March 1955 Rapga Pangdatshang arrived in India. There was widespread suspicion and speculation amongst the local Indian officials and the high Tibetan officials who had taken up residence in Kalimpong and Darjeeling as to the part Rapga was playing. Not knowing the background to his arrival (that I had sent for him) they jumped to the conclusion that he was an emissary from the Communists taking part in some deep scheme of the Chinese to infiltrate into India and also to influence Tibetan officials in India. On the surface there could be no other explanation, for he had been Governor of Markham Province and a member of the Chamdo Liberation Committee, and no one, least of all a feudal intrigue-minded Lhasa official, could imagine that anyone would forego such a position with its possibilities for a journey into India with no known future.

Within a few days of his arrival in Kalimpong I met Rapga in the house he had built for himself during an earlier exile and was now occupying about ten years later. I learned from him that he had already been on his way to India when he received the parcel of medicines from me; in fact, he had been planning this trip for the past three years and more. He also gave me the history of the Chinese take-over in East Tibet.

After I had left Kham, and when it became clear that no help was forthcoming for Tibet from the outside Powers and none from the Lhasa Government for Kham, he, his brother Topgyay, and the other leaders decided to follow the policy they had already prepared—collaborate with the Chinese as long as possible, keeping the reins of power in their own hands in whatever way they could, knowing that the Chinese would have to work through them in order to influence the tribesmen of Kham and

Amdo, whose racial antagonism to the Chinese the Communists knew only too well. He, Rapga, had anticipated that, by using all kinds of delaying tactics, they might be able—on an optimistic estimate—to hold control over their people's loyalties for ten years, but more probably only five years. With this in mind they sent word to the many chieftains and headmen throughout Kham and Amdo to control their tribesmen's natural belligerence until a later opportunity presented itself when they could all rise against the Chinese in unison.

When the advance units of the Chinese Liberation Army moved into their valley (in Bo, Kham) the Chinese Communist officials attached to the advance units persuaded him to leave for Chamdo with certain important communications from them, and he finally agreed after consultations with Peking to go as an emissary with offers from the Chinese to the Lhasa Government. This was in line with their plans to concentrate and keep what power they could in their own hands.

He arrived in Chamdo one day before the new Lhasa Government-appointee, Ngaboo, arrived to take over the post of Governor of Kham from the retiring Governor, Lhalu. The Governorship of Kham was a routine three-year appointment for one of the members of the Lhasa 'Cabinet' and was looked upon with as much favour as the managership of a salt mine in Siberia—it might be a stepping-stone to higher things but it was more likely to mean the first step into the Tibetan political wilderness. Ngaboo had been looked upon as an *arriviste* by the traditional high office-holders in Lhasa, but his shrewdness and surprising drive (for a Lhasa Tibetan) had carried him into the top councils. He had been campaigning for several reforms in the Government structure, denouncing the cynical lethargy and corruption of the Lhasa Government officials, and they reacted in the traditional Tibetan fashion by appointing him Governor of Kham, in Chamdo, East Tibet. It was an appointment that was to have momentous repercussions for Tibet.

When Rapga arrived in Chamdo he found that Lhalu wanted to reject the Chinese overtures and prepare to fight, but Ngaboo was of the opinion that support from the Lhasa Government would not be forthcoming and that without this they would immediately be defeated. In addition to this, the gap between the ordinary Tibetan and the Government was too great, the attachment of even the Chamdo Khambas to the Governor too nebulous, and the antagonism due to the excessive tyranny and exploitation of the Lhasa Government in recent years too deep to contribute to a stable defence.

Ngaboo's assessment of the situation was confirmed when, after they had wirelessed to Lhasa, the Lhasa Government ordered them to take no action as they were about to enter on negotiations with the Chinese through New Delhi. (Even this decision was not taken by collective Government decision but was later established to be due to intrigue by a Lhasa anti-Ngaboo faction, influenced by Shakabpa in Kalimpong. When the decision of the Lhasa Government was communicated to Rapga he decided to confide in Ngaboo and Lhalu and outlined to them his—and the other Kham and Amdo leaders'—plan to overthrow and re-form the Lhasa Government, to establish a new Government, and then from this newly formed Government to send a rejection of the Chinese Communists' proposals. The new Popular Government drawn from Tsang, U, Kham and Amdo Provinces would prepare to fight the Chinese in Kham, in the meantime negotiating with foreign Powers for help. He was convinced that the Chinese were not prepared to fight openly for possession of Tibet and were only using the army as a threat in the background. Both Lhalu and Ngaboo were impressed by the plan, and they quickly drafted an outline for immediate use.

Before anything could be done the Chinese moved suddenly into Chamdo, surprised the Tibetan Government, and presented an ultimatum in the form of a 'Ten-Point Agreement for Peace'. Resistance was now out of the question and when the ultimatum was forwarded to Lhasa the Government agreed to negotiate, appointing as official negotiators Rapga and another Tibetan official, Yishe-Dargyay, son of the Tibetan Foreign Minister, both of whom knew Chinese. On their credentials as official negotiators the Lhasa Government also inserted instructions that they were to go as slowly as possible, that they must only concede permission for the Chinese to enter Tibet when everything else had failed, and that if they had to concede this permission it should be made clear that the acceptance was only temporary and viewed in the nature of a loan during the period of China's fear of external aggression through Tibet. (This was the reason which the Chinese had given for entering Tibet, not at that time that it was part of their own territory.)

The negotiations in the initial stages were conducted through local Communist officials and consultations by wireless with Peking, but as the talks dragged on the Chinese grew exasperated with Rapga's delaying tactics and finally told him that unless he and his colleague produced their official credentials they would demand another delegation from Lhasa. This was not possible as the Lhasa Government had included their instructions on the credentials, so in due course the Chinese complained and a new delegation was formed to proceed to Peking with Ngaboo as the leader and with several members drawn from Lhasa and Kham. On the way through Kangting, Ngaboo was not permitted to talk with Rapga and his colleagues and from that time Ngaboo was never allowed to converse privately with any Tibetan official. Although only a 'goodwill delegation' sent to hold exploratory talks, Ngaboo's delegation finally agreed under pressure to sign in May, 1951, the 17-Point Treaty acknowledging Chinese suzerainty.

On the signing of the Treaty the Chinese formed the 'East Tibetan People's Autonomous Government' from the leaders of the earlier revolutionary Kham-Amdo group, six of them being appointed Vice-Presidents of a divided Kham and Amdo, Top-gyay Pangdatshang and Hou Wan Seiling (or Abu Abalok, as was his Tibetan name) amongst them. They also proceeded to build and install an extensive administrative system with headquarters in Chamdo but with the chief posts in the hands of Kham and Amdo Tibetans. For a year or more the Kham officials under the Pangdatshangs, and also many in Amdo, refused to take any payment from the Chinese for the work they were doing, but under constant Communist pressure Rapga finally advised them to do so as that money was in many cases their sole means of livelihood.

He himself continued to refuse payment, maintaining that he intended working only for a little while as he had not been keeping well and wanted to visit his son in India shortly and also his wife's relatives.

He worked constantly with this end in view, holding together the anti-Communist forces in Kham, together with other groups in Amdo. When local irritation flared up into open fighting he and other leaders strove to pacify the local chiefs with the promise of a co-ordinated uprising with all other Tibetans throughout Tibet sometime in the future, and also the promise of a share in a new Government with interests in all the areas of Tibet and not limited to Lhasa only.

In 1953 he resigned from his political activities on the grounds of ill health, retiring to one of the Pangdatshang estates to work on a book on the history of Tibet. After two years of this he thought it would be safe to make arrangements to visit Lhasa. He was helped in this by the Chinese desire that he should act as one of the representatives from Kham to the newly resuscitated 51-member Political Consultative Committee drawn from all over Tibet. Quite apart from the trouble they were experiencing having it accepted by the Lhasa officials, the Kham and Amdo Tibetans were furious that they had only been allocated eight seats out of the fifty-one represented—another five of which were Chinese. The Chinese hoped that Rapga would use his influence on the Khambas to accept, and reluctantly agreed to his request that he visit Lhasa and India for a few months to settle his affairs first of all as a *quid pro quo*. He had been on this arranged trip to India when he had received my letter.

He had been warned by the Chinese that under no circumstances was he to agree to meeting officials in India, particularly Western officials. Nor was he to see Patterson, who was an agent of the imperialists. He pointed out that he had known Patterson and had been friendly with him before he had met any of the Chinese Communists and that he could not as a friend refuse to meet me. He also ignored the other warnings after his arrival in India and was soon in discreetly arranged consultations with many officials, both Indian and Western.

An American Proposal

If the Indian Government had secretly hoped for a quiet, scholarly organizer of anti-Communist propaganda in Tibet they were shatteringly disappointed. Rapga refused point-blank to list numbers of Chinese soldiers in different places, or collect information, or write articles and pamphlets for clandestine distribution. These were tasks that could be done by any lesser fry who might be interested. He was only interested in complete revolution, overthrow of the Chinese Communists, reform of the Tibetan Government, and recognition of the new Popular Government by the other nations of the world. He had made the journey to India with this in view and would accept nothing less. If the Indian and other Governments were not prepared to help or co-operate in any way, then, of course, the Tibetans would be disappointed but it would in no wise affect their determination to revolt, and the outside countries would just have to adjust their policies accordingly. The anti-Chinese feeling in East Tibet was now so high that the Kham and Amdo leaders would either have to lead their people in the fighting against the Chinese or be killed by them as collaborators. No amount of talking or writing could stop the inevitable uprising, and it was because of this that he had made the trip to Lhasa to co-ordinate the Kham-Amdo Tibetans with the anti-Chinese Mi-mang Tsong-du in Lhasa in a mass uprising.

While in Lhasa he got into touch with one of the leaders of the Mi-mang Tsong-du, a revolutionary friend of former years, but the contact had to be made through writing as he was being closely watched by the Chinese. However, he was able to communicate something of the situation in East Tibet, and suggested a Lhasa participation in the revolt when it came. There were about 100,000 Tibetans in East Tibet, well armed, who were ready to take part in the revolt.

His information rocked the Indian Government, who had only hoped to salvage some prestige from the earlier diplomatic débâcles by working quietly to counteract the steady flow of Chinese Communist propaganda against India. A Tibet up in arms, denouncing China as an aggressor, would seriously embarrass India, now the Afro-Asian champion of the 'Five Principles of Peaceful Co-Existence' signed over the presumed dead national corpse of Tibet. An Asian nation being ruthlessly suppressed by another Asian nation, China, while a third Asian nation, India, connived, and at the same time advocated a policy of non-aggression, non-interference, etcetera, was something which would destroy the prestige of both nations not only in Asia but throughout the world.

When urgent pleas to Rapga to modify the Kham-Amdo aims failed to move him, officials changed their tactics to pointing out how hopeless the Tibetan position was, quoting, of all things, the newspaper-concocted fiction that the Tibetans were inadequately armed with obsolete weapons against a nation which had just held the whole of the armed might of the United Nations in Korea. Rapga pointed out that he and the Tibetans involved were more likely to know what arms they had, and their chances against the Chinese, as they were on the spot and their lives were forfeit, and it was their confident opinion that they could inflict such losses on the Chinese in East Tibet in three months as to make them anxious to negotiate. This admittedly would not be due to military pressure alone, but the fact that they would not wish to make an international issue out of Tibet. His idea, therefore, was to use the revolt as a pistol to the head of the Chinese to force them to withdraw from Tibet in exchange for certain concessions. He and the others were prepared to gamble their lives on the outcome, but they wanted a recognition by the outside Powers of the Tibetan uprising and claims for independence, and help in forcing reforms on the Government in Lhasa to make it more representative of the whole of Tibet.

Rapga also agreed to meet an American representative who arrived on the Tibetan border to discuss the situation with him. I acted as interpreter. When Rapga had again outlined the above the American expressed sympathy with Tibet in their predicament but pointed out the difficulties involved in any supply of military equipment or personnel to Tibet, particularly in view of its contiguity with non-violent, neutralist, anti-American India. Rapga agreed with him, and expressed his own doubt that India would do anything with her present policy and attitude *vis-à-vis* Tibet and China. It was because of this that he felt it was absolutely

An American Proposal

essential that Tibet revolt and present India and other countries with a *fait accompli*.

The American argued with Rapga that co-operation with the Indian Government was essential and that Tibet's future friendly relations with India depended upon this. He also stressed its importance from the point of view that in the event of Tibet making a claim to independence before the United Nations it was imperative that she have the support of India, and through India the Afro-Asian and Middle East support. Recognition by the U.S. and other Western Powers would be almost automatic, but if the West took the lead in such recognition it would immediately antagonize the Communist bloc and thus jeopardize Tibet's chances. Rapga saw the value of this point immediately and agreed to give it more consideration than he had done in the past. The American representative went on to draw up a programme of assistance that he would suggest to the U.S. authorities on his return. Briefly the programme was as follows:

A ten-year period in which Tibet would require help, as revolution against an occupying power, the overthrow of a feudal-collaborationist Government and establishment of a new Government and State of sufficient stability and authority to be recognized by the U.N. would require that as a minimum no matter how soon the actual revolution took place. The U.S. representative then supposed, for the sake of planning, that an initial period of five years be assumed in which the preliminary stages of revolution, overthrow of reactionary Government and establishing of tutelage Government would be required, for which representatives from districts all over Tibet, including instructed clergy, should be included in a Political Consultative Committee.

Keeping in mind that a combination of factors might precipitate the revolution at any time, perhaps in the next few months, it was agreed that Rapga should aim in the first year at organization. This was to include the primary organization of a national entity and the resolution of inter-provincial disputes, the inter-family jealousies and feuds, and the inter-religious divisions (Dalai Lama versus Panchen Lama). The purpose of this period of organization would not just be 'anti-Communist' in emphasis or simply in order to draw a line of demarcation which would serve to indicate who, among the officials and leaders, should be considered for the new Government, but to propagate simple instructions through slogans on such things as land reform; reform of forced labour, forced deportations, forced trade, and all forms of enforced tax imposed by the old feudal and new Communist régimes; Government participation and administration; and other such principles which could be easily grasped by the people of Tibet to associate them in loyalty to the new Government in its proposed reforms.

All this would have to be planned and initiated so that there would be no hiatus in the transition period of changing from the old Government to the new and so that the Tibetans could ultimately carry out all forms of adminstration themselves without the help of other countries.

They also discussed the economic possibilities of Tibet, its mineral resources, possibilities of oil and uranium being found, and in a more immediate context the possibility of taking up the question of Tibet's export of wool in the talks then being held between the U.S. and China at Geneva.

The foregoing programme was only a very tentative outline of proposals suggested by the U.S. representative which he said he would put before the appropriate officials on his return to the U.S. He would also suggest that a special American agent be appointed, who would have no contact with the U.S. Embassy but who, he gave Rapga to understand, would be officially appointed to handle Tibetan affairs. He would not only be the channel of U.S. financial help but would advise on political, diplomatic and economic questions which might arise, and on any problems connected with propaganda, printing and radio. In the meantime Rapga could go ahead doing what he could in the matter of organizing and giving assurance and hope of support to loyal anti-Chinese Communist elements inside Tibet.

Chapter Fourteen

CRISIS IN LHASA

Floods, famine and an unprecedented food shortage served to increase the anti-Chinese feeling in Tibet; public demonstrations and placarding of walls gave way to ugly and dangerous local uprisings. Rumours of a mass uprising were widely current and Tibetans in Lhasa clamoured for arms to be given them by the Government or the monasteries where arms were known to be stored. The Chinese could not help but know of the rumours and general unrest and they issued warnings about the consequences of an armed uprising.

In August 1955, during a great public festival in Lhasa, the Dalai Lama made a speech to his people. The speech, heavily censored for foreign press consumption by the Chinese, was wildly acclaimed by the Tibetans. I heard rumours of the famous speech in Kalimpong and through a Tibetan friend managed to obtain a copy of the original. Here is the full text:

'Tibet is a country in which religion and political life are joined together. On the unity of religion and political life depends our life. If there is no religion we cannot maintain our political life, and if there is no political life our religion also cannot exist alone. The main point is that this kind of political life and religion cannot be separated in any way. We can best understand this by looking to the history of Tibet. For example, the Emperor Me O Nam Sung paid great attention to the joint development of both political life and religion. While carrying out religious reforms he also established order in political life and in this way fully developed the spirit of religious and political unity. As a result of this unity the development of the political society of that period attained the highest point. A few generations later Emperor Lan Ma destroyed religion and paid particular attention to the development of political life alone, as a result of which the development of society received a great setback and the country became weak and defeatist. Afterwards our country invited from India very many great Buddhist teachers and philosophers to come to Tibet and give us teaching and again put into good order our religious path. This resulted in a renaissance of our religious life and a great development of religion took place. With the spread of Buddhism there was great development and progress in Tibetan society as well. This is a bright example from our history.

'At present and in future we ought to carry out many new changes both in our religious and political life and this is the urgent task which faces us. But in what way can we make progress? Today our Tibetan people are facing many difficulties from every side. We have no strength of our own and we have no political experience. We have no means to progress in any way. It is because of this that the Chinese Communists have sent their men here to help us in the reconstruction of Tibet. But we must be definitely assured that the Chinese Communists have not come here to control us, or to become our masters, or to oppress us. We should adopt a friendly attitude towards them.

'If the Chinese Communists have come to Tibet to help us it is most important that they should respect the Tibetan people's own social system, culture, customs and habits, and honour the wishes of the whole people of Tibet, and not obstruct and do damage to the high principles of our nation. If the Chinese Communist personnel in Tibet do not understand the conditions and harm or injure our people, you should immediately report the facts to the Government. The Government will certainly take steps to make them correct their ways. If the Chinese Communist men do not correct their ways our Government can immediately ask for their expulsion.

'I hope all our Tibetan people will take upon themselves the responsibility for carrying out the various tasks allotted to them. For example, if the members of a family can themselves control and carry out the affairs of the family that family may be said to be a self-managed family or an independent one. A country is also in the same position as a family. I sincerely hope that the officials of the Government and the people will stand at their posts, will remain determined in their attitude, carrying out their responsibilities and using their full strength in performing their duties.

'Today I am very pleased with the officials of the Government and the people and thank them for working extremely hard for the welfare of their district, Government and country. But there are some officials and people who have a very narrow outlook and cannot take a broad view of things. For their own selfish advancement and under the attraction of glittering gold they do not care for the good of the country and the people, they practise oppression and deceit, they give trouble to the people and harm the Government, and thus are responsible for great harm to the country. I would request such people to correct their former mistakes and, becoming new men, atone for their misdeeds in the interests of the country and the people. Besides them there are some few people who disregard their national culture and history, consider themselves to be progressives, and who have changed their ways to doing what they like in a very confused manner. I regard such ideas as mistaken. Progress cannot be attained suddenly in a confused manner and must be attained gradually in an ordered way. Again, there are Government officials who are envious of each other, create conflicts and bitterness, and cannot co-operate with each other. Because they fritter away their energies they cannot carry out the work of the administration effectively. I desire that they give up their selfish attitude and take a broad view of things, correct each other and become united together. Only by doing so can we create and develop our strength. For example, it is not possible for a single person to lift a big stone using his own strength, but if the strength of several people is pooled together it becomes very easy to lift the same stone. This is a very simple example but I know that all of you will pay special attention to this matter.

'Tibet, consisting of Kham, Tsang, U and Amdo, all consist of the Tibetan people. Their spirit and way of living all have such intimate connections that they cannot be separated from each other. I hope that all of you will deeply think over this matter, love each other, and be united with each other, and not become separated from each other.

'Finally, I hope that the people of the whole of Tibet by their unity and co-operation will increase our strength and put all their energies into the construction of a new Tibet based on the unity of political life and religion.'

In September I had a visit from a Chinese friend who had access to information about all Communist activities in the area. He informed me that the Chinese Communists in a secret meeting had appointed two people, whose names he had not been able to find out, to approach me and see if they could discover what contact I had with Kham. They were convinced that Rapga and I were at the root of all the restlessness and uprisings in East Tibet. Also, when information about the presumed contacts had been obtained, I was to be quietly liquidated.

A few days later I had a visit from two high Tibetan officials who, after the usual social chit-chat, began to question me about my experiences in Kham, the people I knew there, the means I used for keeping in touch with those people, whether my Khamba servant wrote to his family, and so on. I was able to avoid anything that might have resulted in the unfortunate demise of one of my many Tibetan friends in Kham.

A few nights later I was awakened by a shout from some friends who were spending the week-end with my wife and me, to find that thieves had broken into the house. The three friends, all schoolteachers, occupied two guest bedrooms on the other side of the house. One thief had quietly entered, gone through the two rooms picking up whatever was at hand, and then slipped out through a previously opened window where an accomplice was waiting when he was discovered. That they were not ordinary thieves out for valuables was apparent when they went off with a brief-case containing papers and left handbags and valises belonging to the schoolteachers untouched. Also, when I had roused Loshay, my Tibetan servant, and we had scouted around the house for signs of them, we found the brief-case only two hundred yards away, opened, with the papers scattered everywhere. Although they had been disturbed and must have heard us in our search for them, they had taken time to open and inspect the contents of the brief-case. I concluded that they had not known we had guests, had assumed by the rooms having occupants that those were the rooms used by me and my wife, and that they were Communists searching for the information required by their leaders. They were never found.

In Lhasa events had reached a critical stage. The Mi-mang Tsong-du had presented an appeal to the Dalai Lama to get rid of the Chinese Communists or they would rise in revolt. Again, through a Tibetan friend, I was able to obtain a copy of the appeal:

'We Tibetan people make the following appeal because we oppose the Chinese Communists who are destroying all our customs and systems, and also because of the complete breach of the 17-Point Sino-Tibetan Agreement signed by them. The chief object of the Sino-Tibetan Agreement was to oppose the imperialists, reconstruct Tibet, and also to solemnly honour the political and religious power of the Dalai Lama. Besides this, the main principle on which the Agreement was based was not to oppose or harm the original social system of Tibet and Tibetan customs and habits. In order to win the support of the people by cheating and deception, the Chinese Communists have already paid a very heavy price. At the same time, if we look back on Tibetan history for the past several centuries we find that Tibet has always been a completely free, independent and self-governing country. No foreign power has ever carried out aggression against us or occupied our country. Moreover, we Tibetan people from the earliest times to the present have always been devoutly honest, good and faithful followers of religion, peace-loving and supporters of righteousness.

'The internal policy of Tibet has always been to have peace and calm, to promote the good of the people, and to raise their standard of living. Our external policy has always been to live peaceably with our neighbours and to have profitable intercourse with them. Tibet has never increased her armed forces or tried to extend her power outside Tibet. Because the Tibetan people are devoutly religious and sincerely love peace our country is known as "the Buddhist country" by everyone.

Crisis in Lhasa

'But speaking about the present situation in Tibet we declare that our religion is facing a very grave crisis which has thrown us into the very deep valley of darkness and destruction. The Dalai Lama has been robbed of his political and religious powers. The future of the Tibetan nation is facing as grave a danger as a candle-light in a severe storm. The root cause of this crisis is the oppressive ways in which the Chinese Communists have been forcing Communist ideas upon the Tibetan people, the most deplorable policy of violence practised by the Chinese Communists, and the failure of the Chinese Communists to implement any of the promises made by them to the Tibetan people. In order to save our country from this dangerous future we have already, on a previous occasion, made a formal protest to the Chinese Government and the Dalai Lama.

'Formerly, under the Dalai Lama, there were Regents, Kashag (Parliament), and various other Government organizations which carried out the adminstration of the whole of Tibet. But since the occupation of Tibet by the Chinese Communists all the former organizations of the Government have ceased to function and the Chinese Communists have established a large number of illegal organizations in their place to carry out the administration. For example, the Communists have set up a Food Department, which is not only unnecessary but is also wasting the public money and increasing their burden. We feel that all such organizations are unnecessary and we do not wish to submit to them. The Chinese Communists have not only increased administrative organizations but they have also established organizations such as the "Patriotic Youth League" and the "Chinese Schools", with the sole object of forcibly indoctrinating the youth of Tibet in Communism, and thus to destroy the culture and civilization of the nation. Moreover, in opposition to the will of the people the Chinese Communists have destroyed the social system of Tibet in which political and religious life are joined together, and have also destroyed the religion of the Tibetan people. Therefore we, in the name of all the people of Tibet, have come forward to appeal to the Dalai Lama. We request that the Dalai Lama stop the organization of the "Patriotic Youth League", close the "Chinese Schools", and prevent the indoctrination of the Tibetan people in Communism by the Chinese Communists. We are also resolved not to accept the establishment of the proposed Regional Autonomous Government in Tibet as we already have the Tibetan Government of the Dalai Lama. At the same time we also request the Chinese Communist Military Representative in Tibet to allow us to go to Peking to lodge this protest. If the Chinese Communists disregard the people's wishes, by force, oppression and violence suppress the earnest appeal of the people, and do not allow us to go to Peking, we, in the name of all the people of Tibet, are fully resolved to shed our blood and sacrifice our lives to oppose the Communists and we shall definitely not co-operate in any of the activities of the Chinese Communists in Tibet.'

At the same time Peking began to give more official and public prominence to Tibet and its problems. Without giving any hint of anti-Chinese troubles there the Peking *Shih Shih Shou Tse* (Current Affairs Handbook) of April 30th, 1956, gave a glowing report of progress in Tibet. According to the *Shih Shih Shou Tse*, People's Banks had been opened in Lhasa, Shigatse, Chamdo and other places and in the previous four years had issued more than 1,700,000 yuan of non-interest agricultural loans, and more than 100,000 yuan of non-interest pastoral loans, as well as various amounts of low-interest handicraft loans and commercial loans. One hundred thousand farm implements had been issued, and 2,000,000 yuans' worth of tea, cloth and daily necessities. Twenty-seven primary schools had been established with a total enrolment of 2,000 Tibetan students. Books and stationery were supplied to students free of charge, and subsidies and living expenses were given to the really poor. Twenty-four film projector teams showed films for servicemen and civilians. Broadcasting stations were set up in various cities and towns. Four thousand Chinese medical workers had been sent to Tibet with 5,000,000 yuan for hygienic enterprises. Hospitals were built in Lhasa, Shigatse, Chamdo, etc., and 13 medical centres and medical teams were formed in the various cities and towns to visit outlying areas.

They also issued a copy of a speech on the same day in the *Jan Min Jih Pao*, purported to have been made by the Dalai Lama at

145

the inaugural meeting of the Preparatory Committee for the Autonomous Region of Tibet, in which he said:

'Tibet is the centre of Lamaism, in which religion the whole Tibetan population has a deep belief. The Tibetan people treasure and protect their religious beliefs as they would their lives. During the past few years the People's Liberation Army units and the working personnel in Tibet have strictly adhered to the policy of freedom of religion, carefully protected the lamaseries, and respected the religious belief of the Tibetan people. They have also donated much to the Tibetan monks each year. All this has greatly helped remove the apprehension that previously prevailed among the broad masses of the Tibetans, particularly among the lamas, as a result of rumours and investigations made by agents of the imperialists. On this basis, the fraternal co-operation between the peoples of the Han and the Tibetan nationalities has been increased and consolidated with each passing day. Likewise with the guidance and assistance of the Chinese Communist Party and Chairman Mao, the various domestic circles in Tibet have now been united. . . . On April 29th, 1954, the "Agreement between the People's Republic of China and the Republic of India on Trade and Communications between the Tibet Region of China and India" was signed in Peking by the delegates of the Central People's Government of our country and the Indian Government, bringing to an end the remnant privileges of the British and re-establishing on a new basis the relations between our motherland and India concerning Tibet. It has played a notable role for the motherland in establishing fair trade and commerce between the Tibet region of China and India on the basis of equality and mutual benefit and respect for each other's sovereignty. With unity in foreign affairs and the abolition of the special privileges of the imperialists the national defence of our South-western frontier has been all the more consolidated. . . .

'Our motherland is now engaged in socialist construction with great fanfare, with all the brotherly nationalities marching on the great road to socialism. By socialism we mean a truly happy society, and Tibet has no other alternative but to take the road to socialism. . . .'

Crisis in Lhasa

In Kalimpong Rapga tried desperately to co-ordinate all the mounting anti-Chinese feeling into some semblance of national unity for a general uprising. It was a frustrating hopeless business trying to get Tibetans resident in Kalimpong and Darjeeling together to discuss anything, let alone to organize themselves for a rebellion. Each was suspicious of the other's motives, and only the usual two or three family cliques would get together, and usually that was to discuss how best they could come out of the situation without loss of money, prestige or 'face', not how they might contribute. Rapga tried to get an urgent letter containing information on the situation in East Tibet and suggestions for revolt to the Dalai Lama through a member of the Dalai Lama's family who was, however, too afraid of the possible consequences of discovery to touch it. Rapga then tried to get his older brother, Yangpel, to take a letter to Ngaboo, who in time might have an opportunity to present it to the Dalai Lama, but someone must have persuaded Yangpel that it was political dynamite for he sent it back to Rapga undelivered.

It was as I had earlier warned the Indian officials and anyone else who was interested. There was no official of the Lhasa Government in India, and very few in Lhasa, who was prepared to sacrifice ten minutes of his time, let alone wealth, position or life. If someone else was prepared to take risks for them, to get rid of the Chinese for them, to recover their former official position for them, they would be happy to accept with charming smiles and exquisite manners—might even be prepared to pay considerable sums in bribes, depending on what they received— but do not ask them to express a political opinion, commit themselves to a course of action, or take a gamble on life or liberty. The whispered intrigue, the bought loyalty, the Judas smile, were their coins in the political market-place. It would be left to the laughing, reckless, damn-the-odds Khambas to take on the Chinese in a hopeless death-or-glory battle while the Lhasa political vultures waited to gorge themselves on what was left.

I was wearied with the whole problem, the sudden rise in expectation when events looked hopeful for Tibet, the lapses into despair when officials or Governments showed only cynical self-interest. What was I doing, frittering my life away on the problems of an obscure Asian country when there were so many other things of greater value to be done elsewhere? Even if I remained in India I could preach myself to exhaustion in a glorious ministry to thousands of eager listeners and see something of external value developing daily before my eyes. Then there was the added responsibility of my wife. While I was a bachelor I was at liberty to gamble my life away on a vision, a hope, an exultant faith, but had I the right to gamble with my wife's life as well, particularly when her abilities as a surgeon were being wasted in comparative idleness in Kalimpong?

At that moment of disillusion and despair we received a letter from a friend who had been sympathetic to our belief in an abandoned obedience to God and our conviction that His purpose for us was in Tibet. Now he pointed out that we had given the extreme commitment a fair trial and no one would be more disappointed than himself if it failed, but he thought the time had come to dedicate our lives to more constructive purposes before it was too late. We prayed over his letter and advice, and decided that if there was no definite sign of Tibet opening up in three months we would leave Kalimpong, leave Tibet and its problems, and go to work with more sober, more restrained, more conservative principles elsewhere, accepting the misfortune of being born in a generation of small things, having a small God with small purposes for a small people.

Chapter Fifteen

MY WIFE DANGEROUSLY ILL

When the Dalai Lama visited Peking in 1954 he was a spectator to the tumultuous reception given to India's Prime Minister, Mr. Nehru, who was also there at that time. It was inevitable that he should associate Mr. Nehru with a pro-Chinese policy after all that Tibet had suffered at the hand of Indian policy in relation to Tibet, and now with Nehru's obvious popularity in China. What was a revelation to Nehru was the impression of anti-Tibetan bias that existed in the Tibetan mind with regard to India. It was an impression more than a stated attitude, for Nehru had only an opportunity for a private talk with the Dalai Lama lasting about twenty minutes, when he asked the Dalai Lama if there was anything that India might do to help Tibet and the Dalai Lama cautiously replied there was nothing India could do, Tibet was perfectly happy with the Chinese occupation. Perhaps it was the deliberate display of the lack of confidence in Nehru that disturbed him, but following on his return to India the Indian Government took a renewed interest in Tibet and the Tibetan situation. Before he left China he issued a warm invitation to the Dalai Lama to visit India as he had visited China.

In the autumn of 1955 the matter of the Dalai Lama's visit to India was taken up seriously by the Indian Government. An excellent opportunity was provided by the celebrations of the 2,500th anniversary of Buddha's enlightenment to be held throughout India in 1956, and it was fitting that Buddhism's greatest living representative in the god-king of Tibet should attend. However, there were political considerations that by far exceeded the religious. The Chinese Communists were definitely, for many reasons, against the Dalai Lama going to India. He might choose to stay there and not return to Tibet, as he had planned to do in 1951, in spite of the glowing words they had put into his mouth regarding the situation in Tibet. He might be equally, or even more, impressed by India's political system and progress than he had been in China. He would have many opportunities to meet diplomatic and foreign agents from Western countries with all that could involve. Further it gave Tibet—and Buddhism too—an undue prominence when only the year previously, it had been agreed upon in the Sino-Indian Trade Pact that it was an 'integral part of China'.

However, the Indian Government had become exasperated and annoyed with China's propaganda and military manœuvring on India's borders and they were determined to go ahead with the invitation, not only at Embassy level in New Delhi and Peking, but also in a direct approach to the Dalai Lama himself. Accordingly, the Maharajkumar of Sikkim, related through his Tibetan wife to many high officials in Lhasa, but primarily because of his office of President of the Maha Bodhi Society in India, was despatched to Lhasa with an invitation from the Maha Bodhi Society to visit the Buddha's 2,500th celebrations; he was additionally briefed to find out if the Dalai Lama's reaction to an official invitation from the Indian Government would be accepted, when the Indian Government would send its official representative, the Political Officer in Gangtok, Sikkim, with the official invitation.

The Indian Political Officer in Sikkim, Apa Sahib B. Pant, had only been in the job for a year or so but had already succeeded in breaking down a lot of the anti-Indian antagonism built up by his inept predecessors. Unfailingly courteous, with a deep interest in Tibet and its problems, the Tibetans were gradually being won round to confidence in him. He had a growing reputation among the younger generation of India's diplomats, and had been sent as Political Officer to the strategic border countries of Tibet, Sikkim and Bhutan, following on an excellent record of service in South Africa. He felt that Tibetan aspirations should be encouraged, although he was convinced that Tibetan officials were not sufficiently instructed in political affairs to handle full internal and external policies, and that any programme to help Tibet should have both a spiritual and social emphasis. His impression of Rapga was that he was an able and sincere man, but that he over-estimated the strength and ability of the Kham and Amdo tribes-men and underestimated the magnitude of the obstacles in the way of complete Tibetan independence. My own sole objection to Apa Sahib Pant was that he was unduly influenced by Lhasa officials. It was a fault that was difficult, if not impossible, to correct, for his whole social and political contact was in the company of the high Lhasa officials and those of them who came to India for dubious reasons. The rest of the time he was dependent for his analysis of the Tibetan situation on the Tibetan relatives of the Sikkim royal family.

Rapga was growing increasingly impatient with the frustration of the talks and the lack of communication from the U.S. authorities after the high hopes the representative had raised. He was doubtful if India or the Dalai Lama could bring sufficient pressure on the Chinese to permit him to visit India, but agreed that it would provide an excellent opportunity for him to contact the Dalai Lama with his plans. However, he did not think that the Khambas could be held back until that time, and he preferred a quick statement from India or America as to what help or recognition they could give.

Just at this time I developed an acute abdominal pain and had to go to bed for several days. My wife suspected an attack of an obscure condition known as 'diverticulitis', a condition that could be serious. While in bed Rapga called to see me with the news that the uprising had broken out in Kham, but he had no further details.

After a week or so in bed the pain eased and I got up. I was barely mobile when I received an urgent telephone call from a friend asking me to come to a house in the Homes compound where my wife, who had been visiting there, had had an attack of some kind. When I arrived in the house, half an hour later, I found her writhing in pain and unable to speak. After some time I was able to gather from her that she didn't know what had happened but that she didn't think it was a perforation. I was to send for a doctor urgently.

My Wife Dangerously Ill

The Superintendent of the local Mission Hospital was away from Kalimpong, but after some urgent telephone inquiries I was able to contact a local Indian doctor, Dr. Rao, and ask him to come immediately. While we waited Meg grew steadily worse, tearing at the pillows and bedclothes in her agony. When Dr. Rao arrived he was unable to diagnose what was wrong, but suggested that she be given morphine to ease her pain. Meg refused morphia as she felt that it would confuse anyone trying to diagnose what had gone wrong.

In the meantime I got through on the telephone to Darjeeling, forty miles away, to the Superintendent of the Planters' Hospital, Dr. Bromley, whom we had met and whose ability Meg respected. It was nine-thirty before I contacted him, and Meg had been in pain since three o'clock that afternoon. It would take at least two hours to get to Kalimpong, but he promised to be there as soon as possible.

He arrived at half-past twelve. Meg had to be held down by two sisters, the pain was so great. After investigation Dr. Bromley confessed himself baffled but thought that it might be a leaking duodenal ulcer. In view of the doubtful diagnosis he suggested to Meg that he treat it conservatively and not operate, but set up a glucose drip. He would stay the night to watch what happened and if she responded they would know definitely that that was what was wrong.

Next morning Meg's pain had eased considerably and after leaving some more instructions with the Homes Sister-in-charge he returned to Darjeeling. She was still in pain all day Saturday, although it was not nearly so bad as on the previous night, but on Sunday the pain began to increase again. On Monday morning the sister advised me that her condition was grave and that Dr. Bromley ought to be sent for immediately.

It took an hour or two to get Dr. Bromley on the phone. When I did get through he advised immediate operation but suggested that as the abdomen was not his specialty we should get another surgeon to operate if possible. He would put his instruments together and be over in Kalimpong by early afternoon. I told him that I would telephone Calcutta in the meantime to send up a surgeon by the afternoon plane to be in Kalimpong for four o'clock. But when I tried to telephone Calcutta there was some fault in the line and I could not get through. The Postmaster was very good and sent an urgent emergency telegram to reach Calcutta in half an hour and at the same time I sent a telegram to a business friend asking him to make what arrangements he could to bring the surgeon to Kalimpong immediately.

We waited throughout the afternoon and at five-thirty we had a relayed wireless message from the airfield fifty miles away to say that an emergency message had come through to say that the surgeon required for emergency surgery could not find a plane, not even a specially chartered one, and that he would arrive by the first plane in the morning. Dr. Bromley insisted that morning would be too late and suggested that he ask the Civil Surgeon in the Government Hospital in Darjeeling to do the operation. By that time Meg was too far gone to care who did the operation and I told Dr. Bromley to go ahead.

While we waited for the Civil Surgeon to arrive we moved Meg from the small Homes Hospital to the local Mission Hospital in a 15-cwt. luggage van belonging to Prince Peter of Greece. It was the only vehicle in the area capable of transporting her in the bed to the Mission Hospital in the town three miles away. At half-past eight the Civil Surgeon arrived with a convoy of three Land Rovers bringing all that he would require for the major operation ahead, as well as several assistant doctors and his theatre sister. This brought the total of doctors in consultation to eleven, including my wife.

When he had examined Meg thoroughly, and discussed her condition with her, the doctors went into consultation in the Medical Superintendent's consulting room, and were there until about midnight. I paced up and down on the grass outside the hospital, the memory raging within me of that decision, a few nights ago, to leave Tibet because of the waste of Meg's abilities and my own frustration. I saw the futility of running away from God and His planned destiny for such apparently sensible but selfishly human reasons. Had not God given Meg her ability as a surgeon to use for His purposes? If he chose to take away her ability, or even her life now, what emptiness and mockery it made of my decisions. Into that dark night of my soul there shone a gleam of light; if God had removed my illness on my humbling myself to ask forgiveness and return to obedience six years before, then surely He could and would do the same now for Meg. She was too far gone to take any decision for herself, but I could decide on her behalf, and I contracted with God again that whether Meg lived or died I would continue to be His servant in whatever circumstances He chose to further His purposes in Tibet. •

About midnight I was sent for to talk with the Civil Surgeon. As I made my way to the consulting room two of the doctors stopped me and said that under no circumstances should I permit Meg to be operated upon as they felt that her condition being so low, it would result in her certain death. Leaving them, I met Dr. Bromley on the stairs. He stopped me and said that if I had any say in the matter I must insist that my wife should be operated on immediately as it was the only chance to save her life.

When I entered the consulting room the Civil Surgeon told me to sit down while he outlined the situation to me. He said that all the other doctors agreed that it would mean almost certain death if they operated on my wife at this juncture; that it was not just a question of surviving the operation itself but there were three post-operative hurdles she would have to surmount which were impossible in her present condition. He advised a few days' rest to build up her strength; then she should be moved to Darjeeling where there were better facilities for the operation and for her treatment afterwards. Here in Kalimpong there was no anaesthetic machine, there was no plasma, there were no supplies of glucose for the intra-venous drip which would be required, and he could not stay to supervise her condition after any operation. On the other hand, Dr. Bromley had been with my wife from the first attack, had seen her before her symptoms became confused by the many morphia injections to alleviate her pain, and he was insistent that an operation was urgently necessary. He felt that as the situation was so grave he ought to leave the final decision to me as the husband.

My Wife Dangerously Ill

Now that the time for decision had arrived I was quite calm, and even confident. I told the Civil Surgeon that I definitely wanted him to go ahead and operate immediately. Within twenty minutes he was in the theatre and the operation had begun. It was a wonderful Himalayan night in the serene calm of the snow-covered Kanchenjunga. For three hours I stood on the upstairs veranda outside the theatre and let my soul be bathed in the peace and majesty of the Almighty. Nations and their policies seemed so small when viewed from the presence of God.

At half-past three the door of the theatre opened and the Civil Surgeon appeared, pulling off his gloves. 'You can thank God and Dr. Bromley that we decided to operate,' he said, 'for in another three hours your wife would have been dead. She had an intestinal obstruction and eight feet of her bowel was already gangrenous.'

Her condition was extremely precarious and on the third day after the operation I was sent for at 11.30 a.m. and told by the doctor that the end was near and she wanted to see me. When I entered the room and knelt by the bed she was too weak to lift her head. She gave a faint smile and with a shallow breath after every word she whispered her last messages to her family and me. I had to bend over her face to catch what she was saying finally, and I faintly made out, '—and-don't-let-anyone-stop-you-from-going-to-Tibet-Commit-me-to-God.' I was to learn later that she too had experienced a remarkable sense of peace on making the decision regarding our not leaving Tibet.

The calm of the night of the operation was still with me and I shook my head. 'You cannot die', I assured her, 'for God has told me so. He just wanted to teach us the lesson we have learned. I will pray, but it will be to ask God for strength to enable you to live.' I prayed beside the bed, and then left the room. Outside on the veranda several people came to see me and quietly assured me that they were praying for my wife. The Mother Superior of the Convent told of special prayers being offered morning and even-ing in the Convent. Tibetan priests were offering up prayers in the local monastery. Hindu shopkeepers in the bazaar were pray-ing before their shrines. The headmaster of the Homes School led a special prayer meeting on her behalf.

For four hours she lay at the very edge of death and then in the late afternoon she slowly edged back to a slight improvement. She had another near fatal collapse the next night and then another slow recovery. There were other crises when supplies of plasma, or glucose, or special medicines were not available and had to be rushed from Darjeeling or Calcutta, but all the time from that first crisis there was a gradual, if slow, improvement.

While Meg was fighting her way back to health I heard further rumours of the uprising in Kham and heard of the London *Times* correspondent's report from Nepal that 900 Chinese had been killed in the fighting. But I had enough to occupy me in the hospital and I was in no position to interest myself in and find out more about the rumoured uprising in Tibet.

It was two or three weeks later when Meg was well on the way to recovery that I got the details from Rapga and others, and was able to form a picture of what had happened.

It appeared that a few months before, following on a series of local uprisings in Kham and Amdo, the Chinese arrested Hou Wan Seiling, supposedly for his outspoken opposition to the Communist policy of land reform, and he was taken from Amdo to somewhere in China. Instead of quelling the uprisings, this arrest of a popular Tibetan leader resulted in even more violent anti-Chinese demonstrations and uprisings until the Chinese were forced to send in more troops in an attempt to disarm the rebellious tribesmen. When this failed, they finally agreed to release Hou Wan Seiling from imprisonment and send him back to his people. Coinciding with his return the notorious Golok tribe captured a large detachment of Chinese soldiers sent to disarm them, and cut off their noses, returning them thus mutilated to the Chinese garrison as a warning of what would happen to others. The Chinese then sent three regiments into the area to punish the Goloks, but the Goloks, probably assisted by an infuriated Hou Wan Seiling, annihilated between seven to eight thousand of the Chinese troops.

In Kham the revolt flared up in Litang, Batang and De-ge. Chinese soldiers garrisoned in the 14,500 feet monastery town of Litang, in attempting to disarm the turbulent monks and Litang townspeople, were attacked and over 200 were killed. The large Chinese arsenal and treasury located in Litang was also looted and the arms and ammunition divided amongst the fighting Khambas. The Chinese sent bombers from airfields in China and razed the town and monastery to the ground, but this only served to fan the hatred of the Tibetans against the Chinese and drive them into the mountains where the Chinese foot troops dare not follow.

In Batang the leaders of the revolt attacked and killed over a thousand Chinese and Sino-Tibetan Communists and also destroyed the houses and buildings belonging to the Chinese soldiers, officials and fellow-travellers. However, before they could take over the Post Office a Communist official was able to send a message to China asking for help, and in a few hours three waves of bombers came over and dropped three bombs each. For several days successive waves of bombers came over and bombed the town and local monasteries until it was a shambles. Again, instead of being intimidated, every able-bodied Tibetan between childhood and old age took to the mountains and from there made savage, pitiless raids on the Chinese soldiers who were left camping in the open outside the town.

Although I was approached by several newspaper reporters for any details I might have of the rumoured uprising I did not want to endanger the success of the revolt or embarrass any Government who might want to use the situation to help Tibet. I ought to have known that foreign policy is in the final analysis only national self-interest and it was to the selfish interest of every country to keep the matter as quiet as possible. India could make no protest or gesture of help, because the Indian Government was already involved in conniving in the Chinese occupation of Tibet and its integration with China through the Sino-India Trade Pact with its 'Five Principles of Peaceful Co-existence'. America dare not help because of the strong anti-American feeling in India which necessitated an ultra-cautious diplomacy, and any help, military or otherwise, would have to come through Indian territory. Britain could not help, for since Independence she had no more interest in Tibet and could only support Indian policy.

When Meg had sufficiently recovered to move about the Civil

Surgeon advised a return to the U.K. and possibly another operation there. He had only done an emergency operation to relieve the obstruction, but the gangrenous bowel might have to be resected. With this unexpected visit to the U.K. being found necessary I decided to see what could be done for Tibet in official or public circles.

On arrival in London Meg went into St. James's Hospital where she had formerly worked, under the care of her former chief, Norman Tanner, and I set the wheels in motion to find help for Tibet. I got into touch with a foreign editor friend of one of the leading newspapers and gave him the whole story. He in turn got into touch with the Foreign Office and fixed appointments for me with the officials concerned. It was also through him that I was able to broadcast on 'The Revolt in Tibet'. For a short time it looked as if the wheels might pick up momentum, but gradually they bogged down in the unscrupulous mire of power politics. It was advisable to keep the matter quiet just now as Mr. Nehru was arriving for the Commonwealth Prime Ministers' Conference and mustn't be embarrassed with a public outcry over Tibet; Mr. Chou-En-lai was about to pay a visit to India and relations between China and India mustn't be disturbed by giving the situation in Tibet too much prominence. It looked as if the Dalai Lama would come to India for the Buddhist celebrations and, if so, it was better that the matter be kept as quiet as possible to leave room for possible negotiations during his visit.

That Tibet was a country where thousands of people were dying without aid—not even of the medical kind—and being ruthlessly ground to oblivion between the upper and nether millstones of Chinese and Indian policy did not seem to come within the purview of official consideration. Everyone seemed thankful that its peculiarly remote situation was such that it could be conveniently shelved with the minimum of possible repercussions.

Chapter Sixteen

THE DALAI LAMA RETURNS
TO TIBET

With no knowledge of how to go about publicizing her predicament, Tibet nevertheless made some attempts to bring the situation to the attention of the world.

Several influential Tibetans arrived in Kalimpong and one of them, Tubetan Ningje, Abbot Commissioner of Gyantse, was particularly outspoken. He said that it was his intention to publicize in India and other Asian countries the average Tibetans' aversion to the Chinese Communists and to appeal to these nations to use their good offices to persuade China to remove her occupation army from Tibet so that it might become a free and independent nation again.

He himself was from Gyantse, a large town in West Tibet, between Lhasa and India, but from conversations with eye-witnesses and others he had managed to piece together what had been happening in East Tibet. He described the reports appearing in *The Times* and other newspapers as garbled versions, and gave the true record of events.

A task force of 3,000 Chinese troops had been despatched to a place called Dzachuka, a rebel area in East Tibet, to collect arms and ammunition from the local people who were known to be in sympathy with the rebel elements in the mountains. These people, mostly militant lamas and nomadic tribes with large herds of yaks, cattle, sheep and horses, had from the beginning resisted the introduction of the Communist-sponsored land reforms and had also protested against the heavy imposition of taxes by the Chinese authorities.

When the Chinese tried to disarm the people forcibly they met with violent resistance and many Chinese were killed. The disturbance then spread to other areas, at first to the neighbouring Golok, then to Nyarong, Tao-fu, Ha-ko, Litang, Chatreng and Mili, involving over 2 million inhabitants of East Tibet in guerrilla warfare. The rebels blew up bridges and roads on their eastern side to keep reinforcements from entering from China, and did the same on the western side to disable the Chinese there.

The Chinese, to prevent the rebellion from spreading, erected pill-boxes and barricades all over Tibet, especially round monasteries and important towns, and by air raids on the large towns of East Tibet tried to bring the Kham Tibetans back to subjection.

It proved an impossible task, as Rapga had foretold, and in July 1956 Peking was forced to send a peace delegation, with no less a person than Deputy Premier Chen Yi as its leader, to investigate the causes of unrest; and to report back to Peking with recommendations from the Prime Minister, Chou En-lai himself.

The clumsily fabricated reports put out by Peking were so obviously contrary to what was actually happening inside Tibet that the *Manchester Guardian's* 'Student of Soviet Affairs' was led to head an article:

'NO' REBELLION IN TIBET, AND IN ANY CASE, IT IS OVER—NEARLY

The Peking account began with 'a categorical denial of the rumoured rebellion in Tibet', then went on to concede that there was a rebellion but alleged that reports in the West were based on 'distorted and falsely exaggerated delayed information'. The rebellion occurred 'not in Tibet but in Western Szechwan . . . on the borders of Tibet . . . many months ago . . . and at the end of February. . . .' It was 'provoked by Government reforms to restrict the landlords' and did not apply to lamaseries, so reports that lamas were 'taking part in the rebellion were untrue. . . .' And 'the rebellion has now been settled in the main'.

This was followed a few days later by an ironical article written by Taya Zinkin in the *Manchester Guardian*:

Ever since the Chinese Communists 'liberated' Tibet they have had troubles there and ever since that time they have been trying very hard to pretend that everything was for the best on the terrestrial roof.

However, there is enough trickle of trade and pilgrims into India for much of the happy picture conjured up by Peking not to stand examination, and the Indian papers have had one long series of alarming news about Sino-Tibetan peaceful co-existence, news which has missed the bull's-eye of Indian reactions because both Tibetans and Chinese are yellow-skinned. . . . Colonialism in this part of the world, to be identified, has to be hetero-chromatic, or at least across salt water, and Tibet is only across the hills from China. . . .

Indians do not get elated about such news because they tend to equate them with their own troubles with the Nagas, who are simply being tiresomely resistant to the benefits of being taught Assamese or of recognizing Shillong as their State's capital. This is why even the *Statesman* of Calcutta, which is reporting the revolt of Kham, has given the matter only a few lines. In fact, it is very probable that the revolt in Kham is the key battle between Tibetan autonomy and Communist colonialism. If Kham is too difficult to squash the Chinese may come to loose terms with the Dalai Lama, if not it will be only a matter of years before Tibet ceases to have an entity of its own except phonetically. . . .

In September the Chinese Deputy Prime Minister, Chen Yi, who had led the peace delegation to Tibet, submitted his report to the Central Government in Peking. He said that while it had been agreed that Tibet should take the road to socialism, it was a long road, to be travelled slowly. Democratic reforms were to be carried out, but peacefully, and they were to leave room for guarantees for the 'political position and living standards' of the 'Tibetan nobility and the lamas'. The state would continue to support religious schools.

The Dalai Lama arrived in India on December 25th for the celebrations of the 2,500th year since Buddha's enlightment. He brought with him a large entourage of monks and lay officials, and thousands of pilgrims. At the same time leaders of the Mi-mang Tsong-du, Alo Chondze and Jayang Dawa, arrived to appeal to India and the United Nations for help.

The Dalai Lama was given a warm reception in India, the Indian Government observing a fine distinction between him and the Panchen Lama by providing the former with four outriders to the latter's two when they travelled by car, and by a similar finely discriminated protocol throughout their visit. An ugly incident occurred at the nearest airfield to Kalimpong, where thousands of Tibetans had gathered to welcome the Dalai Lama with gifts and ceremonial scarves. As the scarves were presented and tossed to him from the crowds, someone had taken the opportunity to enclose a stone in a scarf and had thrown it at the Panchen Lama, who received a nasty cut on his cheek. Security arrangements were tightened and no further incident occurred, but the Panchen Lama did not venture to visit Kalimpong.

The Chinese Government had been very insistent that no foreign agents should be permitted to visit the Dalai Lama except on formal occasions when there would be no opportunity to formulate intrigues, and the Indian Government was punctilious in this in every way. I had thought of returning to India so that I could have some talks with him, openly or otherwise, but was officially discouraged because of the possible embarrassments that might result. However, Rapga had a private forty-minute meeting with him during his visit.

Nor was this the only meeting with political significance. On his arrival in India the Dalai Lama requested sanctuary from the Indian Government for himself and for other members of his entourage, and for help in their struggle for freedom from the Chinese occupation. This was an unexpected bombshell to Indian officialdom, which had been publicly accepting the official Chinese handouts that everything in Tibet was peaceful and progressive with cordial relations existing between the two. In addition to this embarrassment was the presence of the Chinese Premier, Chou En-lai, in Delhi to see that nothing untoward occurred during the Dalai Lama's visit.

After a series of consultations a meeting was held attended by the Dalai Lama, his brothers, Mr. Nehru and Chou En-lai to sort out the situation. Chou conceded that there might have been unfortunate incidents in Tibet but said these were due to the too strict interpretation of policies by local officials and had nothing to do with Peking's proper attitude. If the Dalai Lama and the Tibetans objected to anything then they ought to be frank with him and he would see what could be done to mitigate oppressive policies when he returned to Peking. In the meantime the Dalai

The Dalai Lama Returns to Tibet

Lama should not delay in India, or contemplate taking sanctuary here, but should return to Tibet to assure the Tibetans that the Chinese would in the main withdraw and only help as a friendly neighbour.

The Dalai Lama and his brothers were reluctant to accept this, knowing only too well what promises from Chinese had been in the past, but Nehru added his persuasion, assuring them that India would use every sort of influence she possessed to see that the promises were fulfilled, until at last the Dalai Lama agreed.

He would return, but another—the third—of his brothers would remain in India, and also one of his trusted officials, Luk-hang, the respected former Prime Minister who had defied the Chinese when they had first entered Tibet and rejected their claims to suzerainty over the country. He also refused to accept Chou's advice not to visit Kalimpong, where 10,000 Tibetans, including many Kham rebel leaders, had gathered to welcome him, and where it was known that they wanted him to remain and organize help from India and other countries in their struggle for freedom.

Chou returned to Peking in January, 1957, and observers there noted that 'an atmosphere of dejection surrounded the usually buoyant Chinese leader'. When he was asked about the rumours current in India that the Dalai and Panchen Lamas were being approached by United States agents in efforts to influence them against returning to Tibet, he admitted that this was true, and went on to add that if the two Lamas did not return, and the uprisings continued in Tibet, China would be forced to adopt the policy of forceful repression that she had endorsed in Hungary.

Before the Dalai Lama left Delhi he tentatively arranged that Nehru should pay a visit to Tibet in 1958 for the celebrations to be held there in connection with the Buddha Jayanti. Then after ten days in Kalimpong, where he had final discussions with those to be left behind, he returned to Tibet in spite of the pleas of thousands of his subjects.

Chapter Seventeen

THE BRETHREN

I spent Christmas Day 1956 with Lois Mitchison, who had just returned from Peking where she had been a freelance newspaper correspondent. She had received permission to visit Mongolia. Shortly before she left Peking she asked for permission to visit Tibet and was told that it was not possible at that time but that if she applied again in the spring of 1957 she would get permission then.

I got into touch with Guy Wint, Foreign Editor of the *Manchester Guardian*, and suggested that I make application to Peking to visit Tibet to do a series of articles for that paper and also to extend it to a visit to China. He thought that there would be no harm in trying but was doubtful if I, with my record, would be given permission. Accordingly I sent a formal request to the Peking Government, in January 1957, through the office of the Chinese Chargé d'Affaires in London, for a visa to visit Tibet and China for six months.

I received a courteous reply from the Second Secretary in the London Office, asking for any copies of my writings available. I sent word to my publishers and received another letter from the Second Secretary acknowledging receipt of my two books, *Tibetan Journey* and *God's Fool*.

I waited through February and March and in April wrote another letter to see what progress, if any, was being made with the application.

I had a short note in reply to say:
Dear Sir,

I have received your letter of April 3rd and am writing to inform you that we have had no reply from Peking regarding your application for a visa.

The Brethren

What I had in mind was a motor trip over the new China-Tibet highway; three months in Tibet and three months in China, going north from Lhasa to the Sinkiang border through Sining to Peking, returning via Shanghai, Chungking, Chamdo and Lhasa. In this circular tour of over 10,000 miles I would have had an opportunity to observe the changes in the life of the people of both countries and to collect material for articles, a popular travel book, and another book on which I was working on the development of the indigenous Christian churches under Communist rule. That there would be risks involving possibilities of liquidation—by accident, of course—I knew, but I was confident that King David's—'a thousand shall fall at thy side and ten thousand on thy left hand but it shall not come nigh thee'—was equally applicable to me in my God-given service. In any case, it would be interesting to prove the point, and it meant that I was on the offensive and the Communists on the defensive even in a small personal way, a pleasant change from a back-pedalling Christianity.

Most of my time in the U.K. had been spent in helping to nurse back to health my sister, who had had a severe nervous breakdown. However, I had also found time to take up some important matters arising from my earlier denunciations of missionary policy in general and Brethren activities in particular, controversies over which had increased following the publication of my book *God's Fool*.

Shortly after leaving the U.K. in 1954 I had received a most peculiar letter from the Secretary of a group of Brethren Assemblies in my home district who had formed themselves into a committee known, but not acknowledged, as the 'Mid-Scotland Brethren'. Like so many other activities of Brethren, this had been formed in earlier years for the unobjectionable purpose of arranging annual conferences or gospel tent campaigns, but had gradually crystallized into a rank of the hierarchy of the Establishment where certain local elders could use personal prestige and power to influence the climate of opinion in the district to further their own ambitions and opinions. In its earlier conception there was nothing wrong with it from a Scriptural point of view, but in

165

its present practice it was a pernicious cog in the national and international machinery of Brethrenism to suppress effectively anything that was not in conformity with the opinion of the 'Establishment'.

The Secretary was an old friend of my family and he addressed me by my first name:

Dear George,

At a business meeting held a few days ago in connection with the Mid-Scotland work I was asked to write you to ascertain whether you are still engaged in full-time Missionary Work in fellowship with the Assemblies. You will no doubt write me in due course as to this.

I trust you are both keeping well,

Yours sincerely,

GEORGE VEITCH.

As a business letter it was unexceptionable but as a supposed spiritual communication from representatives of Brethren Assemblies to a known rebel it was a petard aching to be hoisted. Why this should be so may be gathered from my reply:

Dear Mr. Veitch,

Many thanks for your letter which I received a few days ago.

Would it be possible to be a bit more explicit? I find the wording of your letter vague and the possibility which prompted its despatch disturbing. You say 'At a business meeting, etc., etc. . . .' If the meeting was in connection with the Mid-Scotland work, wasn't my own assembly represented? If so, why wasn't any question regarding me or my ministry addressed to them? If not, why were they not approached first of all? Surely in matters relating to the Lord's work I am answerable to them before any other? In the event of any defection from the ministry to which I was commended, surely they would be the first to know, particularly when my father is one of them? If I still have the confidence and commendation of my own assembly what is the reason for the above-mentioned letter? What is meant by 'full-time Missionary Work'? 'Full-time' in the modern sense of the term, or

The Brethren

'full-time' in the Pauline? 'Missionary Work' in the modern sense of the term, or 'missionary work' in the Scriptural sense? What is the meaning of 'fellowship with the Assemblies' (please note that all the capitals are your own) in the light of my having the commendation of my own assembly as stated above? Do you doubt their authority, or ability to spiritually discern the mind of God, or spiritually discipline in the case of disobedience? Or do you disagree with the autonomy of the local assembly?

All those questions arise out of the question addressed to me in your letter and as I am only seeking to conform to a simple obedience to the Word of God you will understand why I cannot give you a straight answer to your question any more than could the Apostle Paul. If there has been any gossip, any unfounded rumour, let the individual concerned approach me direct according to the Scriptures. If there are any witnesses with any derogatory report concerning my ministry, from the 'mission field', let them approach my assembly. Until this is done I cannot, in accordance with the Scriptures, enter into any controversy over something couched in ambiguous terms, of which I know nothing.

I then went on to suggest a meeting with all the Brethren concerned to go into the implications of their letter and received a letter from the Secretary saying: 'I . . . personally approve your suggestion for a meeting with the Brethren in Mid-Scotland. You will no doubt make contact with me on arrival and we can make the necessary arrangements for the meeting.'

Within a month after I arrived in the country (I had to spend a month in London with my wife in hospital) I wrote to the Mid-Scotland Brethren. Mr. Veitch had 'resigned' from the group in the meantime, but another brother who had known my family for many years was Secretary. He wrote in reply to my letter:

Dear Mr. Patterson,

I wish to take this opportunity to acknowledge your letter of the 4th inst., and regret the delay in replying.

Unfortunately it is rather an awkward time to call a meeting due to holidays. . . . It may therefore be towards the end of September before we could have a meeting with you and if you can inform

167

me if such a time would fit in with your movements, I think a meeting can be arranged. . . .

I wrote again in August, for several reasons, and received the reply: 'Further to my letter of 20th July and yours of 8th August, I wish to advise you that I laid the correspondence before the meeting of district Brethren in Camelon on Friday evening, 14th inst., with your request for a meeting.

'They are of one mind that the present time is not opportune for such a meeting and they decided to await publication of your second and third books, after which the matter will again be considered. . . .'

So the fantastic situation arose in which I could not get the self-appointed leaders of Brethren to hold a meeting to discuss my implied, but not stated, violation of Scripture, and their un-Scriptural conduct and correspondence, while at the same time they perpetuated their disapproval and forbade me Brethren plat-forms to speak from. It was such a palpably dishonest and un-Scriptural action that had I wanted I could have caused consider-able disruption and even division amongst many Brethren assem-blies. However, while I did not agree with the commonly accepted fear of 'division' amongst Brethren, I was not prepared to lead another faction or clique. If what I had to say was of God, then let the Holy Spirit of God cause it to burgeon into a new sweeping demand for a return to the simple obedience to the Word of God and liberty to practise what it taught. The 'Estab-lishment' had so blatantly over-reached themselves in their paro-chial tyranny and authoritarianism that never again would any spiritual-minded individuals be influenced by what they said. They had been shown up as sterile traditionalists, without even the courage to face an issue over the Word of God, in a meeting before witnesses, and as soon as driving, Spirit-filled young men and women emerged from the torpor induced by their parrotted maunderings they would be swept away.

I went to Netherhall, a Christian Conference Centre which was very much the haunt of the Establishment, to talk with David Haxton, the manager, a close friend for many years although one who was very much against a spiritual revolution and against making a public issue of the Mid-Scotland Brethren's actions. He admitted that their position was weak, even untenable, but argued that they were the best that Brethren had and if they were removed only worse could take their place. It was a shattering indictment of my generation—although I did not wholly agree with him as I maintained that there were some, though very few, who were head and shoulders above the more public figures of the 'Establishment'—but I had to agree entirely with his conclusion. I also accepted his advice to withdraw my name from the Brethren 'Prayer-Lists'—the euphemism employed for accredited missionaries recognized as approved by the Establishment for financial support, as I was now militantly committed to opposition, removal of the 'paternalist-compound' missionary system, and engaged in increasing literary and political activities. He was very grieved that one who had showed such youthful promise (and I owed a lot of it to his influence) should get bogged down in what to him was fruitless controversy, and even worse, that my spiritual experience and ministry should be lost to my generation amongst Brethren through being consigned to the wilderness; if I would only conform I might accomplish all I wanted in more acceptable ways. I could not agree with him, for I pointed out that the very fact that the 'Establishment' had the power to consign me to the wilderness by refusing to have me speak in Brethren assemblies was a pernicious thing and served to underline the parlous state into which the Brethren movement had fallen. And also, if I had any spiritual ministry to give God would see to it that it was given irrespective of whether the Establishment provided platforms or not.

This was what happened. Although there were many places under the influences of the men with charcoal grey suits and charcoal grey minds there were many more who were opposed to their stultifying influence. I could have been fully occupied in those places had I wanted, but I chose under God's direction to speak more to select groups in houses—drawn from Brethren assemblies and other denominations—who were spiritually concerned about conditions in Britain and elsewhere and who wanted to know how those conditions could be altered. They were hungry for a vision and a task and I was hungry to help them. God had given me something to say, and the ability to say it, and it was up to Him to give the increase.

Chapter Eighteen

A DEFEAT FOR CHINA

On August 2nd an outline of propaganda for the Tibetan Working Committee of the Chinese Consultative Political Organization was published in the *Si Tsang Jih Pao* (Tibet daily) in Lhasa. It announced a directive from the Central Committee to postpone democratic reform in Tibet for six years. However, 'to be able to live happily the Tibetan people must necessarily take the road to socialism, and to enforce democratic reforms is the unavoidable path the Tibetan people have to follow in gradually passing into a Socialist society'.

The report boldly admitted that after the resolution to implement democratic reforms in Tibet had been passed the previous year 'facts had proved that only a few of the upper-strata personages support it, while the majority still harbour varying degrees of doubt and are actually against it; and that although a small portion of the masses enthusiastically demand reform, the large portion of the masses still lack such enthusiasm'. On this account therefore, it was concluded that conditions for reform were still inadequate at present. Because of this it had been decided not to implement the democratic reform in Tibet during the period of the Second Five-Year Plan. 'As to whether the democratic reform will be implemented during the Third Five-Year Plan period or not, the question will be decided according to the actual conditions in Tibet then.'

In view of the fact that there was to be no reform in Tibet in the next six years it was also decided that the present organs and personnel—particularly the Han cadres—of the Tibet Autonomous Preparatory Committee were far too many, and that they should be transferred to the motherland to take part in socialist reconstruction there.

A Defeat for China

The previous year, in anticipation of major reforms, the Chinese Communists had made 'political and economic arrangements for some of the upper-level personages'. Since there was to be no reform, the Peking Government decided, there would be no change in the original income of these upper-level personages, and therefore the State, in principle, should not continue to issue salaries to these personages. However, those who could be spared should remain at their posts and continue to receive pay. Proper assistance should be rendered to 'patriotic personages who really have livelihood difficulties'.

In regard to schools, 'certain upper-level personages are even dissatisfied with our opening schools. At the same time the unreasonable phenomenon of drafting people into schools appeared in certain localities, causing many complaints from the students' parents. From now on, the schools in various places should be appropriately readjusted according to the principle of voluntariness and to actual conditions. . . .'

From now on, the report concluded, People's Liberation Army units and working personnel stationed in Tibet would continue faithfully to implement the agreement on the peaceful liberation of Tibet, strengthen unity with the people of Tibet of all strata, assist the Tibetan people to do all the beneficial things which could be done, and strive for the consolidation of the unity of the motherland. 'If any imperialist element or any separationist takes the opportunity of our reduction of our establishment, or under any pretext in the future, to try to conduct sabotaging activities and manufacture revolts, then we will give him this solemn warning: "We are determined to implement the agreement on the peaceful liberation of Tibet, but if someone dares to violate any one of the seventeen articles of the agreement and manufacture revolts then the People's Liberation Army has the responsibility to suppress the revolt, and will certainly join hands with all patriotic citizens in dealing firm and telling blows to the rebellious elements." '

Over 1,000 people attended the public announcement of the above decisions—Tibetan and Chinese leaders of various government departments, monasteries, political cadres and youth

A Defeat for China

associations. The implications were explained and the warning against further revolt stressed.

A few days before my wife and I returned to India, on October 12th, 1957, it was reported in the *Manchester Guardian*, from Hong Kong, that China had withdrawn 91·6 per cent of her Communist officials from Tibet and had temporarily abandoned her attempt to turn the country into a Communist province.

With all the typical Chinese 'face-saving' verbiage it was still an admission of defeat. Seven years previously China, and every other nation, would have laughed to scorn anyone who suggested —as I had done—that the Tibetans could force the Chinese to withdraw from Tibet, yet here was a withdrawal, in any language, due to pressure of events which they could not control.

What had actually occurred was very much greater, and very much worse from the Chinese point of view, than might be gathered from the reports in either the Chinese or foreign newspapers.

When I arrived back in Kalimpong and had several talks with my Tibetan friends it was to find that the tragedy of Tibet was entering its final phase. Just short of an improbable victory over the Chinese in their struggle for freedom, they were now tragically divided amongst themselves.

The revolt in Kham, it transpired, had not only continued but had also intensified. There had been a temporary lull following the discussions with the Chinese peace delegation, and while the talks were going on during the Dalai Lama's visit to India, but when the Chinese callously vitiated this agreement by concentrating reinforcements in East Tibet the Khambas flared up into more bitter fighting than ever. In 1956 the Khambas and Amdowas had approached the Lhasa Government officials with the suggestion that they join them in the revolt, but the Lhasa officials had refused to help, even with guns and ammunition.

When the Chinese made their peace overtures to the Khambas, after the revolt had become uncontrollable, they had suggested that Ngaboo, their usual Tibetan representative in Lhasa, be appointed leader of the 'peace delegation'. The Khambas were so embittered by the Lhasa Government's pusillanimous attitude that they told the Chinese that if Ngaboo arrived in Kham for talks he would be the first one to be shot. The second Chinese suggestion for a leader, another Tibetan official called Karmapa, got the same reply, and the Khambas said they would only recognize Topgyay Pangdatshang as their representative. The Chinese were forced to agree to this. Knowing the temper of his people, Topgyay held out for an unconditional withdrawal of the Chinese—troops and officials—and eventually the Chinese were forced to agree.

When the Lhasa officials in the Dalai Lama's entourage returned to Lhasa they had made arrangements with private dealers in India to send in large supplies of arms and ammunition—not for use but for profit. After arriving in Lhasa they proceeded to sell the guns for rupees 6,000 (£500) per gun and bullets at rupees 30 (£2 10s.) per bullet to their fighting fellow-countrymen in East Tibet. At the same time they strenuously denied to the Chinese Communist officials in Lhasa that they had ever talked about removing the Chinese from Tibet while in India. The Chinese produced the 'peace' document, agreed on with the Khambas, and changed a significant sentence about their withdrawal 'according to the desire of the people of Tibet' to 'according to the desire of the people *and officials* of Tibet'. The Lhasa officials willingly agreed to append their signatures to the altered document and follow it up with an invitation to the Chinese Communists to remain in Tibet. When the Indian Political Officer, Apa Sahib B. Pant, went to Lhasa shortly after the Dalai Lama's return, those same officials who had spoken so vociferously to him and other members of the Indian Government about Tibetan freedom now either refused to meet him or else met him always in the company of other Chinese Communist officials so that they would not be suspect.

In Kham the Chinese deliberately broke their 'peace' agreement. Having successfully driven a wedge between the Lhasa officials and East Tibetan leaders, they calmly announced that the conditions of the 'peace' agreement applied to 'Tibet, west of Chamdo'. All territory east of Chamdo was not Tibet but Szechwan province of China and, as such, the terms of the agreement did not apply to Tibetans inhabiting that area. The troops with-drawn from Lhasa were then sent to Kham and, supplemented by troop reinforcements from China, the Chinese Communists launched an all-out attack to exterminate the tribesmen of Kham and Amdo.

The Khambas were not intimidated. Furious at the betrayal by the Lhasa officials and Chinese Communists, they swore to kill every Chinese in Tibet and then deal in the same fashion with the traitorous Lhasa Government officials. They left the towns, after destroying buildings and everything of value, and took to the mountains where Chinese dared not follow. From there they launched their sudden ruthless attacks on isolated Chinese garri-sons and troop detachments, taking no prisoners. They blew up roads, bridges and airfields so that the Chinese could not send in reinforcements by their much-publicized motor road, and any supplies had to be air-dropped as the planes could not land.

In keeping with my policy to attack the Chinese Communists when and where I could, I immediately sent off a letter to Peking asking for the visa I had applied for several months earlier. I wanted to see what the situation was like for myself, but if the Chinese refused the permission because they were afraid to let me move in the area and amongst the Tibetan friends I knew so well, I decided to publish a series of articles on the situation with the material I had. I applied in December 1957 to the London Chargé d'Affaire's office and received in reply.

Dear Sir,

This is in reply to your letter of 4th December. In reply, I am sorry to say that I have not yet had any instruction from the authorities concerned in Peking regarding your application for a visa.

I sent off a 90-word cable in February direct to the Ministry of Information in Peking, to see if that would produce anything, asking for an urgent reply as I would like to leave in March.

I had already had several pleas from some Kham leaders of the revolt who had ridden incognito to India to see if they could get outside help, and also to see if they could arrange for secret supplies of arms and ammunition through their own channels that would serve to by-pass the extortionate prices being demanded by the Lhasa officials. When their pleading for help and publicity became too much to put off longer, I sent off a last cable to Peking, requesting an urgent reply to my application for a visa—even if it was a refusal. I waited until March 31st, to give the Peking authorities every chance to reply, and when no reply came I sent off, on April 1st, the series of articles I had prepared beforehand entitled 'TIBET—AN ASIAN HUNGARY'. I sent copies to the *Manchester Guardian* and Guy Wint of *The Twentieth Century* in Britain, and to the *New York Times* and *The Reporter* in the U.S.A. It was a last despairing gesture on behalf of a dying country whose tragic destiny was strangely interwoven with my own. Not quite the last.

Chapter Nineteen

TIBET BECOMES UNITED

On April 5th, 1958, Gordon Shepherd, Special Correspondent of the *Daily Telegraph*, visited Kalimpong, Darjeeling and Sikkim, and sent in a front page report corroborating the widespread fighting in Tibet. Kingsley Martin, of the *New Statesman and Nation*, also visited the area, but partly because of his left-wing sympathies and partly because he only interviewed leading Tibetans through Indian official interpreters —before whom the disillusioned Tibetans were reluctant to be frank—he received a less urgent impression.

I was completely cynical about the proposed visit of Mr. Nehru to Tibet, although I knew how much importance the Tibetans were attaching to it. They knew that if he saw for himself how hated the Chinese had become because of their oppressive measures and how completely they were trying to dominate the country, he would as a humane and just man be bound to protest and use his influence on their behalf. I warned the Tibetan leaders not to place too much hope on this very bruised reed, for while Mr. Nehru's motives and intentions might be unimpeachable I was convinced that the Chinese were only using him as a front to screen their activities in Tibet. So long as it was believed abroad that the Chinese were willing to welcome Mr. Nehru to Tibet the report that there was widespread revolt against the Chinese in that country would be discredited. It did not cost the Chinese anything to have it published and anticipated; they could always fabricate an excuse to postpone his visit when the time arrived.

In the meantime 200,000 Chinese troops were occupied in eliminating every particle of opposition in Kham and Amdo. Thousands of villages, nomad encampments and towns were attacked with gas and high explosive bombs and then, when all able-bodied Tibetans had fled to the hills, the Chinese began to move in on a massive programme of complete absorption. A figure in the region of three million Chinese was given as involved in their colonizing move, every village being forced to house and feed half the number of its previous inhabitants in Chinese settlers and being forced to mate with them in the plan of mass 'Hanisation'. The programme was ruthlessly and efficiently organized and initiated, each district and area being completely covered before the Chinese moved on to the next area in a new wave of colonization. The villages were heavily garrisoned and protected during the process, with scouts and patrols on all the high parts of the mountains to warn of any impending Tibetan attacks.

For the Kham and Amdo tribesmen were now equally merciless in their fighting. In addition to their natural fighting qualities they had nothing more to live for—their homes were gone, their lands confiscated, their herds slaughtered, their parents, wives and children either killed or raped or starving—and all that was left to them was the horses they rode, the guns they carried and a raging thirst for revenge against a hated enemy.

Within a few months they had destroyed 500 miles of roads, 400 miles of railways, hundreds of bridges and thousands of Chinese. From the time the fighting started in 1956 until mid-1958 over 40,000 Chinese died in the fighting in East Tibet. The Khambas in return lost about 15,000, the disparity in the numbers of casualties being accounted for by the fact that they refused to meet the Chinese in open places where the advantage would have been with the highly disciplined, well-armed and mobile Chinese troops. Instead, they blew up convoys on the roads, machine-gunned from unassailable positions the tightly packed Chinese troops at river-crossings and various passes, rode out on fast marauding raids against isolated units, and used every possible natural advantage that was theirs at an average altitude of 15,000 feet. The Chinese might have more and better guns, might have held up several armies in Korea, but at 15,000 feet the Chinese soldier was only a poor gasping creature struggling to carry his load and rifle. The Tibetan fighter, who could run for days without discomfort, could live for a month on what he had in his saddle-bag or on his back, and could fire his gun with deadly accuracy at all times.

No prisoners were taken on either side. With all the roads and bridges destroyed there were no supplies coming in from China to the isolated Chinese forces in Tibet, and air-dropped supplies could only be irregular at the best of times and circumstances. When Tibetans were seriously wounded they were killed rather than let them fall into the hands of the Chinese who were torturing prisoners for information or killing them horribly as examples to others not to join the rebels. The Tibetan rebels had no medical aid of any kind, were continually on the move, and could not burden themselves with prisoners, so all Chinese were put to death.

The Tibetans believed that they could hold out longer than the Chinese in these circumstances; accordingly crops were destroyed and herds of yaks, cattle and horses either driven off or slaughtered so as not to provide food or transport for the Chinese. Gradually what the Tibetans had hoped for took place. The Chinese occupation personnel became discontented with their circumstances in Tibet, began protesting and even sympathizing with the Tibetans. The Chinese authorities moved swiftly and 5,000 Chinese merchants, troops, officials and others—1,068 in Lhasa alone—were arrested. Nor were these only from the lower ranks, for amongst others Puntshok Wangje, Tibetan Communist leader for 20 years, number-one puppet in the take-over and Vice-President of the Tibetan People's Political Consultative Committee, was arrested too for protesting at Chinese atrocities and expressing sympathy for the Tibetan struggle for freedom.

My sources of information on the situation inside Tibet were unimpeachable. From the Dalai Lama's brothers, through former Prime Ministers and Cabinet Ministers to the guerrilla leaders or their delegates who poured into Kalimpong, I was able to talk with them freely as a friend and sympathizer. They were in desperate need of help and pleaded with me to publicize their predicament, thinking that if their position were known then some country must come to their aid. They did not ask for troops to be sent or even for guns, although these would have been useful. But they urgently needed ammunition, for two years of guerrilla fighting had seriously depleted their stocks.

Poor Tibetans! No one had ever told them about *realpolitik*. They still believed in British justice, United Nations principles, American anti-Communism and Indian moral indignation. No one had thought to teach them the political facts of life.

Mr. Nehru, giving no reason, postponed indefinitely his visit to Tibet. To three urgent pleas, presented by the Dalai Lama's brother to the Indian Political Officer in Sikkim on behalf of help for Tibetans from East Tibet, the Indian Government replied with advice that the Tibetans should not resort to violence in their campaign for freedom but should emulate India in her struggle with Britain and initiate civil disobedience and non-violent campaigns against the Chinese. India could not recognize Tibet's struggle for freedom. That would mean that India would be morally obliged to help with arms, which in turn would mean that she would be violating her principles of non-violence, also the 'Five Principles of Peaceful Co-existence', and committing herself to the possibility of perhaps having to send men as well as materials to Tibet and so to war with China.

The Tibetan self-exiled officials in Kalimpong and Darjeeling, while disappointed, were not now surprised at this, for they had become accustomed to India's vacillations and political betrayals in relation to Tibet and her own relations with China. But the guerrilla leaders and others from East Tibet were made of sterner, simpler stuff. If the Tibetan exiled officials could do nothing, if the Indian Government would do nothing, then they must appeal to other countries. In the meantime, there was no point in any Tibetans waiting on the borders of Tibet for help that would never come, so all those not committed to an active participation in Tibetan liberation from the Chinese Communists would have to return immediately to Tibet to fight with their fellow-countrymen there and, if necessary, die beside them.

For the first time in a millenium Tibet became a fully united country again. Thirty thousand rebel refugees from East Tibet

Tibet Becomes United

had had to fall back on Central Tibet in the fighting, and entering
Lhasa they made the situation look ominous for the Chinese there.
The Chinese ordered the Lhasa Government authorities to send
them back to East Tibet immediately, but the Government instead secretly supplied the rebels with food and arms and helped
them to escape to the mountains north, south and south-west of
Lhasa. Within a month 23 rebel groups were operating against
the Chinese between Lhasa and the Indian borders.

This indication of unity between the Lhasa Government and
the rebels was conveyed to the Tibetan official guerrilla leaders and
delegates in Kalimpong, and it started a similar movement there.
Previously, in addition to the divisions between the great feudal
families from Lhasa, there were also leaders from different anti-
Chinese groups—the most famous being the Mi-mang Tsong-du,
from Lhasa and West Tibet, known to the West by occasional
newspaper reports—and the much more powerful East Tibetan
guerrilla organization of Chu-Zhi-Kang-Druk, linking all units in
East Tibet against the Chinese. They had all met together and
formed a new representative group called CHUL-KA SUM. This
name had formerly been given to the three provinces of Tibet—
Kham, Amdo and U-Tsang—and signifies a racial, cultural, religious and economic entity; this was what the Tibetans were fighting for. Once more it was chosen as a symbol, and also a sign to
the outside world that the new revolt was no longer an East or
West Tibetan affair but an expression of unity and defiance from
the whole of Greater Tibet.

My effort to help the Tibetans with publicity had not met with
any success. Although I had written for newspapers and journals
in the past, had published three books which were well reviewed
in leading periodicals, and had been asked to send reports on the
Tibetan situation to the *Manchester Guardian*, it seemed that either
my right hand had forgotten its cunning or that there was a baleful
spirit abroad doing its utmost to stifle the news of Tibet's desperate plight and need for help. For more reasons than conceit I
was inclined to the latter, for not only did I give editors full
authority to write up the information I sent to suit their own
high standards but I found that the regular correspondent of the

181

Statesman of Calcutta, who had also been sending articles to his editor, could neither get them printed nor get an explanation as to why they were not being printed.

At the same time this baleful spirit—who must have had some connection with the printer's devil—saw to it that editors of the most respected papers printed the most utter drivel about the situation in Tibet from correspondents whose sources were either questionable or non-existent.

I became more and more reluctant to face my Tibetan friends. What could one say? In a world where not only news of Hungary or Poland, but of Suez, Lebanon, Jordan or Iraq—with a handful of casualties—could make front-page news for weeks and evoke passionate dissertations on freedom from every tuppenny ha'penny demagogue, a small peaceful country on the borders of the greatest moralizing country in the world was fighting against the most feared country in the world, inflicting deadly damage, bringing the proud Communist country to her knees to admit mistakes and concede withdrawal. Yet there was not even a line of print to acknowledge her struggle and her courage.

If Edith Summerskill was ashamed of being British in Egypt and Barbara Castle ashamed in Cyprus, I was sick to the back teeth not only of being British but of the whole human race—of politicians. I might also have added editors, but suddenly I had a cable from the *Daily Telegraph* asking me for all I could give on the situation in Tibet and on July 31st Tibet was on the front page. The *Spectator* printed an article I wrote in fury and frustration on the 'Unrecognized Revolution'. The *New Statesman* carried an article in which it referred to 'former missionaries busy drafting and sending appeals for help on behalf of fugitive nobles in Kalimpong'.

I was the only 'former missionary' in a position to advise the Tibetans, and certainly the only one in a position to 'draft and send appeals', but I never had or will have any intention of asking for help 'on behalf of fugitive Tibetan nobles in Kalimpong'. My interest in people is as creatures of God with destinies to fulfil, my responsibility towards them is that of a fellow-creature, and my interest in Tibet was in the people and country as a whole, not in social strata or passing political ideologies. Further, if the 'appeal' in question was the one addressed to the United Nations I had no direct part in it. It was a document drafted, discussed and issued by the Tibetans of the CHUL-KA-SUM themselves,[1] although several of the members had read articles I had written on the historical and political status of Tibet.

On August 4th a meeting of all leaders from all parts of Tibet was held in Kalimpong to decide on what was to be done in view of India's refusal to help and her non-co-operative attitude. The guerrilla leaders and delegates had been advocating an extreme course of action by proposing an attack on Sikkim and Bhutan with an uprising of Tibetan nationals in sympathy in Kalimpong and Darjeeling. There were about 20,000 guerrillas between Lhasa and Sikkim, and 7,000 of the best fighters most feared by the Chinese on the border of Bhutan. They had only enough food for about two months at the most in Tibet, and a major attack on these areas, coupled with an uprising in Kalimpong and Darjeeling where there were another 10,000 Tibetans, would get them all the publicity they wanted, at the same time giving them supplies of food.

The Tibetan exile-officials were very much against such an extreme step, knowing something of the complications involved, but they were a minority—and a not very respected minority, in most cases, at that. However, they managed to persuade the guerrilla leaders to forego such action for the present and they counter-suggested an appeal to the United Nations. As their earlier appeal to the United Nations, in 1951, had been shelved and ignored, they decided that copies should be sent to every country represented on the United Nations, as well as to religious societies and reputable newspapers. A copy would also be sent to India as a matter of courtesy, although no help was expected from that source.

On August 5th over 300 copies of the Appeal and Manifesto were sent out, amongst those going to Britain being one for the Queen and one for the Prime Minister. The following is a copy of the Appeal sent to the Indian Government, and which, with

[1] See Appendix B, page 211.

183

relevant alterations, was sent to all other countries as well:

Dear Sir,

Tibet is essentially an independent country with sovereign powers. Its people being religious and peace-loving, no stock of modern war-weapons were kept within its boundaries. In the year 1950 the Chinese Communists invaded our land with about 500,000 of their so-called 'liberation army' and overpowered our frontier guards. Later they settled some four million Chinese immigrants in the eastern and north-eastern regions. These settlers, along with their powerful armies, have attempted to destroy our religion, culture and traditions.

We Tibetans, both in Tibet and in India, have tried our utmost to make the Chinese recognize their shameful injustice to us and we have asked them several times to stop oppression and suppression of our people. We have also approached you, Mr. Nehru, in the past, asking you to use your influence with the Chinese on our behalf, but all these efforts proved vain. We have already explained the Tibetan situation to you and know that you are well aware of the facts. In spite of this we are attaching hereto a Manifesto describing the plight of our people. In it you will read of the merciless treatment of our people by the Chinese, and how many had to flee to the far-off deserts and valleys. It is for these reasons that our people are now fighting for freedom. There are hundreds being killed daily by the Chinese in these battles.

There is trouble also in Lhasa, the capital of Tibet. Recently some 30,000 people from the southern areas had to leave their property, families and settled life to save themselves from the brutal treatment of the Chinese overlords. Now without homes, these people are also out in the deserts and it is feared that there may be uprisings in the south and central areas as a consequence.

Not only have the Chinese Communists occupied our country and set about exploiting our people, but they have also made Tibet into a huge arsenal for their future offensive towards her neighbouring countries and the world at large. They are building army barracks, forts, bridges and airfields at strategic places and their immense programme for constructing great roads and railways is mainly to accelerate the movement of their armed forces.

It is in view of the above-mentioned facts and because of your close and cordial relations with China that we request you to kindly make the Government of China realize the desperate situation in our country. We request you to endeavour to make the Chinese immediately stop their offensive which they are launching against the patriots in Don-Kham and Amdo in the eastern regions, and to make the situation in Central Tibet easier.

India, a country which was under British domination for over 150 years, achieved her independence just after World War II. Similarly, a number of other countries which were under foreign yokes for generations have attained their independence within the past few years. On the contrary, the independence of Tibet, an essentially free country which, as history proves, was at no time under any foreign domination, was violated by China, her next-door neighbour. Can the peace-loving countries of the world justify the atrocious actions of the Chinese Communists in Tibet while its people are fighting tooth and nail in a struggle for their very existence?

Since yours is a country which prizes its freedom, we look to you to do what you can to help. Therefore our appeal to you is this. Please request the Government of China on our behalf to allow Tibet to regain her independence and to withdraw all their armed forces and immigrants from the whole of Tibet.

The Appeal was signed by seven people—Lukhang, the respected former Prime Minister, and two representatives each from Kham, Amdo and U-Tsang Provinces, so that it represented the whole of Greater Tibet.

India's reaction was immediate. Local officials were instructed to forbid the Tibetans in Kalimpong and Darjeeling to hold any more meetings, forbid them to talk with newspaper correspondents, and forbid them to take part in political discussions or activities of any kind on the threat of immediate expulsion from India. As the Indian Government was the only authority which could issue affidavits or stateless passports to the passport-less

Tibetans, this threat meant an immediate return to Tibet for execution at the hands of the Chinese.

Britain wasn't much better. The *Manchester Guardian* of August 5th, under the headline 'REPORTS OF TIBETAN MASSACRES AND RIOTING DISCOUNTED', printed an article from its New Delhi correspondent, quoting Indian 'official sources', in which it was not only said that the reports of large-scale rioting and massacre in Tibet were 'grossly exaggerated' but that they were 'stories from Tibetan *émigrés* who have settled down in Kalimpong and other towns on the Indian border'. This was obviously to be the Indian line. The *Statesman* of Calcutta printed the same report—from a stranger in Kalimpong without sources, while ignoring its own regular correspondent who refuted the report. Obviously it could hardly carry a report on a war in Tibet against Chinese aggression while giving front-page coverage to the statement from Kruschev and Mao in Peking on August 4th that:

'the policy of peace of China and the Soviet Union has won increasingly extensive sympathy and support of the peoples of the world. . . . India, Indonesia, the U.A.R. and other countries and people of Asia, Africa, America and Europe who uphold peaceful co-existence are playing an ever more important part in consolidating peace. The forces of peace have already grown to unprecedented strength. . . . China and the Soviet Union give firm support to the just struggles of the peoples of the U.A.R., the Republic of Iraq and the other Arab countries, as well as the national independence movements of the peoples of Asia. . . .'

When the leader of the Opposition challenged Mr. Nehru about Panch Shila, 'The Five Principles of Peaceful Co-existence', in the light of the recent revolt in Tibet, Mr. Nehru, in his usual rambling evasive way, replied: 'Acharya Kripalani has said that Panch Shila was born in sin. According to the Christian doctrine we are all born in sin. Panch Shila was included in the treaty between India and China in regard to Tibet.' He went on to say that about the policy of Panch Shila itself there was nothing new. It had struck him in an odd moment to apply it in regard to foreign affairs because it fitted in with their way of thinking. He admitted that there were other countries who could not get along with the idea of Panch Shila because of the way it had come into existence but, 'if one examines it from the purely practical point of view', he went on, 'there is no other way that nations can behave toward each other. The only other way is the way of conflict.'

On the subject of Tibet Mr. Nehru was equally straightforward. India could not have challenged China's action or claim, either in law or in fact. (Although he failed to mention that India could challenge Britain over Suez, but not Russia over Hungary, Britain and America over Jordan and Lebanon, but not Egypt over Israel.) In the circumstances India's action was 'the only legal, constitutional and available action'. He admitted that there had been internal trouble between Tibet and China. 'We had some trouble over this matter when Chiang Kai-shek controlled the destinies of China. The world community as well as the Government of India, before or after independence, had always acknowledged the suzerainty of China over Tibet. We came into the picture not in a particularly good way when Colonel Younghusband . . . invaded Tibet and forcibly established positions there and gained certain rights for the then Government of India. . . . Whether Tibet was free to act for herself or was functioning under the suzerainty of China, I do not quite understand how India or the British acting through India had a right to put their platoons and companies of troops at odd places in Tibet on the plea of protecting their commerce. . . .'

The fact seemed to escape Mr. Nehru's notice that the Chinese had put 500,000 troops and 5 million settlers in Tibet, and, unlike Younghusband, showed no sign of withdrawing them; that their 'official' reason for being there was a political agreement forced on a Tibetan cultural mission with no authority and sealed with a seal forged by the Chinese Communists in the market-place of Peking.

The United Nations acknowledged receipt of the Appeal—and busied itself about getting the British out of Jordan, America out of Lebanon and Quemoy, and British fishing-boats out of Icelandic waters.

Britain indicated a lively interest in the matter, but was reluctant to embarrass India in a difficult situation.

Tibet Becomes United

America, which had shown such lively interest in the past—
even to the extent of considerable cloak-and-dagger interviews—
showed the same promptitude and ability to help that she had
manifested with Hungary and Poland.

And India? The Indian Government imposed silence on all
Tibetans in India, and to ensure that no word of what was happening in Tibet should reach the world outside they put security
police to watch all Tibetans—and me.

'All tragedies', said Byron, 'are finished by a death, all comedies
are ended by a marriage.' It is fitting, therefore, that the final
words on the tragedy of Tibet should be about death. Since the
final despairing Appeal was issued to the United Nations on
August 4th, 7,000 Tibetans were killed in East Tibet as the
Chinese Communists retaliated by throwing in another 300,000
troops. An average of over 100 Tibetans a day are dying up to the
time of writing, not including the old men, women and children
who are throwing themselves into the rivers to avoid death by
starvation or capture.[1]

'Commonplace people dislike tragedy,' said John Masefield,
'because they dare not suffer and cannot exult. The truth and
rapture of man are holy things, not lightly to be scorned. A care-
lessness of life and beauty marks the glutton, the idler, and the
fool in their deadly path across history.'

---

[1] Estimates of the population of Tibet vary considerably. The Chinese Communists have given a figure of 1,273,969, although no Tibetan knows of any
census having been taken. British Political Officers' estimates lie between three and
five million. The Tibetan estimate is fifteen to twenty million, the basis of calculation
being that there is one lama to every 200 of the lay population, and that there are
known to be 100–150,000 lamas.

APPENDIX A

Before Buddhism was introduced into Tibet, a country seven times the size of Britain or a third of the U.S.A., it was a land noted for its warlike people. They had overrun large parts of Turkestan and India and penetrated into China as far as Sianfu in Shensi. In the middle of the 9th century a treaty of peace was concluded between China and Tibet on a footing of equality. They had already exacted heavy tribute from the Chinese Emperor, including the marriage of his daughter to a Tibetan King.

It was through the influence of this Chinese princess and a co-wife, also a princess, of Nepal, both ardent Buddhists, that Buddhism entered Tibet. From being one of the chief military powers of Asia Tibet gradually deteriorated into a nation largely robbed of vitality through the ramifications of the parasitical priesthood which developed and fastened on the vitals of the country. The form of Buddhism which was introduced into Tibet became mixed up with the earlier black practices of shamanistic Bonism, and gradually became a cloak for the worst forms of aggressive demon-worship by which the poor Tibetan was put in constant fear of attacks by thousands of malignant devils both in this life and the world to come. The 'lamas', or priests, multiplied rapidly, soon usurped authority in matters of state, and finally gained full control, overthrowing the king and assuming the kingship from among themselves. The 'priest-king' structure in Tibet, as in other lands, proved a retrograde movement, and the lamas ruled the country entirely in their own interests, keeping the 'laity' in ignorance and abject servitude, until the former virile Tibetans became the most priest-ridden people in the world, with fully a third of the nation's manhood being absorbed into the parasitic structure.

Appendix A

About the middle of the 14th century a great reformer called Tsong-ka-pa was born. He revived the religion in a purer form, introducing laws of discipline, insisting on the celibacy of the priesthood, forbidding the consumption of alcoholic liquor, and restricting the proliferation of lesser gods and devils in the Tibetan religion and the worship the magic-loving people gave to them. Some time after the death of 'The Perfecter of the Priesthood', as he was called, the first indication of a new process became evident, when priests began to claim that the spirit of 'The Perfecter of the Priesthood' had passed into another priest, who, it was claimed, therefore had a right to succession. The idea appealed to the Tibetans, who were used to the process of transmigration anyway, and the new suggestion that it was possible for someone to waive his right to Buddhahood in order to return and help others still struggling on the upward path gained wide support and was soon established.

Under the third High Priest the title of 'Dalai Lama' was introduced for the first time. He had been the means of converting Mongolia to Buddhism and received from them the Mongolian title of 'Dalai Lama', or 'All-Embracing Lama'; this became one of his, and his predecessors' titles, although the Tibetans preferred other titles of their own.

The fifth in the line of Dalai Lama was a remarkable personality, and although of high spiritual status, he chafed at the limitations of his secular power. He therefore persuaded a powerful Mongol chief to espouse his cause; the Mongol invaded Tibet, defeated the king of Tsang, one of the largest provinces in Central Tibet, and gave the sovereignty of all Tibet to the young fifth Dalai Lama in 1641. He now used his unique power to crush all opposition and to establish himself as a sovereign, able to help or punish his subjects not only in this life but also in the life to come. He was a priest, an incarnation of the god Chen-re-zi, and a secular ruler—a priest, a god and a king. Every Dalai Lama since the 'Great Fifth' has sought to ensure for himself the same recognition.

China's claim to the position of Suzerain of Tibet appears to date from the early days of the Manchu Dynasty in the latter half of the 17th century. Lamaism, or Tibetan Buddhism, had by that time already spread over vast areas of Central Asia from Ladakh to Manchuria; the early Manchu Emperors, by adopting Lamaism as their State religion and recognizing the Dalai Lama as its head, secured a hold over Tibet, Mongolia and the other Lamaistic countries of Asia which lasted until the fall of their dynasty two and a half centuries later in 1911. But it was the Manchu Emperor, rather than the Chinese Government, who was for more than two centuries recognized by the Tibetans as their Suzerain, and up to the last days of the dynasty the Emperor was represented in Lhasa by a Manchu and not a Chinese.

Early in the 18th century Tibet was invaded by the Dzungarian Mongols, and the Manchu Emperor immediately despatched two armies to the help of the Tibetans. One army advanced by the northern Sinang road from Kansu, the other by the southern Tachienlu road from Szechuan, and they succeeded in reaching and occupying Lhasa and expelling the Mongols. This was the first of three successful advances into Tibet, each of which assured the dominion of the Manchu Emperors over the country for a short time afterwards. On this occasion a Manchu Resident and a garrison of Chinese soldiers were left in Lhasa, while communications with China were assured by stationing small detachments of troops along the Chamdo-Batang-Tachienlu road. The 'boundary' between China and Tibet was then demarcated by a pillar, erected in 1727, on the Bum La (home of the Pangdat-shangs, which should really be phoneticized Bum-da-tshang, and where I stayed for a night—see my *Tibetan Journey*), a small pass two and a half days south-west of Batang. The country to the west of this point was handed over to the rule of the Dalai Lama under the suzerainty of the Manchu Emperor, while the Tibetan chiefs of the States and tribes to the east of it were given seals as semi-independent feudatories of China. This arrangement lasted for nearly two centuries, until the Chinese forward movement initiated in 1905 as the result of the British advance on Lhasa in 1904.

During the latter part of the 18th century Chinese power was on the wane until, about 1790, the Nepalese invaded the country and sacked Shigatse, a town in Western Tibet. Roused to action, the Manchu Emperor despatched an army into Tibet which defeated and expelled the Nepalese and even pursued them into their own country. The Manchus decided to use this opportunity to consolidate their position in Tibet; by two Imperial Decrees in 1793 two Ambans were appointed, given equal rank with the Dalai and Panchen Lamas, and made responsible for the superintendence of the administration of the country.

In 1860 the Tibetans of Nyarong in East Tibet, under the leadership of one Gombu Nyamjyel, an ambitious and warlike chief, invaded and conquered the neighbouring States, including De-ge and the Five Principalities of Hor. The Chiefs and the peoples of De-ge and of the Hor States appealed to both the Chinese and Tibetan Governments for assistance against the Nyarong invaders. The Chinese were preoccupied with the T'aip'ing rebellion and other troubles with foreign countries, and so were unable to take any action toward restoring order in the Tibetan States under their nominal protection; but the Dalai Lama responded to the appeals of the Chiefs by sending a Tibetan army into Kham in 1863 under the Kalon Pulung, by whom the disturbances were suppressed. The administration of Nyarong was then formally taken over by the Lhasa Government, who appointed a Commissioner named Punrab, known in Tibetan as the Nyarong Chichyab, to govern the country, and also to superintend the affairs of De-ge and the Five Hor States, which had been freed from the Nyarong invaders and restored to independence under the rule of their native kings.

The *de jure* Tibetan claim to Nyarong, as opposed to the former *de facto* acceptance of it, and to a lesser extent to De-ge and the Hor States, dates from this time (1865). Nyarong appears to have been annexed by the Dalai Lama with the full approval of the Manchu régime. The Peking Government were unwilling to accept the responsibility of administering the area and formally handed it over to the rule of the Dalai Lama, in whose hands it remained until forcibly annexed by the Chinese under their General Chao-Erh-feng in 1911. In 1894 the Tibetans of Nyarong rose again and invaded the State of Jala; the Chinese Viceroy of

Szechuan despatched a Chinese force which suppressed the disorders and occupied Nyarong, and he proposed to the Government in Peking that he take over the administration of Nyarong with Chinese officials. The Dalai Lama protested against any Chinese annexation of Tibetan territory, the Viceroy's proposal was rejected by the Peking Government, and the Tibetan Governor reinstated.

In 1886 the Tibetans raided the Sikkim frontier, to be expelled a year or two later by a small British expedition. As a result of these events the Sikkim Convention was concluded in 1890 between Great Britain and China. A set of Trade Regulations for the control of commercial relations between India and Tibet was signed three years later. No Tibetan representative took part in the negotiations for the Sikkim Convention, Britain dealing with China as the acknowledged Suzerain of Tibet. These events brought Britain for the first time on to the scene of Sino-Tibetan relations.

At the beginning of the 20th century the portion of Central Asia inhabited by Tibetan-speaking peoples, and labelled TIBET on European maps, consisted of three separate entities: firstly, the Central or Lhasa Government-controlled Kingdom of Tibet with its provinces and dependencies; secondly, the semi-independent Native States of Kham under Chinese 'protection'; and thirdly, the Kokonor Territory under the control of the Chinese Amban residing in Sining in Kansu.

The Kingdom of Tibet, ruled by the Dalai Lama from Lhasa with the nominal assistance of the Chinese Amban, extended north to the Altyn Tagh and Tsaidam at Kokonor, and east to the Bum La, the frontier pass near Batang. It included the frontier provinces of Markham[1] and Gonjo, the Lama-ruled dependencies of Draya, Chamdo and Riwoche, and the outlying province of Nyarong situated amongst the Native States under Chinese 'protection'. This was the Dalai Lama's realm in which his temporal power, as apart from his spiritual power, reigned supreme. The powers of the two Chinese Ambans had waned until their positions were only nominal.

[1] See *Tibetan Journey.*

Appendix A

The Native States on the Szechuan Border east of the old Sino-Tibetan frontier on the Bum La sent periodical tribute missions to and were under the nominal protection of Chengtu and Peking. Some, such as the great kingdom of De-ge and the Five Hor States, had come under the direct control of Lhasa, while others such as Jala (Tachienlu or Kangting) and the territory of Batang and Litang remained, owing to their relatively open situation on the 'main road' to Lhasa, more under Chinese influence. However, the powers of the small Chinese military officials and commissariat officers stationed at these places had dwindled to vanishing point, while the soldiers of the frontier garrisons were often unarmed or existed only in the official imagination for the purpose of fixing pay-rolls.

The Kokonor Territory (Amdo Province to the Tibetans and Tsinghai Province to the Chinese) comprised the whole of the upper basins of the Yangtze and Yellow Rivers and part of the Mekong headwater country. In many places uninhabitable desert, it was thinly peopled by Mongolian and Tibetan tribes, loosely termed Amdowas as those in the southern province were termed Khambas, the Mongolians under the Princes of their Banners and the Tibetans under their own small Chiefs and Headmen, the whole area being nominally under the control of the Sining Amban on the Kansu border.

Although the whole of this vast region of mountain and desert was inhabited by Tibetan-speaking people, and had been for centuries, at no time had they ever been unified under the control of a Lhasa Government exercising temporal authority, and the rise and fall of local rulers together with the occasional entrance of the Chinese into the scene had made confusion worse confounded as far as delineation on any map was concerned.

Each of the three occasions on which China sent armies into Tibet followed on the invasion of that country by a third party—the Dzungarian Mongols in 1720, the Nepalese in 1790, and the British in 1904—although the reason was more to keep other countries from having too direct an interest than out of any altruistic desire to help Tibet. As long as Tibet remained isolated and unvisited the Chinese were satisfied with a nominal control, but the opening up of relations between Tibet and her neighbours to the south immediately provoked the Chinese to action.

In British-ruled India the Sikkim Convention concluded between Great Britain and China in 1890 defined the boundary between Sikkim and Tibet, and contained a reciprocal agreement on the part of both contracting parties to prevent acts of aggression across the border. During the years following its signing, however, it became more and more apparent that little or no progress had been made in opening up friendly relations between India and Tibet, and that little satisfaction could be expected from this agreement concluded with China over the heads of the Tibetans, for the latter appeared to consider that as they were not directly a party to the Convention there was no need for them to carry out its provisions. All attempts by the authorities in India to open friendly relations with the Tibetan Government were frustrated, peaceful messengers were maltreated, and letters returned unopened. The Sikkim Convention had been concluded with the Chinese Government on behalf of the Tibetan Government at the request of the former, but when the Tibetans failed to observe its provisions and recourse was had to diplomatic representations in Peking the Chinese Government were found to be unable to influence the Tibetans in any way. At length, in 1903, the British Government, realizing the hopelessness of continuing to attempt to deal with the Tibetans through the Chinese Government, and the absolute necessity of establishing direct relations with the Lhasa Government if trade were ever to be opened and the frontier secured by proper treaty relations, despatched a Mission to negotiate a commercial agreement with the Tibetan authorities direct.

Whatever the advice given to the Tibetans by the Chinese Amban in Lhasa may have been, the Tibetans refused to receive any communication from the Mission, which met with repulse after repulse until, having started as a peaceful embassy, it eventually reached Lhasa in August 1904 as a military expedition. The Dalai Lama fled for the north before the British expedition reached Lhasa, but a Convention was, however, concluded with the remainder of the Tibetan Government in the summer of 1904.

Under this Agreement Tibet undertook to recognize the Sikkim Convention—which she has faithfully observed ever since—while provision was also made for the opening of Trade Agencies in Gyantse, Gartok and Yatung. The British troops withdrew from Lhasa immediately after the Agreement was signed, leaving the territorial integrity of Tibet and the independence of the Tibetan Government unimpaired. The Chinese Government at first endeavoured to revive their claim to be the sole medium of communication between the Government of India and the Tibetans, and to replace the Anglo-Tibetan Treaty by a new Agreement, but eventually the Lhasa Convention was duly confirmed by an Agreement between Britain and China signed at Peking in April 1906.

In August 1907 Britain and Russia signed an Agreement under which both parties undertook to respect the territorial integrity of Tibet and to refrain from interfering in the internal affairs of the Tibetan Government. In 1908 a set of Trade Regulations governing Indo-Tibetan trade was signed in Calcutta between British, Chinese and Tibetan representatives.

Britain's object in concluding these various agreements was to assure the territorial integrity of Tibet and to safeguard her existence as a peaceful autonomous buffer State between the three great Atlantic powers—Russia, India and China. The fact, however, was overlooked that China had through these very Agreements obtained a free hand in re-establishing and consolidating her position in Tibet without the possibility of foreign interference. They were not slow to take advantage of the situation, and turned their attention in the first place to annulling the advantages of direct intercourse between India and Tibet obtained under the Anglo-Tibetan Treaty of 1904. The Tibetans were gradually led to believe that, though the Peking Government had not had time to send an army to expel the British from Tibet at the time of the 1904 expedition, yet it was fear of Chinese displeasure which had caused the British to withdraw their troops immediately after signing the Treaty, and that China had since compelled Britain to sign another Agreement cancelling the Lhasa Convention, acknowledging the right of the Chinese to control Tibet, and prohibiting all intercourse between British and Tibetans except through the medium of the Chinese authorities. Thus within a few years of the signing of the Lhasa Convention of 1904 most of the advantages of direct intercourse with a responsible Tibetan Government had been lost.

The Dalai Lama left Lhasa for Mongolia at the time of the British expedition to Lhasa and arrived in due course at Urga, where he lived with the Lama Pontiff of Mongolia for a year. From there he went on to the great Kumbum monastery on the Kansu-Kokonor border for two years, and then moved on to Peking. Here the involved and elaborate Imperial protocol necessitated his kneeling in the Imperial Presence and so indicating his vassalage to the Throne.

The reception accorded to the Dalai Lama by the Manchu Court during his visit to Peking was scarcely calculated to improve the relations between China and Tibet. From this time it became apparent that it was the intention of the Chinese Government to assume full control over Tibet (hitherto, as far as its internal relations were concerned, an autonomous State) and to deprive its 'king-priest' of all temporal authority. This object was attained a few months after the Dalai Lama's return to Tibet at the end of 1909.

China's new policy in Eastern Tibet was inaugurated in 1904, following on the British expedition to Lhasa and the signing of the Anglo-Tibetan Agreement, by the creation of a new post of Imperial Resident at Chamdo, in East Tibet, with instructions to curtail gradually the powers of the native rulers and lamas and bring the country under the more direct control of the Chinese Government. At the same time a start had been made in the introduction of the new order by converting Tachienlu,[1] hitherto the capital of the semi-independent Tibetan State of Jala, into the seat of a Chinese magistrate controlling a Chinese district. In April 1905 the Tibetans of the neighbourhood and the lamas of the great Batang monastery rose in open revolt and attacked the Chinese. The events at Batang were the signal for a general uprising of all the big monasteries on the border of South-West

[1] Later to be renamed Kangting by the Nationalists: see my *God's Fool*.

Appendix A

Szechuan and North-West Yunnan, and isolated Chinese garrisons were everywhere overwhelmed and put to the sword. The Chinese launched a punitive expedition under the leadership of a general called Chao Erh-feng, in the course of which the great Batang monastery, one of the largest in Eastern Tibet, was razed to the ground, those of the lamas who failed to escape were killed, two native Chiefs were beheaded, and the surrounding Tibetans punished with execution and burnings. From this time on, up to his execution by the Szechuan revolutionaries at Chengtu in 1911, 'Butcher' Chao Erh-feng remained the central figure in Tibet.

In November 1906 Chao Erh-feng returned to Chengtu, the capital of Szechuan, where he was received in state as a victorious general and appointed to the newly created post of Frontier Commissioner. He was then placed in independent control of a vast tract of country extending from the borders of Kansu and the Kokonor in the north to those of Yunnan, Burma and Assam in the south, and from Tachienlu in the east to the confines of Central Tibet in the west, with the duty of bringing under closer Chinese control the congeries of semi-independent Tibetan States, nomadic tribes, and lama principalities which occupied the region. It appears, however, that while Chao Erh-feng had definitely determined to introduce the ordinary Chinese provincial administration into the whole of Kham, Peking had by no means committed itself to such far-reaching action, and the history of the next few years shows the Manchu Government somewhat reluctantly acquiescing in the ruthless interpretation of its forward policy by the powerful Viceroy on the frontier.

In March 1908 an Imperial Edict was issued appointing Chao Erh-feng to be Imperial Commissioner for Tibet. In the autumn of the same year he left Chengtu with several battalions of new troops and advanced by the North road toward De-ge, which for various reasons he had chosen as his first victim amongst the powerful semi-independent Principalities of Kham. The frontiers of De-ge, the largest, wealthiest and most important of the native States of Eastern Tibet, extended from the neighbourhood of Jyekundo in the north to within a few marches of Batang in the

Appendix A

south, and from Chamdo and Draya in the west to Kantze and Nyarong in the east. It had existed as an autonomous State for a thousand years or more, and the family of the chief were supposed to trace their ancestry back for 47 generations. Chao Erh-feng appeared on the scene with his army when the State was torn by internal dissension, the younger of the two brother claimants to the chieftainship being in armed rebellion against the elder. Chao Erh-feng offered the elder brother the assistance of his troops against the younger, and then having expelled him from the State and the Chinese troops having entered and occupied the capital, he deposed the elder brother. The elder brother was exiled to Batang but the younger brother fled to Lhasa, was attached to the Dalai Lama's suite when he fled to India, and eventually received an official appointment in Central Tibet on the Dalai Lama's return to Lhasa. I mention this item of history because he was the father of the Prince of De-ge (who was my host for ten days[1]), Commander-in-Chief of the Tibetan forces in South-East Tibet, who figured so prominently in the Chinese Communist attack in 1950.

Having secured De-ge, Chao Erh-feng was now in a position to advance on Chamdo, the most important centre in Kham and a strategical point in the junction of the main roads from Yunnan, Szechuan, and Kansu to Central Tibet. Towards the end of the year 1909 several thousands of Chinese troops were concentrated at Batang and De-ge Gonchen, and soon after Chamdo, then Draya and Markham, were occupied without difficulty, the local Tibetans not knowing (because of the confusion of orders amongst the leaders and the officials in Lhasa) whether to fight. The local people of the Tibetan frontier States including Chamdo, Draya, and Markham petitioned the Lhasa Government for permission to oppose the Chinese, but the Lhasa Government, reluctant to take up arms against their powerful enemy, refused permission and attempted to stop the advance by negotiations with the Amban in Lhasa. He temporized, assuring the Tibetans that Chao Erh-feng would not advance farther and that if any troops

[1] See *Tibetan Journey; When Iron Gates Yield* by Geoffrey Bull; *Captured in Tibet* by Robert Ford.

entered Tibet it would be merely for the purpose of doing police work on the main roads. In desperation the Tibetan Government, in December 1909, sent telegraphic appeals through India to the foreign powers of Europe and America and the Chinese Government in Peking; the messages had no effect, for Chao Erh-feng marched into Lhasa on February 12th, 1910, the Dalai Lama only just managing to escape down the road to India within sight of the Chinese advance guard. During the remainder of that year Chao Erh-feng consolidated his position, marching his troops as far south as the Mishmi country in North Assam, substituting Chinese magistrates for the former Tibetan officials, and proposing to the Peking Government that Giamda Dzong, within a few marches of Lhasa, should be recognized as the new boundary between China and Tibet. Peking at first refused its consent, but agreed to the proposal about a year later. When Chao Erh-feng finally left Tibet in August 1911 the work begun in 1905 was outwardly completed, and there was not a Tibetan ruler left in Eastern Tibet.

The whole edifice of Chinese control was, however, a hastily constructed framework imposed on an unwilling people taken by surprise, and the greater part of it collapsed completely after the revolution in China in 1911, during which Chao Erh-feng was beheaded by the revolutionaries. Just before the revolution occurred Chao Erh-feng's assistant proposed to Peking that Eastern Tibet should be converted into a new Chinese Province to be called (H) Sikang (or Western Kham), which later Chinese Governments accepted; so, at the whim of a lesser Chinese official, the largest and most populous province of Tibet, Kham, became 'Sikang' on all Chinese and European maps.

By the summer of 1912 the Chinese had already lost control of most of these districts as the Tibetans began gradually to realize what the revolution in China meant to them. By the end of 1912 Chinese authority had ceased to exist in Tibet, and the Dalai Lama having returned from his exile in India the country became once more an autonomous State. The new Republican Government of China tried to placate the Tibetans and recover their position in the country but the Tibetans, intensely hating the Chinese because of the excesses they had inflicted upon them, insisted that every Chinese official and soldier should leave. In Eastern Tibet the fighting was particularly bitter, as each rebellion against the Chinese was followed by greater atrocities, and the Lhasa Government troops only went as far as the Mekong-Salween divide, not wishing to get involved in further border disputes with the Chinese Government. However, in 1917 a Chinese General violated the nebulous frontier agreements and the Tibetan Government troops inflicted a crushing defeat on his forces, advancing deep into Eastern Tibet by the summer of 1918 and looking like taking over all the country up to Tachienlu formerly claimed by them. At this juncture, however, the Chinese capitulated and appealed to the British Consular Agent stationed in Western China for his mediation. The Tibetans were persuaded by him to stop their advance and the fighting ceased.

Meanwhile, on the Indian side of the Tibetan border, ever since the conclusion of the Anglo-Tibetan Agreement of 1904 and the subsequent withdrawal of the British troops, Britain had stood aside watching the ebb and flow of China's attempts to restore her position in Tibet by force. The Dalai Lama, by this time 34 years old, had been given sanctuary in Darjeeling, when he fled to India in 1910, on condition that he refrained from any participation in politics. It was during this time of enforced inactivity that he was to make a friendship which would leave its mark on Tibet for many years—that with the British Political Officer, Charles Bell. He returned to Tibet in 1912, following on the revolution in China and overthrow of the Chinese army in Tibet, to find that Russia was beginning to take a direct interest in Tibet by sending arms to the Chinese troops fighting in Eastern Tibet. He sent a private message to Bell in India to the effect that he did not desire relations with Russia provided that Britain could help Tibet without Russian co-operation.

In the summer of 1913 a conference was held at Simla, in India, with plenipotentiaries from China, Tibet and Britain, to attempt to decide the political status of Tibet. The terms which the Dalai Lama wanted were:

1. Tibet to manage her own internal affairs.

2. Tibet to manage her own external affairs, consulting on important matters with the British.

3. To have no Chinese High Commissioner, no other Chinese officials, and no Chinese soldiers in Tibet.

4. Tibet to include all the country eastward as far as Tachienlu (Kangting). All these districts are purely Tibetan, but some of them had been seized by China and brought under more or less Chinese control during the last 200 years.

The discussions lasted for six months and in April 1914 a Convention was agreed upon and initialled by all three plenipotentiaries. The Tibetans, in accordance with the Dalai Lama's wishes, had claimed all the Tibetan-inhabited territory up to Sining in Kansu in the north, and Tachienlu in Szechuan in the east, and produced whole libraries of historical evidence from Lhasa in support of their claims. The Chinese, ignoring the old records and the Manchu settlement of 1727, went back no further than the time of Chao Erh-feng's greatest successes and claimed the neighbourhood of Giamda Dzong as the boundary between China and Tibet. The British representative in his character of middleman proposed, as a working compromise between the divergent claims of the two sides, that Tibet as it was generally taken to be on the European maps should be divided up into two zones, namely, Inner Tibet—the part nearer China—to be under more direct Chinese control, and Outer Tibet to be under the autonomous Government of Lhasa. The Dalai Lama was to retain full religious control over Inner Tibet as well as the right of appointing local chiefs throughout the territory.

Two days after the draft of the Convention had been initialled the Chinese Government telegraphed repudiating it, but Tibet and Britain recognized it as binding upon themselves. The Dalai Lama objected to the proposal for dividing Tibet into two, but accepted it reluctantly when Bell pointed out that as long as the name 'Tibet' was retained, when the Tibetan Army grew strong enough to insist on Tibet's rights they could regain the rightful possession of this part of the country. China, having repudiated the Convention, was of course entitled to none of the advantages which the Convention would have conferred upon her.

Appendix A

During the three years following the close of the conference in India peace reigned on the frontier between China and Tibet, though civil war and political strife in Western China, reacting on border affairs, prevented the Chinese from making any progress in consolidating their position in Tibetan-inhabited districts on their western borders. Thus the Dalai Lama was able to offer one thousand troops to help Britain in her war with Germany as a token of Tibet's friendship.

By 1920 the Tibetan Government had at length yielded to the political pressure always being applied by the Chinese and had agreed to allow a Chinese diplomatic mission to proceed to Lhasa. On the arrival of the mission in Lhasa it took every opportunity to induce the Tibetan Government to negotiate with them alone and leave out the British. The Tibetan Government thanked them for their proclaimed interest in their religion, but pointed out that when negotiations were conducted in Simla in 1913–14 the Chinese broke them off without coming to an agreement; again, during 1919 when the Chinese themselves reopened negotiations they broke them off again; and therefore in those circumstances the Tibetan Government did not think that any useful purpose would be served by sending delegates to China to negotiate an agreement. The Chinese Government, however, not to be outdone in the international field at least, and having been long accustomed to the white races and their points of view, still write in their records and maps that Tibet is part of China. The Tibetan Government, having had very little contact with the white races and only a few Tibetans being able to read or write any European language, have published no records and produced no maps, thereby conceding the advantage to China by default.

In 1927 Russia began to take a greater interest in Tibet and sent Mongol agents to Lhasa with supplies of guns and money, and for some time managed to have a Russian with considerable influence stationed in Lhasa. But it was a passing phase and by 1931 Chinese influence was again in the ascendant. The Thirteenth Dalai Lama was failing physically and his favourite, a Tibetan called Kun-pel La, wielded tremendous influence on both civil and military affairs. When the Dalai Lama died in 1933 Kun-pel La

Appendix A

continued to exercise power for a brief period, but in the intrigue that followed on the Dalai Lama's death he was arrested and imprisoned. Later he managed to escape through Bhutan into India and settle in Kalimpong.

In Kalimpong he met and became associated with Rapga Pangdatshang, of the famous Pangdatshang family, leaders of the fighting Khambas of East Tibet. He had also fled to Kalimpong after taking part, with his younger brother Topgyay, in an unsuccessful rebellion against the Lhasa Government in Kham and then against the Chinese army sent against them.[1] They collaborated in establishing a 'Democratic Reform Party' to take over power in Tibet with a view to unifying the whole country under a representative Government in Lhasa in place of the old feudal régime with its self-seeking powerful families and warring tribes, but as this was not acceptable to the British authorities—and to the Tibetan officials in Lhasa, needless to say!—and as they were known to be sympathetic towards the anti-British Indian Congress Party the British authorities had them expelled from India and sent to China. In his attempts to win unity and independence for Tibet, Rapga, an astute and far-sighted politician, joined the Commission for Mongolian and Tibetan Affairs in China, but when he finally came to the conclusion that the Nationalist Government of Chiang Kai-shek was also committed to the policy of absorbing the people of Tibet into China he publicly resigned from his post in February 1948, publishing his protest in the Chinese newspaper *Takung-Pau*, and returned to Kangting in Kham, where he arrived in time to take part in the plans of his brother Topgyay for another rebellion against the Lhasa Government.

It was at this point in history that Tibet's destiny and mine met and merged for better or for worse.

Several years before, after a period of intellectual and spiritual struggle, I had committed my life to the direction of God at all times and in all circumstances to prove whether the principles outlined in the Bible were applicable in a modern world. Under this divine direction I left for Tibet via China in March 1947 with

[1] See my *God's Fool*.

204

a companion, Geoffrey Bull, who had had a similar experience.

Although I was associated with a group known as Plymouth Brethren I was under no control by them as a body, for this independence of movement was part of their beliefs. The Plymouth Brethren movement was a 19th-century protest against a dead ecclesiasticism that could neither justify its existence from the Scriptures it claimed to acknowledge nor defend itself against the rising tide of attacks by the neo-Catholic movement led by the brilliant Cardinal Newman, and the rapidly multiplying schools of materialism and 'free thought'. Those early Brethren believed that in proportion as the Christian body ceased to be a spiritual structure in the primitive apostolic sense, the fine suppleness and freedom of fellowship, participation in privilege and discipline, proper to a spiritual structure, must give place more and more to the coarser character of an organized legal structure. If one thing could be added outside the inspired revelation of the whole truth contained in the Scriptures then, on the same premise, one hundred or one thousand other things could likewise be added —with no confidence in any.

The early days of the movement—which later came to be known as the 'Plymouth Brethren' because of a strong group in that city, although this was a misnomer and rejected completely by those who were associated in such groups—had been revolutionary and far-reaching in its impact on contemporary religious thought. An Episcopalian minister in the Church of Ireland, John Nelson Darby, with a brilliant record in classics and law before entering the Ministry, had become more and more disturbed by the anomalies practised in the Church, which were in direct contradiction in many instances to what the Scriptures taught. The most disturbing factor of all, so far as he was concerned, was that those anomalies could not be set right without involving the collapse of the complete structure particularly in those matters relating to Communion and Baptism. During the period of his difficulties he heard of a few people who met together in a room in Dublin to carry out the simple commands of Scripture with regard to these very matters, and he went along to investigate. He was so impressed by the integrity of their Scriptural approach and practice that he gave up the clerical calling to associate with them. With some of the most brilliant minds of that generation and many others grown disillusioned and weary of organized religion they founded groups of believers, without ordained ministers, practising only New Testament principles of church gathering in Bristol, Plymouth and other towns throughout the country in a rapidly spreading movement.

At first an open freedom of fellowship with every believer was encouraged amongst them, but gradually, as in all similar movements in history, the corrupting human element began to creep in and certain people with their own personal emphases in doctrine began to exert undue influence, at first in their own local group and then in a widening circle of others, until from healthy controversy with those holding different emphases in doctrine it was only a step to arbitrarily excluding all those who would not agree or submit to some specific opinion. Then all these schools of thought subdivided into a multifarious collection of sects, each tenaciously holding on to its own particular 'Scriptural teaching'.

In the spiritual revolution of the 19th century a 'new' factor had been introduced into missionary activity when George Muller of Bristol ran his famous orphanage without soliciting public support and devoted his energies to praying to God to provide, through whatever channel He saw fit, all that was required to meet the daily needs of over two thousand children. This followed the 'novel' example of Anthony Norris Groves who abandoned a lucrative dental practice to travel to Persia and India to preach, moving step by step as God directed him, and without a 'Home Board' behind him to send out money as required, depending entirely on God to provide in whatever way He chose.

It was in the spirit of these early 19th—or rather, to be more correct, early first—century principles of missionary activity that Geoff Bull and myself left for China and Tibet in 1947. The missionary emphasis of Plymouth Brethren had started with the work of Anthony Norris Groves. It continued to blossom in the Scriptural manner for some time, but gradually the Brethren had forsaken the simple principles of Scripture in the responsibility of

Appendix A

the servant to God alone and the autonomy of the local church in identifying itself with its own member going abroad as a missionary. Soon several people were collecting items for news interest and prayer, then becoming a 'forwarding agency' for monies contributed by Christians. Finally there appeared a 'Council' for interviewing candidates and advising on practices abroad. The same hierarchies emerged in the various countries to which their missionaries went, until it became impossible for the new missionary to move anywhere except to where he was directed by the authoritarian senior missionaries.

After a period of disillusionment and conflict Geoff and I arrived in Kangting in late 1947 on our way to Tibet, as God had directed, to accomplish whatever it was He had for us to do there. In studying the language and making occasional expeditions into East Tibet with medical treatment and preaching, we met and became friendly with the Pangdatshang family.

When the Communists began to overrun China in 1949, spreading westwards as well as towards the south, Topgyay and Rapga Pangdatshang decided to move deep into the mountains of East Tibet to avoid the decisions they knew the Chinese Communists would force on them as leaders of the Khambas of East Tibet. Also, with two other leaders of the Amdo Tibetans in North-East Tibet, they had planned a revolution against the Lhasa Government, but had been frustrated by the quick overthrow of Chiang Kai-shek and the rapid advance of the Communists. The machinery of this revolution was still there, however, and ready to set into motion, but the astute Pandatshang brothers knew that the Chinese would want to use this for their own purposes.

They were correct in this. But before approaching them the Chinese Communists announced from Peking radio that the two Pangdatshang brothers and the two Amdo leaders had joined the Chinese People's movement; then they made their official approach and offers. But by that time the Pangdatshang brothers had left Kangting for the mountains deep inside East Tibet, where it would take months to contact them, and they had taken Geoff Bull and me with them. They expected to fight and warned us, but asked if we would accompany them to treat the wounded and help in any way we could. They offered to provide all food and travel requirements if we agreed, but after we had decided to go with them we stipulated that we keep an account of all that we received from them so that we could repay this later in India.

In January 1950, when our food and medical supplies had run short and we were discussing the possibility that one of us should go to India to replenish them for the struggle ahead, messengers arrived in our remote valley with the ultimatum from the Communists to the Pangdatshangs. There was the usual long Communist preamble on 'democracy' and 'liberation' and the new freedoms the people would enjoy under the new régime, and then came the important contents.

They had learned of Pangdatshang's plans for a revolution against the reactionary feudal government in Lhasa and they approved of his plans and desire to further the interests of his people. He was to go ahead with those plans and they would supply him with arms, ammunition and necessary financial assistance; the only difference was that it would not be a factional uprising as planned before but a 'people's' revolution against the Tibetan Government. He was not to consider fighting against the Communist army or resisting their orders in any way, for they were not viewing him simply as an intransigent war-lord to be punished in a foray, after which they would withdraw their forces, as had been done in previous years; nor would they be put off in their intentions if he linked up with the Tibetan Government against them, for they intended to 'liberate' the whole of Tibet as part of their plan to liberate the whole of Asia. Within one year Tibet would be liberated; within three years Nepal, Sikkim and Bhutan would be liberated; in five years India would be liberated, and thus the East would be secured for Communism.

The Pangdatshangs were in a quandary. To the west the Lhasa Government was antagonistic and suspicious because of their past history, to the east the Communists demanded collaboration and revolution against their own countrymen. There was no way out. Topgyay was known as the leader of the Khambas and as such would be held responsible for them. If he ordered them to fight they would fight; if he ordered them to submit they would submit; if he gave no decision at all and the Chinese came in, the Khambas, with their centuries-old hatred of the Chinese, would still fight without the leadership of Topgyay, and the Communists would still hold him responsible for the fighting.

There remained only one possibility. Topgyay had to remain in East Tibet to lead the Khambas. Rapga could not go to India for he had been expelled from there and would be arrested on his return. That left myself. Could I make the journey across an unknown part of Tibet to reach India in two months, inform the authorities there—British, Indian, and Tibetan—of what was about to happen, and get word back to the Pangdatshangs before the Chinese attacked? The Pangdatshangs calculated that they had six months before the Chinese decided they would wait no longer for the Pangdatshang's decision and go ahead on their own.

I prayed, and as I prayed God spoke: 'I have brought you to this place as I promised but this is not the end of my promise. There are still greater things ahead. I told you that I would send you to Tibet, and other countries of Asia, to communicate to those who have never heard the knowledge you have learned of me, and that no one would be able to stop you from accomplishing my purpose for you as long as you obeyed my voice. I have brought you to Tibet but this is only a very small part of the work I have yet for you to do. Not only Kham or Tibet or Central Asia but the whole world must know that I am still the God of Abraham and of Moses, of David and Elijah, the God and Father of the Lord Jesus Christ. What you have done so far is nothing to what I have yet for you to do. The way in which I have led you has brought you into possession of unique knowledge. You are the only person with the knowledge of Chinese Communist plans to take over Tibet and the other countries of Asia. No one else knows, no one even suspects that China is making for India. Therefore you will go to India and take the knowledge you have gained to the authorities there and I will use you to stop the Communist advance, to frustrate the Communist plans for taking over Asia, for I have sent you there and no man or nation can withstand me. I only require that you should be obedient to my every word. There is no living without dying; there is no dying without living.'

It was several days later before Geoff and I agreed that we should separate, he to remain in Tibet until my return, I to go to India on an almost impossible journey with an almost impossible mission in the closing chapters of the history of Tibet.

APPENDIX B

MANIFESTO TO THE UNITED NATIONS FROM THE TIBETAN CHUL-KA-SUM, AUGUST 5th, 1958

Because very little is known about Tibet many people think that it has always been under the domination of China. They are surprised to learn, for instance, that the Tibetans have had their own passports, currency, etc., and have had direct trade relations with other countries.

If we begin as early as the year A.D. 635 with Tibet's most famous king, Songtsen Gompo, we find ample evidence in Tibetan history that it has always been an independent country and never under the dictatorship of China. True, this king had a Chinese wife and a Nepalese wife, but he obtained them by force, sending soldiers for that express purpose. At that time the borders of Tibet stretched as far as Lanchow in the east to Nepal in the west and included the whole of Sinkiang province in the north. In A.D. 712 we find that King May-Aktsom also procured a Chinese bride, she being offered in order to bribe the Tibetans into peaceful relations on the Chinese border.

During the reign of Tihtsong Detsen (about A.D. 741) pundits came from India to teach Buddhism. At this time relations were not good between China and Tibet and the former used to pay a yearly tribute of 50,000 pieces of Chinese brocade to Tibet. In A.D. 755 the Chinese stopped this tribute, so the Tibetans attacked China and extended their boundary to Shensi province. The then ruling emperor of China fled the country and the Tibetans enthroned an Emperor of their choice.

The year A.D. 877 saw a religious revival and a treaty with China. This treaty concerned the boundary then fixed at Chorten

Appendix B

Karpo. (The actual White Chorten giving the place its name is still standing today.) The details of the treaty were engraved on three separate pillars, one of which is today in Lhasa, another at Sien (Shensi province) and the third at Chorten Karpo itself. The treaty is written in both Chinese and Tibetan.

In A.D. 1244 the first Lama King of the famous Sakya Lama line began to rule. One of these kings was invited to China by the Emperor, a descendant of the Great Mongolian conqueror Genghis Khan. There he was treated as an independent King; he had a strong religious affinity with the Mongols. The fact that the great Chinese Emperor himself escorted Tibet's King a distance of four months' journey on his return to Tibet proves that great respect was paid to him.

The friendship of the Third Dalai Lama (in A.D. 1578) with Altan, King of Mongolia, gained considerable significance when Altan's grandson became the Emperor of China (the first of the Manchurian line) and invited the fifth Dalai Lama to China. On this occasion it is recorded (both by Tibetans and foreigners) that the Chinese ruler escorted the Tibetan King many days' journey on his entry into China. This, together with the fact that the Chinese and Tibetan rulers often conferred honours upon each other, shows the equality of the relationship of the two rulers.

This visit by the Dalai Lama was also used by the Chinese to their own advantage, since they feared the Mongolians' occasional revolts against them, who in turn recognized the authority of the Dalai Lama. Any friendship which ever existed between China and Tibet was based upon religion and both the Mongols and Chinese recognized the Dalai Lama as their spiritual Guide.

The scene began to change in 1908 during the reign of the Thirteenth Dalai Lama, when the Chinese, under the leadership of Chao Erh-feng (known as 'the butcher') attacked Tibet. Many monasteries were destroyed and hundreds of people massacred. After the raid the remnants of the forces were sent back to China via India. Since that time (1912) up to 1950 no Chinese have been allowed into Tibet without express permission.

Tibet, independent and peace-loving, has a theocratic form of Government with His Holiness the Dalai Lama as its sole Ruler.

Its language, culture, traditions are completely different from those of China. Yet, in the year 1949, when the Communists subdued the whole of China, they declared to the whole world through the radio that China wanted to 'liberate' Tibet.

The Chinese suddenly attacked the eastern regions of our country from eight different directions. Being a non-violent and peace-loving country, Tibet had no stock of arms and ammunition, and the legal Government of the country approached the United Nations General Assembly for justice and to check the further advance of the Chinese invasion. Receiving no reply from that Assembly, we approached the Security Council at its session at Lake Success. To our greatest disappointment both of our appeals were ignored and remain unanswered to this day. It was under these circumstances that the Chinese forced our Governor at Chamdo to submit to their dictates and to make the Government of Lhasa surrender. To the Governor was dictated the so-called '17-Point Agreement', which he had to translate into Tibetan. Then he was forced to sign it on behalf of the Government of Tibet by the threat of further troops being sent into Tibet if this was not done. No document is legal without the official seal of the Cabinet duly sanctioned by the Dalai Lama, but the Chinese made a seal of their own for the purpose (and this seal is still in their possession); therefore the agreement was never properly signed.

Since that time the Tibetans have suffered untold agonies. The Chinese Communists have gradually deprived us of all our political rights. Our Government, right from the top to the provincial and district offices, has been made powerless and today we are governed completely by the Chinese. Soon after their occupation in 1951 the Chinese organized the Regional Military Commanders and abolished our National Army, and the Commanders and Vice-Commanders of our own forces were enlisted with the Communists' forces to bring them into line with the forces of occupation. During 1953–54 the Chinese tried to establish their Military and Political Committee to abolish the Tibetan Government. But the bitter opposition of the people prevented this. By the end of 1954 the Chinese managed to take the Dalai Lama to China and there he was forced to agree and confirm that the autonomous state of Tibet would submit to the establishment of the Regional Autonomous Government of Tibet. In 1955 the Dalai Lama returned to Tibet. In 1956 the Chinese, in order to consolidate their hold on Tibet, formed the preparatory committee of the Regional Autonomous Government of Tibet. This Committee is directly governed by the Peking Government. All its members, both Chinese and Tibetans, must be approved by the Peking authorities and all its decisions must first be confirmed by them. They have installed their own agents in that Committee with fifty-fifty representation of Chinese and Tibetans, and have used those Tibetan puppets to influence the decisions of the Committee. Thus politically the Tibetans have been made completely subservient to the Chinese overlords.

Economically Tibet used to be self-sufficient in its food supply. But today millions of Chinese are living on our people and our food situation is desperate. The people in the east and north-east are facing a famine. The Chinese, besides laying hands on our current crops, have forced our people to open our centuries-old granaries. They have also taken away our reserves of gold and silver bullion. In the southern and central regions they have destroyed thousands of acres of agricultural land by giving priority to 'national highways' and to the building of barracks and arsenals. In the east and north-east regions the Chinese have introduced the Communist method of land reforms. In these areas half the population are peasants and the other half nomads. To effect their land reforms the Chinese have imported masses of their settlers and distributed the agricultural land of the Tibetans among them. They have in this way introduced the collectivization of farms. In this process the Chinese have made the despoiled Tibetan farmers work twelve hours a day, with a daily ration insufficient for a single meal. In the distribution of property they have not even spared the Tibetans' personal requisites of everyday life, such as rugs, rooms in the houses and articles of clothing. Our Tibetans are expected to treat these Chinese settlers as their aunts and uncles, and share all their property equally with the immigrants. The nomads too are victims of these so-called reforms.

Appendix B

Their flocks of sheep and cattle, their wool and dairy products are all being confiscated by the alien Government.

In the name of education they have opened schools of various denominations, organized training centres such as a 'Youth League', 'Women's Association', and 'Workers' Party', and they are trying their utmost to enlist as many as possible of our young men and children. In this way they have made thousands of homes unhappy by sending their children to China for the so-called advancement of their education. None of these children are being trained or educated for any constructive purposes. There are no Tibetan engineers, electricians, chemists or doctors. They train our youths to distrust each other. They are trying to indoctrinate the young Tibetans' minds and to strengthen the forces of Communism in our land. As a result they have divided families: son against father, wife against husband, thus alienating Tibetans from their own culture, tradition and homeland.

In the matter of religion they have their own schemes to subvert the very bases of Buddha's Teachings. Our religion teaches love for all and malice for none. The Communists in their struggle to spread the Marxist ideology have used our well-known monk scholars to mislead the simple Tibetans. In this endeavour they made Geyshey Sherab Gyatso, one of the well-known monk scholars, propagate their own doctrine by writing pamphlets and translating their various books and articles. They have also used the Panchen Lama as a puppet to advance their political purposes in Tibet. Pamphlets and articles of propaganda have been spread all over Tibet since 1948–58, and Communism is being preached to all our people. In Kumbum (one of the famous monasteries in the east) the Chinese have actually made our head lamas study Marxist Dialectics. Ordinary monks they try to overcome by such material arguments as this: The monks are made to remain in their cells and try to procure food by prayer alone. If the food is not miraculously produced, this is supposed to prove that God does not exist. Meantime the Communists prevent the monks from using their God-given natural powers to procure food, and torture them by hunger into abandoning their simple faith. The Communists preach day in and day out to our simple people and monks that religion is nothing short of an opium to distract the human mind from hard work. They have used hundreds of these monks as labourers in the building of roads and barracks. They have stopped the monasteries from sharing the usual food reserves and thousands of monks starved to death for this reason. They have forced many of our monks to marry and move to China to earn a living. They have laid hands on the capital of these monasteries and even subjected to tax the very idols and statues. Such has been the battle of Marxist Ideology against our spiritual heritage.

Outwardly they are telling people that they have come to Tibet to protect and help the Tibetans and to build roads, hospitals and airfields. As a matter of fact the roads are being built to connect Tibet with the Chinese mainland in order to transport millions of their armed forces to the far-flung areas of Tibet. In making these thousands of miles of roads they have used Tibetans as forced labourers and thousands of them have died for want of food and proper care. Their hospitals are not meant for these poor victims but are mainly for their armed forces. The Tibetans even in the towns are not allowed to use these army hospitals. The big airfields that they have built are mainly for the purpose of bringing in fuel, arms and ammunition. Tibetans are not even allowed to pass near those airfields, guarded so heavily by our oppressor. All these constructions are mainly for the purpose of consolidating their hold on Tibet and to suppress and preserve the conquered land and people of Tibet.

To us Tibetans the phrase 'the liberation of Tibet', in its moral and spiritual implications, is a deadly mockery. The country of a free people was invaded and occupied under the pretext of liberation . . . liberation from whom and what? Ours was a happy country with solvent Government and a contented people till the Chinese invasion in 1950.

In view of all these facts the Tibetans approached the Chinese with a view to conciliation. But all our efforts went in vain. Instead we are subjected to untold cruelty. The people of eastern Tibet revolted against the Chinese in February 1956. These spontaneous uprisings brought about further repression by the conquerors. They have desecrated religious buildings and destroyed monasteries, razed villages to the ground and killed thousands of our people. They have also used poison gas. Bombs have been thrown on innocent children and women. More than 15,000 people have been injured in these battles. Life in all parts of Tibet has become unbearable. So much so that more than 30,000 people in central Tibet round about Lhasa, the capital, left their hearth and home for the far-off valleys and gorges. It is feared that trouble may also flare up in these areas. Many places in Kham and Amdo are still scenes of upheaval and turmoil. Our patriots are fighting hard in these areas. Some of the Amdos who fled to the mountains are still not giving up their fight for freedom, suffering at least a hundred casualties a day.

INDEX

NOTE: *Names, Indian or Tibetan, are usually given in full, with title or designation or first name first, e.g. Abu Abalok, Apa Sahib B. Pant, as these are more familiar forms. Exception is made for the Pangdatshang brothers, and a few simpler names. G. P. refers to author, G. N. Patterson*

Index

Index

Index

datshang in, after March 1955, 130 seqq.; Dalai Lama's visit to, 149, 161, 162; new promises to Tibet from, 163; rejects Tibet's right to struggle for freedom, 180; Tibet's 1958 Manifesto to, 184–5, 186, 187; silences Tibetans in India, 188

Ingram, Margaret (*later* Mrs. G. Patterson), 105, 120, 121; *see also* Patterson, Mrs. G.

International Communist Intelligence Bureau, 106–7

In Two Chinas (Pannikar), 59–60

Ja Gag, 118
Jala State, 192, 194, 197
Jan Min Jih Pao, 45
Jayang Dawa, 161
Juga, 40
Jyekundo, 19, 20, 118, 198

Kalimpong, 22, 23, *and casual references passim*; G.P. in, after Calcutta talks with officials, 24 seqq.; cyclone in, 35; at Mr. Lloyd's house in, 36 seqq.; earthquake in, 46–9; continued residence in, 58 seqq.; Bakht Singh comes to, 74–5; Dr. Chang comes to, 78; Taktser's escape engineered from, 78–90, 91; Chang Chung Win marooned in, 92–7; Gompo Sham in, 107–9; G.P.'s return to, with wife, 121 seqq.; wife's dangerous illness in, 152 seqq.; Tubetan Ningje in, 159; G.P.'s 1957 return to, 173 seqq.; Kun-pel La in, 204

Ka Meng-yu, 104
Kanchenjunga mountain, 24, 58
Kangting, frontier role of, 18, 19, 20, 37, 38, 41, 55, 79, 101, 117, 128, 197, 207 seqq. *See also* Jala
Kansu, 107
Kantze, 19, 37, 41
Karachi, 75
Karmapa, 174
Kashmir, 104
Kham, Khambas, in the conflict, 17–37 *passim*, 48, 52, 80, 88, 95, 100–8, 122, 130–6 *passim*, 141, 142, 147, 151, 156, 160, 161, 163, 173 seqq., 204, 207 seqq.
Khatmandu, 107
Kingdon-Ward, Jean, 47

Kokonor territory, 19, 194
Konko Lama country, 118
Korea, 33, 44, 136, 178
Kruschev, Mr., 186
Kuomintang, 38, 39, 59, 73, 126, 127
Kumbum monastery, 100, 197
Kun-pel La, 203–4
Kuo-Mo-jo, 68, 74

Laing, John W., 71
Lamaism, history of, 190 seqq.
Lammo La, 106, 107
Lan Ma, Emperor of Tibet, 139–40
Largs, Brethren at, 113
Le Tourneau, Robert, 71
Lha Dun, 118
Lhalu, Governor (Kham), 131, 132
Lhasa, principal references to, 17, 20, 21, 22, 27, 31, 33, 54, 59, 62, 78, 81, 88 seqq., 100, 103, 106, 117, 121 seqq., 130 seqq.; 1955 crisis, 139 seqq.; Mi-mang-Tsong-du's appeal to, 143–5; indolence of, 147; Khambas tire of attitude of, 173 seqq.; some Chinese revolt in, 179; and Tibetan unity, 181; and Manchu dynasty, 191; *see* App. A *generally*
Lhasa Convention, 195–7
Likiang, 19
Litang, 156–7, 160
Li Tsung-jen (former Vice-president of Nationalist China), 99, 104
Liu, Dr. B. L., 99
Liu, Mr. and Mrs. (of Chinese Embassy, Lhasa), 58–9
Liu Po-chen, General, 44
Liu Sha (Tibetan Foreign Minister), 94
Liu Wen Huie (Governor of Sichang), 38
Lloyd, Mr., 26, 36, 37, 48, 58, 78
Loshay (G.P.'s Tibetan servant), 24, 34, 50, 80, 95, 96, 142
Ludhiana Christian Medical College, 105
Lukhang (of Kashag, Tibetan parliament), 98, 163, 185

Ma Bao-feng, General, 109
Mackinder, Sir Halford, 76
Macmahon Line, 123
Ma Feng-Kwai, General, 109
Maha Bodhi Society, India, 150
Manchester Guardian, 160, 164, 173, 176, 181, 186

221

Index

Index

Index

Abdullah, Morag Mary, *My Khyber Marriage* - Morag Murray departed on a lifetime of adventure when she met and fell in love with Sirdar Ikbal Ali Shah, the son of an Afghan warlord. Leaving the comforts of her middle-class home in Scotland, Morag followed her husband into a Central Asia still largely unchanged since the 19th century.

Abernathy, Miles, *Ride the Wind* – the amazing true story of the little Abernathy Boys, who made a series of astonishing journeys in the United States, starting in 1909 when they were aged five and nine!

Atkinson, John, *Afghan Expedition* – The author travelled to Afghanistan in 1838. He had been designated the Superintending Surgeon of a massive British invasion force resolved to place a sympathetic ruler on the Afghan throne. Soon after Atkinson was released from duty, and thus escaped the catastrophe which awaited his comrades. During the subsequent rebellion the British political agent was beheaded and an estimated 16,000 British soldiers and their dependents were slaughtered in a week by the vengeful Afghans. This book is a must for anybody interested in Afghanistan – then and now.

Beard, John, *Saddles East* – John Beard determined as a child that he wanted to see the Wild West from the back of a horse after a visit to Cody's legendary Wild West show. Yet it was only in 1948 – more than sixty years after seeing the flamboyant American showman – that Beard and his wife Lulu finally set off to follow their dreams.

Beker, Ana, *The Courage to Ride* – Determined to out-do Tschiffely, Beker made a 17,000 mile mounted odyssey across the Americas in the late 1940s that would fix her place in the annals of equestrian travel history.

Bird, Isabella, *Among the Tibetans* – A rousing 1889 adventure, an enchanting travelogue, a forgotten peek at a mountain kingdom swept away by the waves of time.

Bird, Isabella, *On Horseback in Hawaii* – The Victorian explorer's first horseback journey, in which she learns to ride astride, in early 1873.

Bird, Isabella, *Journeys in Persia and Kurdistan, Volumes 1 and 2* – The intrepid Englishwoman undertakes another gruelling journey in 1890.

Bird, Isabella, *A Lady's Life in the Rocky Mountains* – The story of Isabella Bird's adventures during the winter of 1873 when she explored the magnificent unspoiled wilderness of Colorado. Truly a classic.

Bird, Isabella, *Unbeaten Tracks in Japan, Volumes One and Two* – A 600-mile solo ride through Japan undertaken by the intrepid British traveller in 1878.

Blackmore, Charles, *In the Footsteps of Lawrence of Arabia* - In February 1985, fifty years after T. E. Lawrence was killed in a motor bicycle accident in Dorset, Captain Charles Blackmore and three others of the Royal Green Jackets Regiment set out to retrace Lawrence's exploits in the Arab Revolt during the First World War. They spent twenty-nine days with meagre supplies and under extreme conditions, riding and walking to the source of the Lawrence legend.

Boniface, Lieutenant Jonathan, *The Cavalry Horse and his Pack* – Quite simply the most important book ever written in the English language by a military man on the subject of equestrian travel.

Bosanquet, Mary, *Saddlebags for Suitcases* – In 1939 Bosanquet set out to ride from Vancouver, Canada, to New York. Along the way she was wooed by love-struck cowboys, chased by a grizzly bear and even suspected of being a Nazi spy, scouting out Canada in preparation for a German invasion. A truly delightful book.

de Bourboulon, Catherine, *Shanghai à Moscou (French)* – the story of how a young Scottish woman and her aristocratic French husband travelled overland from Shanghai to Moscow in the late 19th Century.

Brown, Donald; *Journey from the Arctic* – A truly remarkable account of how Brown, his Danish companion and their two trusty horses attempt the impossible, to cross the silent Arctic plateaus, thread their way through the giant Swedish forests, and finally discover a passage around the treacherous Norwegian marshes.

Bruce, Clarence Dalrymple, *In the Hoofprints of Marco Polo* – The author made a dangerous journey from Srinagar to Peking in 1905, mounted on a trusty 13-hand Kashmiri pony, then wrote this wonderful book.

Burnaby, Frederick; *A Ride to Khiva* – Burnaby fills every page with a memorable cast of characters, including hard-riding Cossacks, nomadic Tartars, vodka-guzzling sleigh-drivers and a legion of peasant ruffians.

Burnaby, Frederick, *On Horseback through Asia Minor* – Armed with a rifle, a small stock of medicines, and a single faithful servant, the equestrian traveler rode through a hotbed of intrigue and high adventure in wild inhospitable country, encountering Kurds, Circassians, Armenians, and Persian pashas.

Carter, General William, *Horses, Saddles and Bridles* – This book covers a wide range of topics including basic training of the horse and care of its equipment. It also provides a fascinating look back into equestrian travel history.

Cayley, George, *Bridle Roads of Spain* – Truly one of the greatest equestrian travel accounts of the 19th Century.

Chase, J. Smeaton, *California Coast Trails* – This classic book describes the author's journey from Mexico to Oregon along the coast of California in the 1890s.

Chase, J. Smeaton, *California Desert Trails* – Famous British naturalist J. Smeaton Chase mounted up and rode into the Mojave Desert to undertake the longest equestrian study of its kind in modern history.

Chitty, Susan, and Hinde, Thomas, *The Great Donkey Walk* - When biographer Susan Chitty and her novelist husband, Thomas Hinde, decided it was time to embark on a family adventure, they did it in style. In Santiago they bought two donkeys whom they named Hannibal and Hamilcar. Their two small daughters, Miranda (7) and Jessica (3) were to ride Hamilcar. Hannibal, meanwhile, carried the baggage. The walk they planned to undertake was nothing short of the breadth of southern Europe.

Christian, Glynn, *Fragile Paradise: The discovery of Fletcher Christian, "Bounty" Mutineer* – the great-great-great-great-grandson of the *Bounty* mutineer brings to life a fascinating and complex character history has portrayed as both hero and villain, and the real story behind a mutiny that continues to divide opinion more than 200 years later. The result is a brilliant and compelling historical detective story, full of intrigue, jealousy, revenge and adventure on the high seas.

Clark, Leonard, *Marching Wind, The* – The panoramic story of a mounted exploration in the remote and savage heart of Asia, a place where adventure, danger, and intrigue were the daily backdrop to wild tribesman and equestrian exploits.

Clark, Leonard, *A Wanderer Till I Die* – In a world with lax passport control, no airlines, and few rules, the young man from San Francisco floats effortlessly from one adventure to the next. When he's not drinking whisky at the Raffles Hotel or listening to the "St. Louis Blues" on the phonograph in the jungle, he's searching for Malaysian treasure, being captured by Toradja head-hunters, interrogated by Japanese intelligence officers and lured into shady deals by European gun-runners.

Cobbett, William, *Rural Rides, Volumes 1 and 2* – In the early 1820s Cobbett set out on horseback to make a series of personal tours through the English countryside. These books contain what many believe to be the best accounts of rural England ever written, and remain enduring classics.

Codman, John, *Winter Sketches from the Saddle* – This classic book was first published in 1888. It recommends riding for your health and describes the septuagenarian author's many equestrian journeys through New England during the winter of 1887 on his faithful mare, Fanny.

Cunninghame Graham, Jean, *Gaucho Laird* – A superbly readable biography of the author's famous great-uncle, Robert "Don Roberto" Cunninghame Graham.

Cunninghame Graham, Robert, *Horses of the Conquest* – The author uncovered manuscripts which had lain forgotten for centuries, and wrote this book, as he said, out of gratitude to the horses of Columbus and the Conquistadors who shaped history.

Cunninghame Graham, Robert, *Magreb-el-Acksa* – The thrilling tale of how "Don Roberto" was kidnapped in Morocco!

Cunninghame Graham, Robert, *Rodeo* – An omnibus of the finest work of the man they called "the uncrowned King of Scotland," edited by his friend Aimé Tschiffely.

Cunninghame Graham, Robert, *Tales of Horsemen* – Ten of the most beautifully-written equestrian stories ever set to paper.

Cunninghame Graham, Robert, *Vanished Arcadia* – This haunting story about the Jesuit missions in South America from 1550 to 1767 was the inspiration behind the best-selling film *The Mission*.

Daly, H.W., *Manual of Pack Transportation* – This book is the author's masterpiece. It contains a wealth of information on various pack saddles, ropes and equipment, how to secure every type of load imaginable and instructions on how to organize a pack train.

Dixie, Lady Florence, *Riding Across Patagonia* – When asked in 1879 why she wanted to travel to such an outlandish place as Patagonia, the author replied without hesitation that she was taking to the saddle in order to flee from the strict confines of polite Victorian society. This is the story of how the aristocrat successfully traded the perils of a London parlor for the wind-borne freedom of a wild Patagonian bronco.

Dodwell, Christina, *Beyond Siberia* – The intrepid author goes to Russia's Far East to join the reindeer-herding people in winter.

Dodwell, Christina, *An Explorer's Handbook* – The author tells you everything you want to know about travelling: how to find suitable pack animals, how to feed and shelter yourself. She also has sensible and entertaining advice about dealing with unwanted visitors and the inevitable bureaucrats.

Dodwell, Christina, *Madagascar Travels* – Christina explores the hidden corners of this amazing island and, as usual, makes friends with its people.

Dodwell, Christina, *A Traveller in China* – The author sets off alone across China, starting with a horse and then transferring to an inflatable canoe.

Dodwell, Christina, *A Traveller on Horseback* – Christina Dodwell rides through Eastern Turkey and Iran in the late 1980s. The Sunday Telegraph wrote of the author's "courage and insatiable wanderlust," and in this book she demonstrates her gift for communicating her zest for adventure.

Dodwell, Christina, *Travels in Papua New Guinea* – Christina Dodwell spends two years exploring an island little known to the outside world. She travelled by foot, horse and dugout canoe among the Stone-Age tribes.

Dodwell, Christina, *Travels with Fortune* – the truly amazing account of the courageous author's first journey – a three-year odyssey around Africa by Landrover, bus, lorry, horse, camel, and dugout canoe!

Dodwell, Christina, *Travels with Pegasus* – This time Christina takes to the air! This is the story of her unconventional journey across North Africa in a micro-light!

Duncan, John, *Travels in Western Africa in 1845 and 1846* – The author, a Lifeguardsman from Scotland, tells the hair-raising tale of his two journeys to what is now Benin. Sadly, Duncan has been forgotten until today, and we are proud to get this book back into print.

Ehlers, Otto, *Im Sattel durch die Fürstenhöfe Indiens* – In June 1890 the young German adventurer, Ehlers, lay very ill. His doctor gave him a choice: either go home to Germany or travel to Kashmir. So of course the Long Rider chose the latter. This is a thrilling yet humorous book about the author's adventures.

Farson, Negley, *Caucasian Journey* – A thrilling account of a dangerous equestrian journey made in 1929, this is an amply illustrated adventure classic.

Fox, Ernest, *Travels in Afghanistan* – The thrilling tale of a 1937 journey through the mountains, valleys, and deserts of this forbidden realm, including visits to such fabled places as the medieval city of Heart, the towering Hindu Kush mountains, and the legendary Khyber Pass.

Gall, Sandy, *Afghanistan – Agony of a Nation* - Sandy Gall has made three trips to Afghanistan to report the war there: in 1982, 1984 and again in 1986. This book is an account of his last journey and what he found. He chose to revisit the man he believes is the outstanding commander in Afghanistan: Ahmed Shah Masud, a dashing Tajik who is trying to organise resistance to the Russians on a regional, and eventually national scale.

Gall, Sandy, *Behind Russian Lines* – In the summer of 1982, Sandy Gall set off for Afghanistan on what turned out to be the hardest assignment of his life. During his career as a reporter he had covered plenty of wars and revolutions before, but this was the first time he had been required to walk all the way to an assignment and all the way back again, dodging Russian bombs *en route*.

Gallard, Babette, *Riding the Milky Way* – An essential guide to anyone planning to ride the ancient pilgrimage route to Santiago di Compostella, and a highly readable story for armchair travellers.

Galton, Francis, *The Art of Travel* – Originally published in 1855, this book became an instant classic and was used by a host of now-famous explorers, including Sir Richard Francis Burton of Mecca fame. Readers can learn how to ride horses, handle elephants, avoid cobras, pull teeth, find water in a desert, and construct a sleeping bag out of fur.

Glazier, Willard, *Ocean to Ocean on Horseback* – This book about the author's journey from New York to the Pacific in 1875 contains every kind of mounted adventure imaginable. Amply illustrated with pen and ink drawings of the time, the book remains a timeless equestrian adventure classic.

Goodwin, Joseph, *Through Mexico on Horseback* – The author and his companion, Robert Horiguichi, the sophisticated, multi-lingual son of an imperial Japanese diplomat, set out in 1931 to cross Mexico. They were totally unprepared for the deserts, quicksand and brigands they were to encounter during their adventure.

Grant, David, *Spirit of the Vikings: A Journey in the Kayak Bahá'í Viking From Arkosund, Sweden, to Odessa, Ukraine* – David Grant takes his kayak on an adventure-filled and spiritual journey from Sweden to Odessa on the Black Sea.

Grant, David, *The Wagon Travel Handbook* - David Grant is the legendary Scottish wagon-master who journeyed around the world with his family in a horse-drawn wagon. Grant has filled *The Wagon Travel Handbook* with all the practical information a first time-wagon traveller will need before setting out, including sections on interior and exterior wagon design, choice of draught animals, veterinary requirements and frontier formalities.

Gray, David and Lukas Novotny, *Mounted Archery in the Americas* – This fascinating and amply illustrated book charts the history of mounted archery from its ancient roots on the steppes of Eurasia thousands of years ago to its current resurgence in popularity in the Americas. It also provides the reader with up-to-the-minute practical information gleaned from a unique team of the world's leading experts.

Hanbury-Tenison, Marika, *For Better, For Worse* – The author, an excellent story-teller, writes about her adventures visiting and living among the Indians of Central Brazil.

Hanbury-Tenison, Marika, *A Slice of Spice* – The fresh and vivid account of the author's hazardous journey to the Indonesian Islands with her husband, Robin.

Hanbury-Tenison, Robin, *Chinese Adventure* – The story of a unique journey in which the explorer Robin Hanbury-Tenison and his wife Louella rode on horseback alongside the Great Wall of China in 1986.

Hanbury-Tenison, Robin, *Fragile Eden* – The wonderful story of Robin and Louella Hanbury-Tenison's exploration of New Zealand on horseback in 1988. They rode alone together through what they describe as 'some of the most dramatic and exciting country we have ever seen.'

Hanbury-Tenison, Robin, *Mulu: The Rainforest* – This was the first popular book to bring to the world's attention the significance of the rain forests to our fragile ecosystem. It is a timely reminder of our need to preserve them for the future.

Hanbury-Tenison, Robin, *A Pattern of Peoples* – The author and his wife, Marika, spent three months travelling through Indonesia's outer islands and writes with his usual flair and sensitivity about the tribes he found there.

Hanbury-Tenison, Robin, *A Question of Survival* – This superb book played a hugely significant role in bringing the plight of Brazil's Indians to the world's attention.

Hanbury-Tenison, Robin, *The Rough and the Smooth* – The incredible story of two journeys in South America. Neither had been attempted before, and both were considered impossible!

Hanbury-Tenison, Robin, *Spanish Pilgrimage* – Robin and Louella Hanbury-Tenison went to Santiago de Compostela in a traditional way – riding on white horses over long-forgotten tracks. In the process they discovered more about the people and the country than any conventional traveller would learn. Their adventures are vividly and entertainingly recounted in this delightful and highly readable book.

Hanbury-Tenison, Robin, *White Horses over France* – This enchanting book tells the story of a magical journey and how, in fulfilment of a personal dream, the first Camargue horses set foot on British soil in the late summer of 1984.

Hanbury-Tenison, Robin, *Worlds Apart – an Explorer's Life* – The author's battle to preserve the quality of life under threat from developers and machines infuses this autobiography with a passion and conviction which makes it impossible to put down.

Hanbury-Tenison, Robin, *Worlds Within – Reflections in the Sand* – This book is full of the adventure you would expect from a man of action like Robin Hanbury-Tenison. However, it is also filled with the type of rare knowledge that was revealed to other desert travellers like Lawrence, Doughty and Thesiger.

Haslund, Henning, *Mongolian Adventure* – An epic tale inhabited by a cast of characters no longer present in this lackluster world, shamans who set themselves on fire, rebel leaders who sacked towns, and wild horsemen whose ancestors conquered the world.

Hassanein, A. M., *The Lost Oases* - At the dawning of the 20th century the vast desert of Libya remained one of last unexplored places on Earth. Sir Hassanein Bey, the dashing Egyptian diplomat turned explorer, befriended the Muslim leaders of the elusive Senussi Brotherhood who controlled the deserts further on, and became aware of rumours of a "lost oasis" which lay even deeper in the desert. In 1923 the explorer led a small caravan on a remarkable seven month journey across the centre of Libya. **Heath, Frank,** *Forty Million Hoofbeats* – Heath set out in 1925 to follow his dream of riding to all 48 of the Continental United States. The journey lasted more than two years, during which time Heath and his mare, Gypsy Queen, became inseparable companions.

Hinde, Thomas, *The Great Donkey Walk* – Biographer Susan Chitty and her novelist husband, Thomas Hinde, travelled from Spain's Santiago to Salonica in faraway Greece. Their two small daughters, Miranda (7) and Jessica (3) were rode one donkey, while the other donkey carried the baggage. Reading this delightful book is leisurely and continuing pleasure.

Holt, William, *Ride a White Horse* – After rescuing a cart horse, Trigger, from slaughter and nursing him back to health, the 67-year-old Holt and his horse set out in 1964 on an incredible 9,000 mile, non-stop journey through western Europe.

Hope, Thomas, *Anastasius* – Here is the book that took the world by storm, and then was forgotten. Hope's hero Anastasius was fearless, curious, cunning, ruthless, brave, and above all, sexy. He journeyed deep into the vast and dangerous Ottoman Empire. During the 35 years described in the book (1762-1798) the swashbuckling hero infiltrated the deadly Wahhabis in Arabia, rode to war with the Mamelukes in Egypt and sailed the Mediterranean with the Turks. This remarkable new edition features all three volumes together for the first time.

Hopkins, Frank T., *Hidalgo and Other Stories* – For the first time in history, here are the collected writings of Frank T. Hopkins, the counterfeit cowboy whose endurance racing claims and Old West fantasies have polarized the equestrian world.

Jacobs, Ross, *Old Men and Horses – A Gift of Horsemanship* - Ross Jacobs is an extraordinary and experienced Australian horseman, trainer and writer. In *Old Men and Horses* he has created three fictional characters whose role in the history of equestrian training will never be forgotten.

James, Jeremy, *Saddletramp* – The classic story of Jeremy James' journey from Turkey to Wales, on an unplanned route with an inaccurate compass, unreadable map and the unfailing aid of villagers who seemed to have as little sense of direction as he had.

James, Jeremy, *Vagabond* – The wonderful tale of the author's journey from Bulgaria to Berlin offers a refreshing, witty and often surprising view of Eastern Europe and the collapse of communism.

Jebb, Louisa, *By Desert Ways to Baghdad and Damascus* – From the pen of a gifted writer and intrepid traveller, this is one of the greatest equestrian travel books of all time.

Kluckhohn, Clyde, *To the Foot of the Rainbow* – This is not just a exciting true tale of equestrian adventure. It is a moving account of a young man's search for physical perfection in a desert world still untouched by the recently-born twentieth century.

Lambie, Thomas, *Boots and Saddles in Africa* – Lambie's story of his equestrian journeys is told with the grit and realism that marks a true classic.

Landor, Henry Savage, *In the Forbidden Land* – Illustrated with hundreds of photographs and drawings, this blood-chilling account of equestrian adventure makes for page-turning excitement.

Langlet, Valdemar, *Till Häst Genom Ryssland (Swedish)* – Denna reseskildring rymmer många ögonblicksbilder av möten med människor, från morgonbad med Lev Tolstoi till samtal med Tartarer och fotografering av fagra skördeflickor. Rikt illustrerad med foto och teckningar.

Leigh, Margaret, *My Kingdom for a Horse* – In the autumn of 1939 the author rode from Cornwall to Scotland, resulting in one of the most delightful equestrian journeys of the early twentieth century. This book is full of keen observations of a rural England that no longer exists.

Lester, Mary, *A Lady's Ride across Spanish Honduras in 1881* – This is a gem of a book, with a very entertaining account of Mary's vivid, day-to-day life in the saddle.

MacDermot, Brian, *Cult of the Sacred Spear* – here is that rarest of travel books, an exploration not only of a distant land but of a man's own heart. A confederation of pastoral people located in Southern Sudan and western Ethiopia, the Nuer warriors were famous for staging cattle raids against larger tribes and successfully resisted European colonization. Brian MacDermot, London stockbroker, entered into Nuer society as a stranger and emerged as Rial Nyang, an adopted member of the tribe. This book recounts this extraordinary emotional journey, regaling the reader with tales of pagan gods, warriors on mysterious missions, and finally the approach of warfare that continues to swirl across this part of Africa today.

Maillart, Ella, *Turkestan Solo* – A vivid account of a 1930s journey through this wonderful, mysterious and dangerous portion of the world, complete with its Kirghiz eagle hunters, lurking Soviet secret police, and the timeless nomads that still inhabited the desolate steppes of Central Asia.

Marcy, Randolph, *The Prairie Traveler* – There were a lot of things you packed into your saddlebags or the wagon before setting off to cross the North American wilderness in the 1850s. A gun and an axe were obvious necessities. Yet many pioneers were just as adamant about placing a copy of Captain Randolph Marcy's classic book close at hand.

Marsden, Kate, *Riding through Siberia: A Mounted Medical Mission in 1891* – This immensely readable book is a mixture of adventure, extreme hardship and compassion as the author travels the Great Siberian Post Road.

Marsh, Hippisley Cunliffe, *A Ride Through Islam* – A British officer rides through Persia and Afghanistan to India in 1873. Full of adventures, and with observant remarks on the local Turkoman equestrian traditions.

MacCann, William, *Viaje a Caballo* – Spanish-language edition of the British author's equestrian journey around Argentina in 1848.

Meline, James, *Two Thousand Miles on Horseback: Kansas to Santa Fé in 1866* – A beautifully written, eye witness account of a United States that is no more.

Moates, Tom, *A Horse's Thought* – This is a collection of the author's popular writings exploring his personal exploits with horses as he sincerely attempts to improve his horsemanship skills. This book combines an abundance of new, previously unpublished material regarding this ongoing odyssey.

Muir Watson, Sharon, *The Colour of Courage* – The remarkable true story of the epic horse trip made by the first people to travel Australia's then-unmarked Bicentennial National Trail. There are enough adventures here to satisfy even the most jaded reader.

Naysmith, Gordon, *The Will to Win* – This book recounts the only equestrian journey of its kind undertaken during the 20th century - a mounted trip stretching across 16 countries. Gordon Naysmith, a Scottish pentathlete and former military man, set out in 1970 to ride from the tip of the African continent to the 1972 Olympic Games in distant Germany.

Ondaatje, Christopher, *Leopard in the Afternoon* – The captivating story of a journey through some of Africa's most spectacular haunts. It is also touched with poignancy and regret for a vanishing wilderness – a world threatened with extinction.

Ondaatje, Christopher, *The Man-Eater of Pununai* – a fascinating story of a past rediscovered through a remarkable journey to one of the most exotic countries in the world — Sri Lanka. Full of drama and history, it not only relives the incredible story of a man-eating leopard that terrorized the tiny village of Punanai in the early part of the century, but also allows the author to come to terms with the ghost of his charismatic but tyrannical father.

Ondaatje, Christopher, *Sindh Revisited* – This is the extraordinarily sensitive account of the author's quest to uncover the secrets of the seven years Richard Burton spent in India in the army of the East India Company from 1842 to 1849. "If I wanted to fill the gap in my understanding of Richard Burton, I would have to do something that had never been done before: follow in his footsteps in India..." The journey covered thousands of miles—trekking across deserts where ancient tribes meet modern civilization in the valley of the mighty Indus River.

O'Connor, Derek, *The King's Stranger* – a superb biography of the forgotten Scottish explorer, John Duncan.

O'Reilly, Basha, *Count Pompeii – Stallion of the Steppes* – the story of Basha's journey from Russia with her stallion, Count Pompeii, told for children. This is the first book in the *Little Long Rider* series.

O'Reilly, CuChullaine, (Editor) *The Horse Travel Handbook* – this accumulated knowledge of a million miles in the saddle tells you everything you need to know about travelling with your horse!

O'Reilly, CuChullaine, (Editor) *The Horse Travel Journal* – a unique book to take on your ride and record your experiences. Includes the world's first equestrian travel "pictionary" to help you in foreign countries.

O'Reilly, CuChullaine, *Khyber Knights* – Told with grit and realism by one of the world's foremost equestrian explorers, "Khyber Knights" has been penned the way lives are lived, not how books are written.

O'Reilly, CuChullaine, (Editor) *The Long Riders, Volume One* – The first of five unforgettable volumes of exhilarating travel tales.

Östrup, J, (*Swedish*), *Växlande Horisont* – The thrilling account of the author's journey to Central Asia from 1891 to 1893.

Patterson, George, *Gods and Guerrillas* – The true and gripping story of how the author went secretly into Tibet to film the Chinese invaders of his adopted country. Will make your heart pound with excitement!

Patterson, George, *Journey with Loshay: A Tibetan Odyssey* – This is an amazing book written by a truly remarkable man! Relying both on his companionship with God and on his own strength, he undertook a life few can have known, and a journey of emergency across the wildest parts of Tibet.

Patterson, George, *Patterson of Tibet* – Patterson was a Scottish medical missionary who went to Tibet shortly after the second World War. There he became Tibetan in all but name, adapting to the culture and learning the language fluently. This intense autobiography reveals how Patterson crossed swords with India's Prime Minister Nehru, helped with the rescue of the Dalai Lama and befriended a host of unique world figures ranging from Yehudi Menhuin to Eric Clapton. This is a vividly-written account of a life of high adventure and spiritual odyssey.

Pocock, Roger, *Following the Frontier* – Pocock was one of the nineteenth century's most influential equestrian travelers. Within the covers of this book is the detailed account of Pocock's horse ride along the infamous Outlaw Trail, a 3,000 mile solo journey that took the adventurer from Canada to Mexico City.

Pocock, Roger, *Horses* – Pocock set out to document the wisdom of the late 19th and early 20th Centuries into a book unique for its time. His concerns for attempting to preserve equestrian knowledge were based on cruel reality. More than 300,000 horses had been destroyed during the recent Boer War. Though Pocock enjoyed a reputation for dangerous living, his observations on horses were praised by the leading thinkers of his day.

Post, Charles Johnson, *Horse Packing* – Originally published in 1914, this book was an instant success, incorporating as it did the very essence of the science of packing horses and mules. It makes fascinating reading for students of the horse or history.

Ray, G. W., *Through Five Republics on Horseback* – In 1889 a British explorer – part-time missionary and full-time adventure junky – set out to find a lost tribe of sun-worshipping natives in the unexplored forests of Paraguay. The journey was so brutal that it defies belief.

Rink, Bjarke, *The Centaur Legacy* – This immensely entertaining and historically important book provides the first ever in-depth study into how man's partnership with his equine companion changed the course of history and accelerated human development.

Ross, Julian, *Travels in an Unknown Country* – A delightful book about modern horseback travel in an enchanting country, which once marked the eastern borders of the Roman Empire – Romania.

Ross, Martin and Somerville, E, *Beggars on Horseback* – The hilarious adventures of two aristocratic Irish cousins on an 1894 riding tour of Wales.

Ruxton, George, *Adventures in Mexico* – The story of a young British army officer who rode from Vera Cruz to Santa Fe, Mexico in 1847. At times the author exhibits a fearlessness which borders on insanity. He ignores dire warnings, rides through deadly deserts, and dares murderers to attack him. It is a delightful and invigorating tale of a time and place now long gone.

von Salzman, Erich, *Im Sattel durch Zentralasien* – The astonishing tale of the author's journey through China, Turkistan and back to his home in Germany – 6000 kilometres in 176 days!

Schwarz, Hans *(German)*, *Vier Pferde, Ein Hund und Drei Soldaten* – In the early 1930s the author and his two companions rode through Liechtenstein, Austria, Romania, Albania, Yugoslavia, to Turkey, then rode back again!

Schwarz, Otto *(German)*, *Reisen mit dem Pferd* – the Swiss Long Rider with more miles in the saddle than anyone else tells his wonderful story, and a long appendix tells the reader how to follow in his footsteps.

Scott, Robert, *Scott's Last Expedition* – Many people are unaware that Scott recruited Yakut ponies from Siberia for his doomed expedition to the South Pole in 1909. Here is the remarkable story of men and horses who all paid the ultimate sacrifice.

Shackleton, Ernest, *Aurora Australis* - The members of the British Antarctic Expedition of 1907-1908 wrote this delightful and surprisingly funny book. It was printed on the spot "at the sign of the Penguin"!

Skrede, Wilfred, *Across the Roof of the World* – This epic equestrian travel tale of a wartime journey across Russia, China, Turkestan and India is laced with unforgettable excitement.

The South Pole Ponies, *Theodore Mason* – The touching and totally forgotten story of the little horses who gave their all to both Scott and Shackleton in their attempts to reach the South Pole.

Stevens, Thomas, *Through Russia on a Mustang* – Mounted on his faithful horse, Texas, Stevens crossed the Steppes in search of adventure. Cantering across the pages of this classic tale is a cast of nineteenth century Russian misfits, peasants, aristocrats—and even famed Cossack Long Rider Dmitri Peshkov.

Stevenson, Robert L., *Travels with a Donkey* – In 1878, the author set out to explore the remote Cevennes mountains of France. He travelled alone, unless you count his stubborn and manipulative pack-donkey, Modestine. This book is a true classic.

Strong, Anna Louise, *Road to the Grey Pamir* – With Stalin's encouragement, Strong rode into the seldom-seen Pamir mountains of faraway Tadjikistan. The political renegade turned equestrian explorer soon discovered more adventure than she had anticipated.

Sykes, Ella, *Through Persia on a Sidesaddle* – Ella Sykes rode side-saddle 2,000 miles across Persia, a country few European woman had ever visited. Mind you, she traveled in style, accompanied by her Swiss maid and 50 camels loaded with china, crystal, linens and fine wine.

Trinkler, Emile, *Through the Heart of Afghanistan* – In the early 1920s the author made a legendary trip across a country now recalled only in legends.

Tschiffely, Aimé, *Bohemia Junction* – "Forty years of adventurous living condensed into one book."

Tschiffely, Aimé, *Bridle Paths* – a final poetic look at a now-vanished Britain.

Tschiffely, Aimé, *Coricancha*: A fascinating and balanced account of the conquest of the Inca Empire.

Tschiffely, Aimé, *Don Roberto* – A biography of Tschiffely's friend and mentor, Robert Cunninghame Graham.

Tschiffely, Aimé, *Little Princess Turtle Dove* – An enchanting fairy story set in South America and displaying Aimé Tschiffely's love, not only for children and animals, but also for South America.

Tschiffely, Aimé, *Mancha y Gato Cuentan sus Aventuras* – The Spanish-language version of *The Tale of Two Horses* – the story of the author's famous journey as told by the horses.

Tschiffely, Aimé, *Ming and Ping*: An adventure book for older children. The title characters go exploring South America together. They meet many tribes of Indians and learn about their way of life. Exhilarating and effortlessly instructive.

Tschiffely, Aimé, *Round and About Spain:* Tschiffely sets off to explore Spain, but this time his steed is a motorbike, not a horse! With wit, wisdom and a sharp eye for the absurd, he travels to all four corners of this fascinating country and makes many friends along the way. So much has changed since the Second World War that that this book is a unique snapshot of Spain as she was in 1950.

Tschiffely, Aimé, *The Tale of Two Horses* – The story of Tschiffely's famous journey from Buenos Aires to Washington, DC, narrated by his two equine heroes, Mancha and Gato. Their unique point of view is guaranteed to delight children and adults alike.

Tschiffely, Aimé, *This Way Southward* – the most famous equestrian explorer of the twentieth century decides to make a perilous journey across the U-boat infested Atlantic.

Tschiffely, Aimé, *Tschiffely's Ride* – The true story of the most famous equestrian journey of the twentieth century – 10,000 miles with two Criollo geldings from Argentina to Washington, DC. A new edition is coming soon with a Foreword by his literary heir!

Tschiffely, Aimé, *Tschiffely's Ritt* – The German-language translation of *Tschiffely's Ride* – the most famous equestrian journey of its day.

Ure, John, *Cucumber Sandwiches in the Andes* – No-one who wasn't mad as a hatter would try to take a horse across the Andes by one of the highest passes between Chile and the Argentine. That was what John Ure was told on his way to the British Embassy in Santiago – so he set out to find a few certifiable kindred spirits. Fans of equestrian travel and of Latin America will be enchanted by this delightful book.

Warner, Charles Dudley, *On Horseback in Virginia* – A prolific author, and a great friend of Mark Twain, Warner made witty and perceptive contributions to the world of nineteenth century American literature. This book about the author's equestrian adventures is full of fascinating descriptions of nineteenth century America.

Weale, Magdalene, *Through the Highlands of Shropshire* – It was 1933 and Magdalene Weale was faced with a dilemma: how to best explore her beloved English countryside? By horse, of course! This enchanting book invokes a gentle, softer world inhabited by gracious country lairds, wise farmers, and jolly inn keepers.

Weeks, Edwin Lord, *Artist Explorer* – A young American artist and superb writer travels through Persia to India in 1892.

Wentworth Day, J., *Wartime Ride* – In 1939 the author decided the time was right for an extended horseback ride through England! While parts of his country were being ravaged by war, Wentworth Day discovered an inland oasis of mellow harvest fields, moated Tudor farmhouses, peaceful country halls, and fishing villages.

Von Westarp, Eberhard, *Unter Halbmond und Sonne* – (German) – Im Sattel durch die asiatische Türkei und Persien.

Wilkins, Messanie, *Last of the Saddle Tramps* – Told she had little time left to live, the author decided to ride from her native Maine to the Pacific. Accompanied by her faithful horse, Tarzan, Wilkins suffered through any number of obstacles, including blistering deserts and freezing snow storms – and defied the doctors by living for another 20 years!

Wilson, Andrew, *The Abode of Snow* – One of the best accounts of overland equestrian travel ever written about the wild lands that lie between Tibet and Afghanistan.

de Windt, Harry, *A Ride to India* – Part science, all adventure, this book takes the reader for a thrilling canter across the Persian Empire of the 1890s.

Winthrop, Theodore, *Saddle and Canoe* – This book paints a vibrant picture of 1850s life in the Pacific Northwest and covers the author's travels along the Straits of Juan De

Fuca, on Vancouver Island, across the Naches Pass, and on to The Dalles, in Oregon Territory. This is truly an historic travel account.

Woolf, Leonard, *Stories of the East* – Three short stories which are of vital importance in understanding the author's mistrust of and dislike for colonialism, which provide disturbing commentaries about the disintegration of the colonial process.

Younghusband, George, *Eighteen Hundred Miles on a Burmese Pony* – One of the funniest and most enchanting books about equestrian travel of the nineteenth century, featuring "Joe" the naughty Burmese pony!

We are constantly adding new titles to our collections, so please check our websites:

www.horsetravelbooks.com
www.classictravelbooks.com
The Equestrian Wisdom & History Series: www.lrgaf.org

CPSIA information can be obtained at www.ICGtesting.com
Printed in the USA
BVOW071023030112

279688BV00001B/32/P